THE
DISTURBING
PROFANE

THE DISTURBING PROFANE

HIP HOP, BLACKNESS,
AND THE SACRED

Joseph R. Winters

Duke University Press   *Durham and London*   2025

Project Editor: Lisa Lawley
Designed by Courtney Leigh Richardson
Typeset in Portrait and Changa by Westchester Publishing Services

Library of Congress Cataloging-in-Publication Data
Names: Winters, Joseph Richard, [date] author
Title: The disturbing profane : hip hop, blackness, and the sacred /
Joseph R. Winters.
Other titles: Hip hop, blackness, and the sacred
Description: Durham : Duke University Press, 2025. | Includes
bibliographical references and index.
Identifiers: LCCN 2024050801 (print)
LCCN 2024050802 (ebook)
ISBN 9781478031857 paperback
ISBN 9781478028604 hardcover
ISBN 9781478060826 ebook
Subjects: LCSH: Hip-hop—Religious aspects | Rap (Music)—Religious
aspects | Music and race | African Americans—Social life and customs
Classification: LCC ML3921.8.R36 W568 2025 (print) | LCC ML3921.8.R36
(ebook) | DDC 781.64/9—dc23/eng/20250519
LC record available at https://lccn.loc.gov/2024050801
LC ebook record available at https://lccn.loc.gov/2024050802

Contents

Acknowledgments

This book brings together (into a kind of cypher) hip hop, blackness, and the unruly side of the sacred. In the process, I aim to contribute to conversations about hip hop's errant and profane religiosity, which directs attention to moments when sounds, images, and cuts unsettle and interrupt desires for purity and coherence, desires that tend to diminish our sense of the violence that these very aspirations facilitate. At the same time, *The Disturbing Profane* aligns itself with efforts to show how black study has, and should be, invested in interrogating the religious grammars that underpin and propel antiblackness, racialized sex/gender mechanisms of power, Western imperialism, and so forth. If the left-hand sacred has been associated with the accursed, then there is some resemblance with blackness, which has been similarly situated as wretched within white supremacist constructions of the human being.

In many ways, this book is my endeavor to come to terms with how I have been formed, unformed, and touched by hip hop, the politics of the sacred, and black study. With regard to hip hop, which involves practices, discourses, and visual and sonic economies, I am thinking about a series of experiences and encounters: the wonder and awe that I felt when my father took me to see groups like Public Enemy, Rakim, or Whodini as a child; the competitive anxiety that arises during cyphers and freestyle sessions at the lunch table, in the parking lot, or during a pregame gathering; the contentious debates and arguments over the quality of various albums, artists, lyrics, and videos; the melancholy and ecstasy that mark habits of solitude when I am listening to rap music, contemplating loss and absence, and sipping on whiskey; the tension and guilt that I have felt when (black) women friends tell me they cannot listen to rap music because it too often feels like an assault on their body/flesh (and I wonder why it shouldn't feel the same way to me); the anxiety I experience when I am about to teach Queen Latifah's "U.N.I.T.Y." or Lil' Kim's verse on "Get Money," knowing that these songs provide a glimpse into how hip hop's prevailing masculinist formations are predicated on verbal and physical animosity against black women; the difficulty of trying to write about tendencies within hip hop to strain against normalization, even as so many rap lyrics are queerphobic and even as the ruling logics, desires, and aspirations prevalent within hip hop bear the traces of inexorable subjection to the order of things. Consequently, hip hop's religiosity involves forms of discursive, visual, and physical sacrifice that both preserve and destabilize the celebratory and affirmative tendencies within the genre. As I hope to show in this book, hip hop refracts the violence and death that enables social life. As an assemblage of practices and discourses that are inseparable from the culture industry and the commodity form, hip hop both aligns with ruling paradigms (that profit from the fascination and aversion to blackness and black sexuality) and testifies to an intractable disturbance that is part of its volatile sacrality.

This book would not have been possible without the brilliance, generosity, and care of colleagues, mentors, friends, and family. First and foremost, I want to shout out Duke University Press, especially my editor Miriam Angress. Alongside my doubts and hesitations about this book (and experiences of writer's block during the early stages of the pandemic), Miriam has been a steadfast and patient supporter of the project. I am more than grateful. I also want to thank Lisa Lawley and Nicholas Taylor for all their hard work in making this project come to fruition.

I would not have written a book on religion and hip hop if it were not for the kindness and generosity of Anthony Pinn, Monica Miller, and Christopher Driscoll. Over the past decade, these prolific scholars have invited me to contribute to edited volumes and participate on conference panels dealing with the complex relationships between hip hop and religion. Without these spaces to develop my thoughts and reflections, this book would not be possible. I also want to recognize Sean McCloud and Candice Jenkins, who, in two different contexts, invited me to write about hip hop in the early stages of my career. Much respect.

I have been fortunate to learn from and with amazing people at various academic institutions. At Princeton University, I was fortunate to be advised by Eddie Glaude, Jeff Stout, and Cornel West in a subfield (religion, ethics, and politics) that enabled me to study religion, race, and critical theory together. I've benefited not only from my advisers but also from conversations with colleagues connected to REP—Andrea Sun Mee Jones, Stephen Bush, Fannie

Bialek, Kevin Wolfe, Clifton Granby, Terrence Wiley, Melvin Rogers, Elias Sacks, David Decosimo, and Molly Farneth.

When I started teaching at UNC Charlotte, my interests in religion and hip hop formed in conversation with colleagues and students. My ongoing conversations with Kent Brintnall on gender, sexuality, blackness, and Georges Bataille have been indispensable. My discussions with David Mozina on ritual and language have made me rethink my relationship to religious studies. I also want to shout out Julia Robinson Harmon, whose insights on Charles Long (and black religion more generally) were timely and prescient. In addition, I want to thank the graduate students who pushed me to think about the sacred and its relationship to cultural and political formations—Ilya Merlin, Carrie Jones, Julie Hawks, Shontea Smith, and Travis Jones.

Since I arrived at Duke in 2015, my discussions with colleagues, friends, and students around religious thought, black religion, black studies, and critical theory have pushed me into unexpected directions. I want to thank my colleagues in religious studies, especially Mel Peters, David Morgan, Leela Prasad, Valerie Cooper, and Mona Hassan. I am also deeply indebted to interactions with colleagues in the African and African American Studies and English departments, most notably Karla FC Holloway, Mark Anthony Neal, Jasmine Cobb, Tsitsi Jaji, Jarvis McInnis, Anne-Maria Makhulu, Michaeline Crichlow, Khwezi Mkhize, 9th Wonder/Patrick Douthit, and Wahneema Lubiano. In addition, I want to send my gratitude to Jennifer Nash, Nikki Lane, Deonte Harris, Henry Pickford, Patrice Douglass, Priscilla Wald, and Ranji Khanna. I also want to acknowledge the tireless work of Marissa Lane, Holly Rich, Wilhelmina Green, and Carol Rush. Thank you for all that you do.

I have been fortunate to work with exceptional graduate and undergraduate students while working on this project. While there are too many to name, I want to single out those who served as teaching assistants and coinstructors for my hip hop courses. Many thanks to Nick Wagner, Scott Muir, Grazina Bielousova, Krishni Metivier, Marvin Wickware, Tyler Bunzey, Mickey D'Addario, Christopher Newman, and Rukimani PV.

It has been a pleasure to become colleagues with my former professors and mentors at Duke (many of whom are no longer at the institution but continue to serve as model scholars, teachers, and persons). Much respect to Bill Hart, J. Kameron Carter, Leela Prasad, Willie Jennings, Wahneema Lubiano, and Amy Laura Hall.

And then there are the people in my life who have been friends and conversation partners over the years (some of whom I wish I could talk to and learn from more often): Ken Walden, Terrence Johnson, Diane Stewart, Jamil Drake,

Corey Walker, Antonia Randolph, Sarah Cervenak, Jon Gill, Sasha Panaram, I. Augustus Durham, Amanda Bennett, Luke Powery, Courtney Bryant, Lisa Yebuah, Karen Rucks-Walker, Michael Fisher, Brandon McCormick, Daniel Barber, Patrick Smith, Xavier Pickett, Youssef Carter, and Angie Hong. Thanks for everything.

Since my last book, I have been able to share my work on hip hop, blackness, and the sacred at various venues. In the fall of 2016, Gail Hamner graciously invited me to Syracuse University to discuss the figure of the monster in hip hop. I received very helpful comments, especially from Megan Ewing and Meina Yates-Richard. In the spring of 2017, Anthony Pinn invited me to Rice University to discuss my work on hip hop and the sacred. The following year, Jeremy Schott and the religious studies graduate students at Indiana University read and critically engaged an early version of the introduction to the book. In the fall of 2020, Jessica Boon invited me to give the McLester lecture at UNC Chapel Hill, where I developed my reflections on these topics. And in the spring of 2021, Harvey Stark facilitated a virtual conversation between me and Vaughn Booker, a discussion that included connections between jazz, hip hop, and the religious. Ahmad Green-Hayes invited me to the Black Religion and Critical Theory Colloquium at Harvard Divinity School in the fall of 2023 to talk about connections between blackness and the unruly sacred. And in the spring of 2024, Ashon Crawley and Michelle Bostic graciously asked me to participate in the Blackness Beyond Protestantism Conference at the University of Virginia, which permitted me to speak about W. E. B. Du Bois's notion of sorrow as a precursor to recurring themes and sounds within hip hop and rap music. These opportunities have been pivotal to sharpening my arguments and ideas.

The chapters in this book sample and elaborate on articles that have been published in other places. Chapter one contains material from "Contemporary Sorrow Songs: Traces of Mourning, Lament, and Vulnerability in Hip Hop," *African-American Review* 46, no. 1 (Spring 2013): 9–20. Chapter two includes a fragment from "Constructing Constellations: Frankfurt School, Lupe Fiasco, and the Promise of Weak Redemption," in *Religion in Hip Hop: Mapping the New Terrain in the US*, edited by Monica R. Miller, Anthony B. Pinn, and Bernard "Bun B" Freeman (New York: Bloomsbury Academic, 2015). And chapter three includes part of the article "The Horrifying Sacred: Hip Hop, Blackness, and the Figure of the Monster," *Journal of Africana Religions* 5, no. 2 (2017): 291–99.

In 2019, I organized an American Academy of Religion panel on Georges Bataille and blackness that included Amy Hollywood, Danube Johnson, Jeremy Biles, Kent Brintnall, and J. Kameron Carter. While COVID-19 interrupted our plans to develop this Bataille and blackness project beyond AAR, I am grateful for this evanescent moment.

During the early stage of the pandemic, I participated in a series of virtual gatherings organized by Kathryn Lum and Vincent Lloyd which included scholars interested in crossing the line and refusing the binary between history and theory. I learned a great deal from these conversations.

I also want to shout out those of us on the steering committee for a Henry Luce Foundation grant that focused on religion as the unthought dimension of black studies. Much respect to Josef Sorett, Tiffany Hale, Monique Bedasse, Alex Alston, and the scholars who participated in the virtual discussions and the culminating conference. In many ways, I hope that hip hop can become one way to make the religious, or a certain genre and subset of the religious, within black studies more explicit and provocative.

My family extends their support and love to me in ways that I can barely describe. To my cousins, aunts, uncles, and extended family, your love helps me get through the world's anguish. To the Winterses, Smiths, Karims, Legettes, Bakers, Reeses, and Freemans, thank you for accepting me in all of my idiosyncracies. To my father-in-law, Willie Legette, thank you for the talks, for the debates, and for challenging me on my theoretical assumptions. More important, I appreciate the laughter during trying times. To my mother-in-law, Alice Baker, I always appreciate your humor, care, and commitment to helping others. Thank you for everything.

To my sister, Mareisha (and Byron), I hope that you find something in this book that makes sense to you. I love you both very much and appreciate the times we can connect, share time, and talk about music, culture, and politics.

Mom, it is impossible to put into words how much I am indebted to you and your generous spirit. I have learned so much from you as a thinker, writer, speaker, justice advocate, and human being. Your encouragement and love (especially when I lack confidence in myself) has been indispensable and life-giving. I am eternally grateful.

To my partner, Kamilah, I am less than a void without you in my life. While writing this book, we have had many (geographical) shifts and changes in our relationship. I will never forget those moments in the fall of 2022 while I was on sabbatical in Denver. You listened to me ramble about chapters in the book, lament yet another deceased rapper, or debate whether I should even finish this project. I have not always been good at balancing care for you with fulfilling academic responsibilities. Thank you for your patience, understanding, and ability to forgive. This book is dedicated to you.

Introduction

Specters and Evanescent Intimacies

When I lived in Charlotte, North Carolina, my friends and I would regularly attend a hip hop club called Republic, a name that invokes community, shared power, and a sense of equality. The latter attribute is complicated in light of the ways that some people clamor to reach the VIP section, to be *set apart* from and above the ordinary masses. On Wednesday nights, the DJ would play a blend of hip hop classics and contemporary rap music—songs by A Tribe Called Quest, Lil' Kim, and DMX to more recent tracks by Nicki Minaj, Future, and Kendrick Lamar—for an assembly of predominately black congregants. Over time, my friends and I made these Wednesday nights a kind of ritual, one in which the combination of song, dance, spectatorship, erotic desire, nostalgia, and alcohol consumption occasioned moments of ecstasy, glimmers of transcendence, where we felt beside and outside ourselves. If ecstasy names a transition from the inside to the outside, then perhaps sweat is one physical mark of this exteriority, of an excess that cannot be contained within the walls of the body. OutKast member André 3000 suggests this dynamic when he alludes to the DJ as one who "sweats out all the problems and troubles of the day."[1] We might think of the body's excretion of sweat as a substitute for tears since, as André 3000 suggests, the DJ's selection of songs enables trouble, concern, and pain to be released. But this release is more like a reexpression of anguish, a reexpression through dance, pageantry, flamboyance, and the collective reciting of music lyrics. There is something about music that prompts the externalization of trouble, even if that trouble is disguised, rearticulated, and embodied in a manner that we must strain to notice. In other words, even if the pleasure in hearing a favorite song or the enjoyment of seeing and being seen by others can give club participants a fleeting sense of release or escape, one can detect the problems that club attendees desire to "sweat out." One notices pain in a glance, a brooding scowl, the intensity of the body's dancing motions, or the efforts to be hypervisible in a social world that relegates certain people to the fringes of human recognition. Moreover, the fraught energy generated and experienced in a club like Republic can take a belligerent turn when the intimacy associated with dance and greeting another becomes a physical collision, an invasion of personal space, or an undesired sexual advance. Consequently, the DJ presides over a terrain, a dance floor, that exists somewhere between worry and enjoyment, violence and pleasure, alienation and connectedness to others.

This interplay between agony and excitement in a hip hop setting like Republic resembles James Baldwin's description of black church worship practices in *The Fire Next Time*. While celebrating the uncanny power and liberation associated with church music, even after being estranged from the institutional church, Baldwin writes, "The church was very exciting . . . on the blindest, most visceral level. There is no music like that music, no drama like the drama of the saints rejoicing, the sinners moaning . . . and all the voices coming together crying holy unto the Lord. . . . Their pain and joy were mine and mine were theirs. . . . [We] all became equal, wringing wet, singing and dancing, in anguish and rejoicing at the foot of the altar."[2] For Baldwin, this black church assembly is organized by a set of tension-filled relationships—sinner and saint, rejoicing and moaning, crying and dancing, possession and dispossession (mine and theirs). During these gatherings, there is an excitement that reverberates through anguish. It is a space where equality, or intimacy, happens momentarily at the intersection of the laugh and the cry, as bodies tremble, dance, and sweat, before God and in response to the shared condition of mortality. As Baldwin's description suggests, this is not a pure domain; in fact, Baldwin speaks about the black church as an institution that contains pernicious hierarchies and other "monstrous things."[3] More specifically, Baldwin connects Christianity's redemptive logic, its evangelical onus vis-à-vis the pagan, to the formation of racial hierarchies and the yearning for purity that undergirds whiteness, coloniality and its afterlife, American innocence, and general aversions to the erotic (and those bodies unduly associated with the erotic). For Baldwin, there is a violent side of Christianity and perhaps religion more generally. One cannot easily disentangle the anguished liberation experienced in a Pentecostal service from this troubling legacy (especially since the former both contests and participates in the latter).[4] By broaching Baldwin's description of black church worship, my intention is not to ignore the differences between a church and a hip hop club. I simply want to highlight, and anticipate, continuities and affinities regarding affective experience and the haunting presence of violence in a manner that forecloses any stable demarcation between the sacred and the profane.[5]

On one particular Wednesday, the strange religious quality internal to hip hop gatherings became especially palpable. At some point during the night, the DJ announced that one person in the crowd, a black male who looked to be in his early to mid-fifties, had just been released from a twenty-year prison sentence. As part of the celebration of his "coming home," he requested to hear 2Pac's classic song "Dear Mama." As I witnessed him walk from the DJ booth to the crowd, I saw people—some of his friends and family perhaps, but mostly strangers—walk up to him and give him a hug or a handshake while we collectively rehearsed the lyrics to Tupac Shakur's song. I could not help but notice the analogy here between the practice of welcoming a visitor or a new member to a church service and the crowd's embrace of this black male just returning to social life. As I looked around and joined in the celebration, I was pleasantly surprised at how many people were visibly moved, touched, and impressed by his presence, a response that was intensified by the enrapturing quality of "Dear Mama." At a moment when many hip hop club participants expected to hear songs with catchy lyrics and beats that incite a "turning up," hearing Tupac's tribute and letter to his mother was a kind of detour. The slowness of the beat, the decelerated tempo, the gentleness of the vocals, and the combination of yearning, gratitude, and pain in this track occasioned a slightly different set of corporal movements, facial expressions, and interactions among the club participants. One noticed an atmosphere of what Kevin Quashie calls "quiet" in his study of black culture and literature. As Quashie points out, quiet is not necessarily silence or stillness; rather, it signifies those desires, emotions, and vulnerabilities associated with intimacy and interiority.[6] For Quashie, the notion of quiet speaks to the introspective qualities of black life and refuses tendencies to exclusively associate blackness with public expressiveness. Since we do not have to accept a simple binary relationship between quiet and expressiveness, we might say that Tupac's "Dear Mama" induced displays of vulnerability and reflection in addition to joy, care, and affection. While I can only speculate about what others were contemplating, my thoughts were dispersed and included things like the state surveillance and containment of blackness (what Tupac called being "trapped"),[7] the difficult position of black motherhood, and the magnetic power and grip that music has on our flesh.

It makes sense that Tupac's voice and music facilitated this homecoming and welcoming-back moment. In his afterlife, Tupac has become somewhat of a sacred figure in hip hop culture.[8] In addition to holographic technologies

that enable Tupac performances three decades after his murder,[9] a predicament that contributes to the fantasy of his immortality, the late rapper continues to be one of the most cited and venerated by contemporary artists and
fans. This veneration is exemplified in Meek Mill and Rick Ross's 2011 song
"Tupac Back." On this track, Mill and Ross do not simply assemble a collection
of quotes and passages from Tupac's corpus; they also show how music conjures, reincarnates, and inhabits the boundary between life and death. Tupac
returns, or remains alive, through remembrance, mourning, mimesis, and
homage.[10] His afterlife is also made possible by hip hop's ongoing investment
in authenticity, a kind of self-grounding realness that betrays itself by solicit-
ing recognition and certification from others. Artists and participants often
secure a kind of authority within hip hop culture by citing Tupac or claiming
to be the sole inheritor of his legacy. According to Michael Eric Dyson, part of
Tupac's allure derives from his capacity to embody and take on the paradoxes
and contradictions of black life, the United States, and late modern existence:
"Tupac is perhaps the representative figure of his generation. In his haunting
voice can be heard the buoyant hopefulness and desperate hopelessness that
mark the outer perimeters of the hip hop culture he eagerly embraced."[11] For
Dyson, Tupac has become iconic not only because he referred to the blackness
of Jesus or because he encouraged black women to remain resilient in the face
of poverty and disregard. His iconic status also derives from his strong identification with, and occasional glorification of, practices and behaviors associated with the thug and outlaw, the figure who does not simply transgress the
law but exposes the violent quality of the legal order. Here one is reminded of
Walter Benjamin's claim that the figure of the criminal, "however repellent
his ends . . . has aroused the secret admiration of the public . . . not from his
deed but from the violence to which it bears witness."[12] Along this line, while
Tupac's music urges positive change and transformation, he also prompts listeners to linger in, and be cut by, painful stories and hyperbolic expressions
of violence—hyperbole that ingests, rearticulates, and amplifies the systemic
violence endured by "undesirable" black masculine subjects. Similarly, Tupac's
musical corpus blends aggressive rhetoric with moments of quiet and vulnerability; claims to being invincible and triumphant are contravened by a gentler
contemplation of suffering, loss, intimacy, and tears. While it is tempting, and
understandable, to separate and minimize the more troublesome aspects of
Tupac's music and life ("I live thug life, baby, I'm hopeless"[13]), Dyson suggests
that the late rapper's iconicity derives from the split character of his persona
and legacy. Consequently, there might be something about Tupac's incoherence and tornness that shifts how we think about religiosity and the sacred.

For James Perkinson, these qualities in Tupac resemble those of West African orishas and trickster figures such as Ogou Acade that tend to encompass both good and evil, beauty and terror, in a manner that refuses clear distinctions among these attributes.[14]

Tupac's noncoherence can be heard in the treatment and depiction of women in his music and life.[15] As Dyson points out, "Although Tupac remained steadfast in his love of women, a troubling sexism seized his microphone and throbbed in hateful lyrics."[16] For Dyson, these hateful lyrics betray "femiphobia," or fear and hatred of women, that according to him is pervasive in hip hop and the broader social world. Among other things, this phobia is directed toward the female body as an imagined site and source of a perilous excess that needs to be contained and surveilled in accordance with masculinist fantasies of dominance and order.[17] One strategy of containment is the proverbial Madonna/whore binary—women are cast as innocent and pure or promiscuous and dangerous—which has been rearticulated in hip hop and black culture as the distinction between queens and bitches (a distinction that an artist like Lil' Kim, the Queen Bee, complicates). According to the latter opposition, black women are either adored as nurturing mothers and faithful companions or scapegoated as the source of black people's troubles, including the errant habits of children.[18] In this schema, the complexities of black feminine desire and experience are obscured along with the conditions that enable and constrain black motherhood—including entrenched heteropatriarchal assumptions that a (black) woman's life is fulfilled through children. In "Dear Mama," one hears traces of the queen/bitch binary even as Tupac simultaneously troubles it. When he croons that his mother was a queen even though she was a crack addict, a complicated juxtaposition occurs. While the queen and the addict couldn't seem more incompatible, both positions are set apart from the ordinary and mundane.[19] The queen stands apart in her elevation above the normal, while the addict is typically viewed as below/beneath the ordinary order of things. Therefore, both figures represent a kind of excess or outside with respect to this order, even if they evoke different affective responses and dispositions. In the juxtaposition of queen and addict, we might read the former position as redeeming the repugnance and opprobrium associated with the latter. At the same time, we can eschew a redemptive logic and think about what it means to painfully contemplate the "and" between royalty and crack addiction, sovereignty and abjection. As Tupac struggles to affirm this conjunction, to embrace his mother, I am mindful of Hortense Spillers's insistence that the claims and rights attributed to motherhood have traditionally been withheld from black women. And as Tupac expresses a vexed relationship to his mother (both estrangement and intimacy) and black women more generally, "Dear Mama" confirms Spillers's claim that "the African-American male has been touched . . . by the mother, handed by her in ways that he cannot escape."[20]

And yet this touch, this hand(ling), is fraught in a genre where prevailing performances of black masculinity rely on endeavors to escape the "feminine within," even as masculine power within hip hop is regularly visualized as possession and containment of women. This sense of being the recipient of the touch is complicated by the fact that black masculine vulnerability to various forms of exploitation and violence can be simultaneously exposed and deflected within this genre, a deflection that redirects violation and injury for the sake of appearing like an untouchable and invincible subject. Or to put it differently, black (cishet) masculine precarity is often dealt with or handled by assuming modes of verbal, symbolic, and physical control over other black men, black women, femininity, the queer, the sissy, and those who have been positioned to bear the burden of death, lack, and permeability. The vulnerability involved in touching and being touched can easily slide into a desire to possess and handle (for artists as well as listeners and spectators invested in maintaining a certain legacy). For some Tupac fans, this desire for self-possession, which involves remembering, identifying with, and lauding Tupac in an unequivocal manner, requires them to keep silent about elements of his life that jeopardize habits of veneration—including Ayanna Jackson's confessions that the late artist facilitated her collective rape and assault. How does the veneration of Tupac implicitly rely on the demonization and silencing of the assaulted black female? What forms of unrecognized sacrifice and erasure enable an instantiation of black masculinity to be elevated to the status of saint, martyr, and prophet?

Republic, the place that occasioned these reflections on Tupac, blackness, motherhood, gender, imprisonment, and the sacred, is no longer there; it has been replaced by a series of establishments that cater to different kinds of audiences and crowds. This replacement is part of a broader set of maneuvers and strategies in Charlotte and other US cities to change the look and appearance of downtown topographies, a conversion that precipitates the removal and displacement of black people and their gathering spaces. (To be sure, the ephemeral presence of Republic and my inhabitation of various spaces in downtown Charlotte was itself derivative of previous iterations of displacing working-class black communities in the process of securing the interests of capital.) While I cannot get into the complexities of gentrification, I simply underscore how this process often entails the language of revitalization. To revitalize is to renew, to bring life and value, or to resuscitate some object that is perceived as defunct, unproductive, dying, et cetera. This rhetoric conjures a legacy of justifying the dislocation of "darker peoples" and the appropriation of indigenous land in the name of redemption, generosity, and new life, a legacy that demonstrates the relationship between religion, race, capital, and settler colonial paradigms. (Here one might think of how the very name Tupac, which derives from the eighteenth-century indigenous figure Túpac Amaru, who organized a rebellion against Spanish colonial rule, inscribes this history of colonial terror.) Similarly, the process of gentrification and the grammar of revitalization show how race and class inform the imagination of social landscapes, how antiblackness and the schemes of capital contribute to the organization of space in terms of life and death, safety and danger, being and nonbeing, or sacred and profane.[21]

The Disturbing Profane is my endeavor to make sense of the kinds of friction-filled thoughts, desires, and affects that the world of hip hop elicits. More specifically, *The Disturbing Profane* is my attempt to flesh out how and why I encounter, and experience, the sacred within hip hop culture, often more intensely than in a church service or a gospel song. This study is my elaboration on the fact that my nights at Republic became analogous to Charles Mingus's Wednesday night prayer meeting. The sacred I have in mind does not connote purity, protection, wholeness, and security; rather, it involves interruption, diremption, exorbitance, and contamination—even as we cannot eliminate yearnings for the more comforting qualities associated with religion and the sacred. In this book, I examine the volatile dimensions of hip hop's sonic and visual components, its fascination with death, violence, anguish, and redemption as well as enjoyment, laughter, and extravagance, contending that within these qualities lies hip hop's strange religiosity. Even, or especially, at its most monstrous and horrifying, hip hop registers and makes audible a general complicity and involvement in pernicious predicaments and arrangements that subjects, for the sake of intelligibility, deny or yearn to be separate from. Despite various forms of containment and through its increasing popularity, hip hop *remains* a disturbing presence in part because it compels us to hear, see, and contemplate the (antiblack and black gendered) violence that structures the world.[22] Consequently, this investigation engages hip hop at the intersection of black studies and religious thought.[23]

Call and Response

This book participates in the rich, generative discussions around hip hop and religion that have emerged in the last three decades. In opposition to those who initially dismissed hip hop culture and rap music as nihilistic and empty,[24] a collection of authors draw attention to the complexities (limitations, possibilities, and contradictions) within these practices regarding social critique, the creative articulation of frustration and pleasure in the face of power and domination, the poetics of rap and rhyming, the relationship between authenticity and commodification, and the reinterpretation of black religiosity. As one of the early proponents of this complexity, Michael Eric Dyson has been steadfast in challenging hip hop's detractors, exemplified in his response to politicians and religious leaders in the 1990s who demanded the censorship of gangsta rap, a genre that included Tupac.[25] In *Between God and Gangsta Rap*, Dyson expresses sympathy with critics, like C Dolores Tucker and Bob Dole, who voiced concerns about the "misogyny, violence, materialism, and sexual transgression" within the more obscene forms of rap music. There is much in gangsta rap's cruel treatment of women and attraction to "gratuitous violence" that Dyson finds alarming. Yet unlike these critics, Dyson also hears in this genre "the complex dimensions of ghetto life ignored by many Americans . . . [and] the pains and possibilities, the fantasies and fears of poor black urban youth."[26] Furthermore, Dyson refuses the assumption, often betrayed in the notion that gangsta rap undermines American values, that American values are pristine and benign. As Dyson suggests, violence and theft have been internal to the idea, and actualization, of America as a perpetually expansive frontier. In addition, as he points out, many of America's religious institutions, including the black church, are breeding grounds for misogyny and sexism. According to Tamura Lomax, "The discourse on black womanhood [as Jezebelian, dangerous, and the opposite of proper womanhood] circulating between religion and culture was reappropriated and reproduced by the Black Church *and* black popular culture."[27] For Lomax, black church and popular culture are two sides of the same coin regarding the production of pernicious images of black women and girls. Consequently, one must interrogate instances when religious leaders like the late Calvin Butts or T. D. Jakes excoriate rappers for pernicious attitudes and dispositions that have a long history in the black church and Christian discursive practices more broadly. Consequently, if gangsta rap contains horrifying features, this is because it tends to mimic, reexpress, and magnify the monstrous qualities and contours of the wider, structuring world that people are trained to diminish, explain away, and deflect elsewhere. Gangsta rap is a distorted mirror of the broader national body and world, a world that, according to Tupac, "eats its babies."[28]

By highlighting the sexism in even the most venerable black church legacies, such as the civil rights movement, one can begin to disassemble the kinds of inflexible distinctions imagined between the church and world, or religion and culture. This not only allows an author like Dyson to underscore the violence that is internal to the religious (and not merely attributable to profane activities), but also prompts him to identify religious desire and practice in domains, like hip hop, that are often associated with the secular and ostensibly nonreligious. Consistent with Dyson's concerns, Ebony Utley shows how gangsta rap is replete with religious sensibilities and commitments even when artists forgo institutional affiliations. Within rap music and hip hop culture, artists regularly exhibit various forms of piety, such as praying on a song or at a concert, acknowledging god at an awards show, or engaging in imaginary conversations with the devil. In addition, as Utley indicates, album covers and videos contain religious iconography, exemplified by the image of a black Jesus riding in the backseat of a car on the Clipse's *Lord Willin'* cover or the related image of a black Jesus, with a red bandana concealing his face, on the cover of The Game's *Jesus Piece*.[29] At other moments, especially in rap music influenced by the Nation of Gods and Earths, rappers actually collapse the distinction between god and human, affirming the divine quality of blackness.[30] In Utley's reading of these kinds of examples, religion functions for gangsta rappers as a "quest for meaning and power"[31] in the face of antiblackness and socioeconomic disparity. As she points out, occasionally god is invoked to make sense of oppressive conditions and experiences, while at other times, god is used to "empower [rappers] to be respectable murderers, misogynists, and agents of mayhem in the hyperbolic rap worlds of their lyrics and videos."[32] In other words, identifying with god and channeling divine power might enable a form of destructive agency, but this agency usually involves "re-establishing hierarchies" and securing authority and control over others, especially women. Echoing Dyson, Utley suggests that if religion and god-talk operate ambivalently in hip hop, then this ambivalence is also internal to the traditions that have formed rap artists and that these artists draw from and reimagine.[33]

Utley provides resources to think about rap and religion as unstrange bedfellows, as interconnected in ways that undercut ordinary demarcations between these categories. Yet Utley's understanding of religion remains somewhat underdeveloped. While she underscores how rap artists invoke and identify with god to "fulfill requests for meaning, power, and respect," it is not clear if the expedient use of divine figures and images primarily makes rap religious, or if the search for meaning, authority, and recognition has its own, stand-alone religious quality. In addition, if rappers seek and identify with divine figures in response to "senseless death" and "mayhem," we might want to push further than Utley does on the relationship between meaning and nonsense or control and disorder. Anthony Pinn indirectly speaks to these lingering concerns in his writings on hip hop and religion. Even though Pinn acknowledges the influence of theistic traditions within rap music, particularly Islam, Christianity, and Rastafarianism, his definition of religion extends beyond particular religions or belief in gods and supernatural beings. According to Pinn, "religion's basic structure, embedded in history, is a general quest for complex subjectivity in the face of the terror and dread associated with life within a historical context marked by dehumanization, objectification, abuse, intolerance, and captured most forcefully in the sign/symbol of the 'ghetto.'"[34] With this definition, Pinn is able to hear in artists like Tupac or Scarface a kind of spirituality defined not by fidelity to a god but by the self's confrontation with terror and absurdity. For Pinn, religion names a perpetual transformation from a dehumanized object to a creative subject and a concomitant "struggle to obtain meaning through a process of becoming."[35] Even though this struggle to find meaning and identity amid systemic violence and injury may include interactions with gods, Pinn contends that humans are ultimately responsible for making something out of nothing, for changing and transforming their circumstances. By reading hip hop through terror, dread, human agency, and the search for meaning, Pinn connects hip hop to antecedent musical traditions, like the spirituals and the blues, that have enabled black people to make sense of senseless conditions, to creatively respond to antiblackness, colonial terror, and slavery and its afterlife.[36] In chapter 1, I also look at the connections between the spirituals and hip hop through the trope of sorrow, especially as this motif is articulated by W. E. B. Du Bois in his tribute to the "rhythmic cries" of the slave.

Like Utley, Pinn focuses on religion as a meaning-making mechanism in the face of senseless violence, even as he provides a more determinate description of what makes rap religious. At the same time, Utley seems more attuned to the dangers and harms of this search for identity and agency, insofar as the empowerment of self and effacement of the (female) other are frequently intertwined in her diagnosis of rap music. (This is a result of power being modeled after the sovereign agent, the subject defined by its ability to control, possess, and impose form on signifiers of the chaotic.) However, the insistence on religion as a meaning-making structure has its limitations.[37] This way of thinking about religion often privileges the self's various strivings and experiences instead of the social conditions that enable and limit these strivings. Similarly, the religion-meaning nexus is connected to an enduring assumption that religion is a universal human quality, which diminishes the ways religious meanings and definitions are historically formed, altered, and authorized within discourses and power relationships. Monica Miller exposes the difficulties in this universalist definition of religion, especially as it pertains to Pinn's earlier work. According to Miller, Pinn's writings on rap and religion reflect a tendency to imagine religion as a perennial phenomenon, expressed primarily in the form of belief and internal striving.[38] Among other problems, this position does not "consider religion as something constructed in and by practices for various interests."[39] By shifting the emphasis from striving, belief, and meaning to practice and power, Miller directs attention to underanalyzed aspects of hip hop's religiosity. Instead of prioritizing the meaning behind lyrics and sonic texts, Miller examines how religious language and imagery authorize certain claims to authenticity, exemplified in KRS-One's *The Gospel of Hip Hop*, or how religion functions as a survival strategy, demonstrated powerfully in RZA's *The Tao of Wu*.[40] For Miller, religion in these examples is not so much a search for meaning but rather an "effect, strategy, and manufacturing of social, cultural, and political interests."[41] The point is not that authors like Pinn or Utley deny how religion functions as a strategy in hip hop. Rather, the point is to shift emphasis away from the quest for meaning, toward other kinds of effects and maneuvers that religious language and ideas enable. Instead of asking what religion *means*, we should be looking at what religion *does*, including, but not limited to, the fabrication of meaning.[42]

From Miller's vantage point, the religion as meaning framework dovetails with prevailing assumptions and fantasies that designate religion as the ultimate source of protecting or rescuing people from the threat of nihilism. Miller identifies in the quest for meaning and identity, even a complex identity, a sanitizing strategy, a desire to regulate youth deviance and resolve social contradictions in a manner that leaves regimes of normalization and propriety intact. This is where and when I enter. *The Disturbing Profane* seizes, and runs with, an insight that reverberates throughout these hip hop / religion conversations and that Miller underscores. For many of these authors, there is much in hip hop that burdens stable distinctions between religion and culture and the sacred and the profane. More important, through this agitation, ideas, figures, personas, and objects of desire, often imagined as pristine and unscathed by life's unsettling features, become susceptible to a wounding. As Imani Perry describes it, hip hop resists conventional divisions between the sacred and the profane, or cleanliness and funk, a separation made popular within civil rights legacies and black respectability politics. In fact, "in the world of hip hop, holy and well-behaved gestures sit next to the rough and funky."[43] Consequently, lines of demarcation that separate the divine from dirt, or the holy from a kind of wildness, are perpetually transgressed, crossed, and redrawn and reestablished within hip hop. This trespass happens, for instance, on André

3000's OutKast track "God," as the rapper talks vividly about oral sex during his prayer in a manner that violates the conventional separation between piety and erotic desire.[44] One may experience this trespass while looking at the album cover for Remy Ma's *Shesus Khryst* mixtape, as we see black female flesh on a cross, imitating the execution of Jesus, an emulation that accentuates Remy Ma's voluptuous body. For some, especially within a Western Protestant culture, the very association of blackness and the feminine with the divine is a sort of tear in the prevailing image of god as white and masculine.[45] As my study extends this insistence on hip hop's unsettling presence, I contend that more attention to the complexity and ambivalence internal to the category of the sacred helps illumine this haunting quality. In the same way that Miller criticizes hip hop scholars for taking the availability and meaning of religion for granted, I maintain that we tend to assume that the signifier "sacred" is relatively clear and stable. The sacred-profane distinction, for instance, is often conflated with the religious-secular contrast, a misleading analogy since secular entities and arrangements, like the nation-state, hold certain figures, objects, and spaces as sacred and sovereign.[46] In what follows, I take seriously the volatility internal to the sacred, namely its capacity to stand in for yearnings for purity and safety and, alternatively, its power to indicate trespass, disorder, and opacity.

The Volatile Sacred

The language of the sacred-profane is complicated and multivalent, and requires renewed study and examination. As there are many ways to define and conceive of the sacred, this study draws attention to emphases and ambiguities within the grammar of the sacred and profane that are pertinent to hip hop, blackness, and related matters. Within religious studies, for instance, the relationship between sacred and profane spaces and objects has been elaborated on by many authors, most notably Mircea Eliade and Émile Durkheim. Even though their respective accounts of religion contain salient limitations and problems, I revisit their ideas to highlight a set of tensions, or unstable qualities, within the category of the sacred. I am particularly interested in how both authors gesture toward the interruptive dimension of the sacred, only to diminish this feature for the sake of coherence and solidity.[47]

In Eliade's account of these matters, he contends that religious people treat and experience sacred space as fundamentally different from profane space. Whereas the former is "strong and significant," the latter is experienced as "without structure or consistency, amorphous."[48] The break between "real and really existing space and all other space, the formless expanse surrounding it,"[49] is made possible, according to Eliade, by a hierophany, or the manifestation of the divine. This manifestation of the sacred creates a world, a home for religious subjects. It provides a well-defined, meaningful foundation, a fixed center, amid chaos and undifferentiated space. Although Eliade seems to imagine a qualitative difference between the sacred (as structure, form, foundation) and the profane (as lack, chaos, formlessness), he does claim that even secular, nonreligious people treat certain spaces or times as if they were sacred—birthplaces, holidays, first romantic experiences. These stand apart as a break from the ordinary, as places and events that give meaning to mundane, everyday activities that would otherwise lack any sense of form or structure. Furthermore, Eliade describes how "thresholds" like a door to a temple or a religious rite of passage indicate some kind of communication between the gods and earthly beings, or a passage from the profane to the sacred domain. A threshold signifies a place where the difference between two entities is both accentuated and elided. The sacred-profane boundary is perhaps more fluid, on Eliade's own terms, than he initially describes.[50]

The manifestation of the sacred, according to Eliade, is first and foremost an interruption into the ordinary, a "revelation of a reality *other* than that which [man] participates through his ordinary life."[51] This interruption is epitomized by the divine creation of the world, an original event that is reenacted by religious communities through ritual and myth. There is a tension in Eliade between the sacred as a kind of alterity with respect to mundane life and the sacred as world foundation.[52] On the one hand, Eliade riffs on Rudolf Otto's notion of the divine as mysterious, terrifying, and alluring.[53] On this reading, the sacred has an unmanageable quality about it, insofar as it both attracts and repels, simultaneously evokes awe and terror. There is something about sacredness that is initially overwhelming and impossible to grasp or pin down. On the other hand, this interruption of the Other, especially when it is identified as a center or foundation, quickly becomes a fixed source of meaning, order, and legibility in the world. Sacred spaces, objects, and rituals enable humans to overcome the chaos and nonsense associated with the profane world. As Eliade points out, this overcoming is demonstrated in religious/colonial projects that seize and occupy lands in the name of bringing life and structure, a process I mentioned above. As Eliade describes, "An unknown, foreign, and unoccupied territory (which often means unoccupied by 'our people') still shares in the fluid and larval modality of chaos. By occupying it, and above all, by settling in it, man symbolically transforms it into a cosmos."[54] This contrast between legible world and uncultivated, chaotic territory maps onto the distinction between civilization and "the chaos, the disorder, the darkness that will threaten our world."[55] While it is not clear whether Eliade endorses the violence that these distinctions work to justify and deny—especially with regard to blackness—it is clear that the sacred for him is ultimately defined over and against that which is fluid, unstable, larval, volatile, and opaque. In fact, humans imitate the gods by creating legible worlds, a creation that requires eliminating figurative "monsters" and other "dark forces" that imperil form, structure, and order. This need to overcome disorder and tumult is animated by a will to purity, or what Eliade calls religious nostalgia. This is a desire to "inhabit a divine world," a yearning to "live in a pure and holy cosmos, as it was in the beginning, when it came fresh from the Creator's hands."[56] The sacred, under this nostalgic description, is associated with purity, origins, and untainted power. These motifs are familiar in the world of hip hop, where some participants associate authentic and bona fide hip hop with its roots in New York City, a place that is considered sacrosanct within cultural imaginaries. In chapter 1, I discuss how Nas's infamous "Hip Hop Is Dead" announcement can be read as a nostalgic attachment to hip hop before it became corrupted, and taken over, by corporate interests. I also show how Nas's mournful claim can be read against the grain of uncontaminated yearnings and heard as a way of refusing the very notion of purity.

Not unlike Eliade, Durkheim (who influenced the former) also develops a conception of religion that contains a moment of disturbance, even though this moment becomes subordinate to religion's unifying function. For the French sociologist, religion does not necessarily involve gods or supernatural beings.[57] And even when these beings are involved, they are not essential to religion. According to Durkheim, religion refers to the ways communities are formed by beliefs and practices that pertain to sacred things, or things set apart by taboos and prohibitions.[58] Religion, he claims, is "an eminently collective thing";[59] in fact, the very distinction between sacred and profane does not derive from divine revelation, but from the social world. Religion functions as a kind of social glue; it is a cohesive force. By conflating religion and the social world, Durkheim does not deny that religious adherents experience transcendence at a temple or during a holy ritual. It simply means that when these practitioners attribute this experience to a deity, they mistake the true source of exaltation—which is communion with others. As Durkheim puts it, "It is true with a truth that is eternal that there exists outside us something greater than we and with which we commune. . . . That power exists, and it is society."[60] Because Durkheim locates religious desire and emotion in social gatherings and communal rituals, he suggests some continuity between a Candomblé dance ritual and a hip hop club, or between a political rally and a church revival. Similarly, because society creates sacred objects, Durkheim identifies affinities between, for instance, a cross and a flag, insofar as these objects are "rallying points" for church communities and nation-states, respectively.

Like Eliade, Durkheim initially associates the sacred with the extraordinary, some interruption into the normal course of things. For Durkheim, a communal gathering like a festival or a concert marks a break with respect to profane time and space. Whereas profane experience refers to individuals engaging the world and performing tasks in a disconnected, humdrum manner, these communal gatherings are occasions for intimacy, connection, being taken outside oneself, et cetera. These sacred experiences are different from routine life at an affective level—connecting with others entails excitement, exaltation, stimulation, and a heightened sense of power and energy. The transcendence of profane life, through communion with others, is an electric experience. In fact, this effervescence (which for Durkheim is the source of religion) is described by the sociologist with terms like loss of self-control, chaotic movements, wild frenzy, and the feeling of being possessed by an outside force.[61] While this energy is initially tumultuous, Durkheim suggests that it must find a stable object, like a flag or a Tupac hologram, for the collective intimacy to endure. As Durkheim puts it, "Without symbols . . . social feelings could have only an unstable existence. . . . But if the movements by which these feelings have been expressed become inscribed on things that are durable, then they too become durable."[62] Because the energies and affects associated with the sacred are volatile, Durkheim indicates that they must be regulated and harnessed for the sake of stability and community. Consequently, once the flag is imagined as a reliable rallying point and source of cohesion, acts of dissent and protest during flag-related rituals—as in the case of Colin Kaepernick kneeling during the national anthem portion of football games in remembrance of black death—are denounced by some as horrifying, terrible, and dangerous.[63]

The play between rupture and stability within Durkheim's understanding of religious life is most noticeable in his distinction between two kinds of sacred realities. Alluding to the "ambiguity of the idea of the sacred," he distinguishes between religious forces associated with life, health, order, and protection, and those associated with impurity, disorder, and death.[64] In other words, if sacredness signifies that which is set apart, this separation includes those life-conferring phenomena that require protection and those objects and forces that represent danger and need to be cordoned off from social life. For Durkheim, the pristine sacred and dark sacred exist in a fluid relationship since, for instance, objects and energies associated with disorder can be incorporated into a ritual and become sources of security and protection. The cadaver is both holy and defiling; ancestors can protect people and harm them, especially when the living are not being properly reverent to the dead. In line with this ambivalence at the heart of sacredness, this book aims to think at the edge of these two forces, at the point where images and sounds of impurity and disorder undermine desires for coherence and protection, especially since these desires are the main source of acceptable forms of violence, and disorder, against communities that bear the onus of embodying death and contingency. This contrast between the secure and volatile senses of the sacred brings to mind Mary Douglas's well-known distinction between purity and dirt. Whereas the former alludes to unavoidable attachments to meaning and coherence (which involves clear concepts and rigid distinctions), the latter connotes matter out of place or that which cannot be captured by structure and form, even as the matter out of place gets incorporated into social practices and rituals.[65] The "quest for purity" and the attachment to the secure form of the sacred line up with Eliade's understanding of sacredness as fixed foundation and nostalgia for pristine origins; the volatile, dirt-bound sacred resembles the dark, unsettling qualities that Eliade defines religious life over and against. It should not be surprising that an array of hip hop artists, including Ol' Dirty Bastard, Goodie Mob, and Snootie Wild, identify with dirt,[66] a signifier for the formlessness from which we originate and an allusion to a history of marking black people as an enduring threat to what Nahum Chandler calls "projects of purity."[67]

Another author who is important for my project and who explicitly embraces the darker sacred is Georges Bataille.[68] As a critical reader of Durkheim, Bataille equates the profane with practices and habits of self-preservation and the sacred with experiences—mystical, erotic, and aesthetic—that cut against and unravel our sense of coherence and presence in the world. If the energy and excitement associated with religion in Durkheim's analysis must find a stable object, Bataille suggests that religious experience is located in the fleeting moment of being overwhelmed and losing a sense of self-possession. For Bataille, religion at its heart is "the search for lost intimacy,"[69] an intimacy that is blocked by the need to set limits and boundaries, but that is available through moments of transgression and the dissolution of form. Religion, according to this definition, is ecstatic and excessive; it transgresses boundaries and constraints, even as it recalibrates. The sacred involves rituals and practices that cut against the idea of an autonomous, separable self. In addition to filth, dirt, blood, tears, and laughter, all of which are markers of excess, the image of the monster is crucial for Bataille. Because of our everyday attachment to form and coherence, religious encounters for Bataille are experienced as monstrous, both horrifying and alluring. In chapter 3, I use Bataille's ideas, in conversation with black studies, to interrogate the figure of the monster in hip hop, especially as performed by artists like Kanye West and Nicki Minaj. Because of its monstrous features, religious experience for Bataille (and hip hop for my project) undermines a general and inescapable investment in transparency, an investment that is intertwined with all too human endeavors to grasp, control, and contain—particularly entities, desires, and encounters that appear volatile and out of line. For Bataille, the sacred encompasses forms of intimate contact and modes of contemplation that "imply a beclouded consciousness" or a drift toward the opaque.[70]

Perhaps what is most crucial in Bataille's thought is his attention to a paradox in the exposure to the exorbitant energies that circulate through phenomena. For Bataille, life consists of an "excess that cannot be absorbed in growth [or productivity]," and yet human subjects are condemned, to some extent, to converting that excess into something useful through production, the construction of meaning, and boundary-making.[71] Consequently, Bataille locates his ethical enterprise in projects (which involve intentions, goals, the desire for fulfillment) that interrupt the very logic of project, that shatter aspirations for fulfillment and coherence. These are projects—aesthetic, mystical, erotic—that expose participants to death, loss, and negation as well as the ecstatic (enjoyment, pleasure, and anguish) and self-dissolving exuberance. As Bataille puts it, in his description of inner experience, "But project is no longer in this case, that positive of salvation, but that negative of abolishing the power of words, hence of project."[72] On some level, this statement by Bataille does not seem to accord with the power and intensity of verbal expression within rap music, or the ways that words, images, and vocal intensities display modes of power and mastery. And yet there are other moments when the power of the word lies precisely in the break or breaking down of meaning, resonating with Bataille's claim that "the poetic is the familiar dissolving into the strange, and ourselves with it."[73] Similarly, there are moments when the musical *production* engenders layers, contradictions, and dissonance that undermine the notion of a coherent, unified product or sound. What is crucial here is that Bataille thinks about the sacred as a kind of profanation, in light of human impulses to preserve self and community at the expense of that which is deemed threatening and unproductive according to this will to coherence. At the same time, I remain mindful of how Bataille works within a tradition that prioritizes the European self that is assumed to have access to the fantasy of being whole and fulfillable. Black studies and the world of hip hop takes us into a domain of racialized and blackened subject-objects that have been positioned as the ex-orbitance, and lack, that the ideal Western subject defines itself against and through.

Opacity and the Rites of Black Noise

As suggested above, there is a curious relationship between the volatile sacred and the concomitant notions of opacity and blackness articulated in black studies.[74] This resonance is exemplified in the work of Charles Long, an author who informs Pinn's understanding of religion, and who explicitly brings together, and thinks at the intersection, of black studies and religious thought in a manner that contributes to an engagement with hip hop and rap music.[75] In conversation with Eliade, Long famously makes a distinction between modern theologies and modes of thought animated by a will to transparency and what he calls "opaque theologies." The former encompasses legacies of the Enlightenment and Euro-American Christianity that have justified violence and erasure of the world's darker peoples in the name of bestowing light, reason, democracy, et cetera. The latter, even as they replicate the imperial tendencies within Christian theology, entails an intervention by those darker subjects who have historically been positioned as indices of chaos in need of the imposition of law. On these matters, Long contends:

> Theologies are about power, the power of God, but equally about the power of specific forms of discourse about power. These discourses are about the hegemony of power—the distribution and economy of this power in heaven and on earth—whether in the ecclesiastical locus of a pope, or more generally since the modern period, the center of the power in the modern Western world. It is this kind of power which is attacked in the opaque theologies, for this power has justified and sanctified the oppression rendering vast numbers of persons and several cultures subject to economic-military oppression and transparent to the knowledge of the West.[76]

In this passage, Long maintains that modern colonial arrangements and orderings rearticulate theological ways of dividing the earth and configuring space—the heaven/earth hierarchy becomes the division between the Euro-American center and its dark periphery.[77] These kinds of divisions carry implications for how those on the periphery are positioned, studied, and subjected to military power. The containment of black and indigenous peoples requires a hermeneutic of transparency, a way of rendering the complexities and alterity of these cultures visible, clear, and governable. As Long suggests, the trope of the opaque does not simply valorize the practices and refusals of oppressed peoples; rather, the language of opacity troubles and inundates the kinds of clear, stable distinctions and binaries associated with yearnings for transparency. Within this alternative logic, for instance, the very distinction between transparency and darkness collapses. This unraveling happens as Long examines how Enlightenment legacies, animated by a will to legibility, harbor a dark, violent underside. Similarly, modern projects defined by *freedom* and *progress* rely on *enslavement* and *domination*; the *civilizing* burden emboldens and authorizes the West to treat its others with *barbaric* tactics. The types of distinctions made between the illuminating progress of civilization and the dark backwardness of the noncivilized (distinctions that are constantly revised and rearticulated) break down in the context of colonial terror and in the face of blackness. As I show in chapter 2, an artist like Lupe Fiasco indirectly expresses this opaque hermeneutic in his refusal of the America-terror binary or, to put it differently, in his analysis of the terror that accompanies the idea of America and its redemptive thrust.

For Long, the opaque communities that subsist on the underside of modernity are not simply figures of lack and deprivation. As he insists, "These bodies of opacity, these loci of meaninglessness . . . were paradoxically loci of a surplus of meaning."[78] In other words, we do not have to think of opacity as the absence or lack of something that is abundant at the center of modern life; the darker regions of the earth have produced "new rhythms," practices, and modes of becoming that contain their own fecundity and complexity. And for Long, these practices and forms of resignification (in response to colonial/racial discourses and frameworks of meaning) encompass a religious quality insofar as they produce certain orientations toward the world, ways of coming to terms with one's place in the temporal and spatial order of things.[79] For black people forced into the contact zone of the Americas, a zone inaugurated by settler colonial genocide and slavery, this religiosity does not only allude to institutions and recognizable traditions. It also includes "folklore, music, style of life" in addition to "experience, expression, motivations, intentions, behaviors, styles, and rhythms."[80] This is what Long alludes to as the extra-church,[81] a kind of surplus or exorbitance to not only Christianity but to recognizable institutions, traditions, and doctrines. With this extra-churchly attention to black experience and aesthetics, Long is offering a notion of religion that highlights a comportment toward the opaque, the untransparent, and those movements and vibrations that muddy stable forms and demarcations. In black aesthetics and music, among other places, we can hear what Édouard Glissant calls a "right [and rite] to opacity."[82]

Saidiya Hartman suggests this in her reading of slave songs and black spirituals as expressions of opacity. According to Hartman, the cries and shrieks of the enslaved subject—in response to torture, forced labor, sexual violence, and dispossession—register an excess of meaning and affect that cannot be easily classified or rendered intelligible. She writes, "Rather than consider black song as an index or mirror of the slave condition, this examination emphasizes the significance of opacity as precisely that which enables something in excess of the orchestrated amusements of the enslaved and which similarly troubles distinctions between joy and sorrow and toil and leisure."[83] Not unlike Long, Hartman examines the entangled relationship between freedom and domination or entertainment and anguish, particularly within the matrix of slavery and its afterlife. This entanglement played itself out on auction blocks and in coffles as captive bodies were disciplined to appear jovial and content, to entertain slave traders and flesh-mongers. The trope of the opaque beckons Hartman to hear the "subterranean and veiled character of slave songs" and the "accumulated hurt, . . . the wild notes, and the screams lodged deep within [that] confound simple expression and, likewise, withstand the prevailing ascriptions of black enjoyment."[84] Crucial here is how the slave song overflows certain affective distinctions—pleasure and pain, anguish and exaltation—a quality I discuss in chapter 1 as I trace the work of sorrow in hip hop. In addition, Hartman's understanding of the opaque upends reliable divisions between the present and past, emancipation and slavery, moving forward and reaching backward, since black subjects continue to be haunted by painful contradictions experienced by enslaved black people. Throughout the book, I note how artists tacitly perform and visualize the aftereffects of slavery in a manner that introduces a sense of the opaque into conventional understandings of time, progress, and redemption.

While Hartman describes the opacity of slave songs, Tricia Rose makes a case for the sonic complexity of hip hop and rap music. In her foundational text *Black Noise*, Rose examines the postindustrial social and historical conditions that bring hip hop into being, while remaining mindful of hip hop's continuity with jazz, blues, and other musical traditions. In her analysis of the elements of hip hop, such as graffiti, rap, and breakdancing, Rose borrows from Arthur Jafa's claim that three tropes connect hip hop practices: flow, rupture, and layering. With particular reference to rap music, she writes, "Rappers speak of flow explicitly in lyrics, referring to an ability to move easily and powerfully through complex lyrics as well as of the flow in the music. The flow and motion of the initial base or drum line in rap music is abruptly ruptured by scratching, or the rhythmic flow is interrupted by other musical passages. . . . Rappers layer meaning by using the same word to signify a variety of actions and objects. DJs layer sounds literally one on top of the other, creating a dialogue between sampled sounds and words."[85] Here we might read the assemblage of layering, flow, and rupture as another way of naming hip hop's opacity. The layering motif resists all too familiar assumptions about the simplicity of black culture; it refuses reductive readings of rap music that render its sounds, images, and meanings instantly graspable, one-dimensional, and easy to dismiss. The layering in hip hop indicates a kind of multiplicity within what might seem like a straightforward, unified composition. We should think of flow as a trope that indicates the excessive, fluid, and unstable qualities of rap, rhyme, and hip hop aesthetics. And at times, this motion of words, beats, sounds, and visual fragments can interrupt something (and undergo an interruption); this tumultuous movement can alter how we see, hear, relate to the world, or imagine progression and linear temporality.

In line with these qualities of hip hop, the title of Rose's text sounds appropriate. *Noise* is associated with the emanation of loud sounds, with vibrations that are unpleasant and discordant to hear. To some extent, noise is the aural counterpoint to opacity, insofar as both register a level of incoherence with respect to the senses and their capacity to receive from, and incorporate, the external world. Of course, the transition from noise to digestible sound depends on familiarity and acclimation. (A longtime listener of hip hop music might not find the beats, lyrics, and vocal tones as discomfiting as a novice to the genre.) Yet I take it that Rose's title, and her concomitant analysis of hip hop as youth rebellion, prompts the reader to think about the general relationship between blackness and noise, or blackness as a kind of noise. As Jennifer Stover points out, black peoples and cultures are often associated with loudness, harsh voices, and disturbing sounds, suggesting that the color line is as sonic as it is visual.[86] This conflation of blackness with noise, especially within white supremacist imaginaries and paradigms, tends to ignore the continuity between noise and Quashie's notion of quiet. Quiet, as described above, is not necessarily incompatible with the discord and incoherence that accompanies noise; it simply locates that discordance in moments of vulnerability, intimacy, contemplation, and the internal life of black selves. Jordan Davis experienced this general inability to acknowledge the overlap between black noise and quiet in the final moments of his life as he was attacked and killed for playing his music too loud, for performing and sounding blackness in a manner that "interrupted the peace" while immediately precipitating his death.[87]

Consequently, there are a series of life and death matters that arise when discussing the conjunction between blackness and sound. Rose's early text on rap and hip hop draws a connection between blackness and noise, or those vibrations that are loud and discordant. And yet the technical term "black noise" refers to the absence of frequencies and sounds, to a kind of silence. At the same time, black noise is associated with sounds that need to be contained below the surface or held at bay in order to prevent a crack (in glass, for instance) or some kind of rupture.[88] Perhaps the very bringing together of blackness and noise compels us to further think about interplay between silence, noise, and sound. Silence, for instance, can be glaring. On the other hand, certain ways of producing sound rely on patterned forms of silencing, muting, and erasing. Silence can also be the occasion or precondition for the emergence and emanation of certain audible vibrations. In this project, I want to think about blackness as a kind of noise, where the sense of discordance does not exclude the ways that blackness can slip out of discourse and be experienced through unsettling silences, pauses, withdrawals, and what David Marriott refers to as effacement.[89]

One also has to tread lightly when making claims about the qualities and features of blackness. By associating black culture and music with opacity and discordant sound, it would seem I run the risk of promoting racial essentialism. Racial essentialism attaches certain traits to black people as a whole, thereby downplaying the significance of differentiation, historical change, and internal conflict. By downplaying difference and conflict, racial essentialism fails to consider how race is articulated through, and mediated by, class, gender, sexuality, citizenship, region, and other sociopolitical factors. Furthermore, by privileging the blackness of hip hop, one might argue that we underappreciate the ways hip hop has always included nonblack participants, consumers, performers, and executives.[90] In this study, I respond to these concerns by making a slight, but crucial, distinction between blackness and black people, a distinction indebted to the work of Fred Moten. As Moten suggests, blackness can be thought of as an unstable movement, a tumult, and a rupture. It names a fugitive drive that antecedes strategies of containment and capture; yet this drive also "brings the law online,"[91] or incites the urge toward order into existence. Blackness names those larval, fluid, and chaotic dimensions of existence and becoming that according to Eliade need to be converted into a well-defined world or cosmos. It marks a tear or wound in world-making endeavors. With Long, blackness is a stand-in for the opaque, for those aspects of being and existence that elude reliable divisions and demarcations, upset general inclinations toward transparency, and fracture what we imagine and insist on as coherent.

To put this another way, blackness is the tumult that has to be managed and contained (and sometimes eliminated) for the order of things to hold sway. Blackness is what the proper human subject—Western, male, white, propertied—depends on for life and vitality, but also contrasts itself against in a manner that justifies the subordination of peoples and regions that depart from the idealized human. According to the machinations and aspirations of the proper and upright subject, blackness appears as wretched, accursed, and monstrous. Following Moten, this study acknowledges a distinction between blackness and black people while affirming a vital, and mortal, relationship between the two.[92] Therefore, black people cannot own blackness even as they have been called, and conscripted, to give form to blackness. In addition, blackness cannot be confined to race. Rather, racial taxonomies have been constructed in ways that regulate and sanction desires, forms of confinement, and hierarchies that comprise the violent relationship between the ideal human, or what Sylvia Wynter calls Man,[93] and blackened subjects. If blackness has generally been associated with a kind of wildness that catalyzes law and order, one must bear in mind that this wild quality has been affixed to blackness through projections, anxieties, and fantasies concerning black sexuality and gender (black people are oversexual; black women are not feminine enough; the Negro race, according to sociologist Robert Parks, is the "lady" of the races[94]). Blackness within modern discourses is often figured as both excess and lack with respect to appropriate expressions of gender, sexual desire, and religious practice. Here I think of Frantz Fanon's description of how a particular white woman's yearning for black men accompanied a desire to "break with her being and to volatilize at a sexual level."[95] This particular woman, as Fanon diagnoses, wants to lose herself in black masculinity, always already reduced to the biological and sexual. Drawing from an author like Fanon, I acknowledge that while the language of blackness or antiblackness risks being totalizing and endorsing a "race-first" approach, blackness talk in this study traverses and unsettles gender, sexuality, the logic of property, and so forth. On the flip side, blackness undergoes what Cathy Cohen calls a crosscut, a wound, a splitting that indicates the different positions (gender, class, sexuality, citizenship) that black people inhabit and the disparate modes of vulnerability to violence that these positions give rise to.[96] Blackness cannot be approached without something like an intersectional analysis, and hip hop's visual and sonic expressions demonstrate this point. To recapitulate, blackness, which is not tantamount to black people, is analogous to the opaque; it subsists as a haunting excess that cannot be readily controlled, explained away, or assimilated into prevailing discourses and imaginaries. And while blackness cannot become black people's exclusive property, black people, under the regimes of slavery and racial capitalism, have been called to give form to the terror, fascination, and (antiblack) violence that blackness elicits.[97]

In *The Disturbing Profane*, I examine hip hop culture at the intersection of two organizing frameworks—the volatile, left-hand sacred and blackness. By drawing from religious theory and black studies, this investigation aims to draw out and critically engage those elements of hip hop that disturb, haunt, and disarticulate prevailing logics and fantasies even in moments when these logics are being replicated and mimicked. In the process, I hope to show how rap music generates lines of thought and affect in unexpected directions. This book endeavors to hear and experience hip hop's layered qualities, its complexity, particularly around themes like death, sorrow, anguish, redemption, the wound, ecstasy, monstrosity, and the relationship between creativity and destruction. Inseparable from the thematic concerns is an appreciation for hip hop's formal and aesthetic qualities—wordplay, flow, sampling, layering, cuts and breaks, exaggeration, flamboyance, and masking. The volatile sacred heard in hip hop, the sacred that unsettles and interrupts, is articulated through hip hop's opacity and its vital relationship to blackness, black sexuality, performance, and so forth. Among other instances, the strange religiosity of hip hop is located in its reenactment and reexpression of the (antiblack) violence and terror that structures and organizes the modern world. In this reexpression, an opening emerges that makes available alternative ways of hearing, relating to, and contemplating this violence. Hip hop is a soundtrack for the dark underside of late modern projects; its ethical promise partly lies in its ability to bring to sound (and silence) and figuratively cut against regimes that have made violence against black people normal, acceptable, and even desirable. In the process, hip hop music similarly exposes and halts ingrained desires to be/come whole, coherent, and settled.

Capital, Aesthetics, and the Dissonant Cry That Remains

It might seem that my argument is late and outdated. Hip hop is no longer a marginal cultural phenomenon, as it was when Tricia Rose wrote *Black Noise* in the early 1990s. As early as the thirtieth birthday of hip hop (people typically locate its beginnings in 1973), Greg Tate acknowledged that "what we call hip hop is now inseparable from what we call the hip hop industry, in which the nouveau rich and the superrich employers get richer."[98] In fact, rap music—the most lucrative element of hip hop culture—is ubiquitous. It can be heard frequently at coffee shops, at major athletic events, on soundtracks to films, in video games, or as the musical backdrop to popular television series. Furthermore, rap music produced in the United States is a useful medium to sell and distribute commodities across the globe, promote a presidential candidate like Barack Obama, and advance the notion of a multicultural and even post-racial America.[99] Consequently, a suspicious reader might argue that while hip hop at one point exhibited a rich complexity, contemporary hip hop culture and rap music have become increasingly predictable and monotonous. In other words, hip hop is no longer volatile or opaque and has become an integrated part of the commodified culture industry. Hip hop seems all too transparent and predictable. It is very comfortably situated within the precincts of capital, wealth accumulation, misogynoir, and neoliberal sensibilities. Consider how Donald Trump, prior to and during his run for president, and Bill Gates have been icons of success, figures that rap artists have pictured as models to aspire to and emulate.[100] Think of how the mantra "if it doesn't make dollars then it doesn't make sense/cents" circulates in hip hop discourses, as if meaning and sense-making are determined by capital and the ability to generate surplus monetary value. Think of how artists are preoccupied with creating and maintaining their brand, their ability to continue being a self-generating lucrative product within the music and culture industry.

In line with these concerns, Lester Spence argues that recent trends in hip hop reflect a neoliberal shift in black culture and politics.[101] Alluding to Jay-Z's line, "I'm not a Business man; I'm a business, man,"[102] Spence draws attention to the ways rap artists are disciplined to think of their pursuits exclusively in terms of capital, profit accumulation, the hustle (work ethic without leisure), and entrepreneurship. For Spence, this exemplifies a broader trend in which institutions and social practices are increasingly compelled to imitate business and corporate paradigms in order to survive. This neoliberal framework, among other problems, exacerbates race and class inequalities and weakens democratic energies and collective efforts to empower marginalized communities. Even realist rap, or rap that claims to be an authentic depiction of black urban communities, tends to reproduce these neoliberal sensibilities through what Spence calls "crack governmentality." This term captures how "realist MCs deploy [narrow constructions] of realness and authenticity as vehicles of urban and human capital and as a technology of subjectivity within subjected places and populations."[103] In the process, emcees are placed in the position of being experts and representatives of urban spaces, the ghetto, and so forth. This presumed expertise proves to be lucrative for record companies at the same time that the first-person perspective in realist rap creates a distance between "the subject and the subjected."[104] Here we might pause and think about the different ways that "the real" or "keeping it real" circulates in hip hop. When rappers make claims, for instance, about the real corresponding to those who are dead or in prison, there is a way that reality as authenticity, or the real as the most genuine and untainted representation of life, hardship, and the proverbial streets, slides into the Real, or that which cannot be easily assimilated into the production of life, meaning, and value.[105]

This study takes Spence's arguments seriously, especially at a moment when the hip hop billionaire has become another "first" to laud and treat as iconic. As Spence suggests, the corporatization of hip hop is not new, even if the mainstreaming of rap music and the inescapability of late capitalist logics and rationalities intensifies the process. The continuity between the recent past and the present regarding hip hop's dance with capital is demonstrated in Eithne Quinn's study of late 1980s and early 1990s gangsta rap. According to Quinn, even as artists like Ice Cube and Ice-T put forth criticisms of state violence against poor black and brown people and the devastating economic conditions that produce the gangsta persona, many of these artists promoted a kind of rugged individualism and street entrepreneurship as the only way to escape the ghetto. Consequently, for Quinn the gangsta genre is equivocal. Agreeing for a moment with an author like Dyson, Quinn acknowledges that the genre gives an expression to "the social ills that resulted from deindustrialization and destructive government policies—poverty, chronic unemployment, political disaffection, and (particularly in the LA area) police repression, the drug trade, and gang activity."[106] On the other hand, gangsta rap "gave rise to captivating stories which could be exploited for commercial gain."[107] Alluding to documentary-style rap videos and St. Ides beer commercials that fabricated a sense of ghetto authenticity (Spence's crack governmentality) while relying on the links between blackness and (sexual) vitality, Quinn suggests that what captivates and fascinates audiences is always fodder for the accumulation of capital. In other words, there is a connection that we have to interrogate between capital, the captivating, the captive, and what holds audiences and performers enthralled to particular images and representations. What is the relationship between surplus value and the surplus desires and expectations that circle around certain performances of black gender? How does the gangsta persona and its offshoots require the subordination of women, queerphobia, and the simultaneous dismissal and adoption of deviant expressions of black masculinity? How does the music and culture industry capitalize on black performance by delimiting the kinds of responses to antiblackness and capitalist exploitation and predetermining the form and articulation of the response? More generally, why are certain ways of narrating and imaging black life and death so exciting, enticing, and prone to routinization? What kinds of affective regimes does the culture industry rely on and reproduce and what kinds of dissonant affects imperil its ability to remain intact? How does gangsta rap both expose and recapitulate the conditions, logics, and fantasies that have been pernicious to black people? It is this both/and that Quinn wants the reader to hear and be attuned to, a kind of doubleness that for her signals "an increasingly non-politicized generation, which has seen traditional forms of protest lose much of their resonance."[108] For my project, this ambivalence in gangsta rap and hip hop more generally points to a constitutive tear or wound that has indirect implications for how we think about the political and its re-lationship to aesthetics.

Among other things, what is instructive about the sorts of criticisms put forth by Spence and Quinn is that they prompt us to elaborate more generally on the relationship between aesthetics, the logic of capital, and popular culture. One author who infamously addresses this nexus is Theodor Adorno. While Adorno is often associated with the rejection of popular culture—including a critique of jazz that resembles hoary attacks against hip hop—his understanding of art and culture is much more subtle and interesting than this dominant perception permits. Influenced by Karl Marx, Adorno claims that the culture industry—a term that depicts culture (particularly radio, film, television, and advertising) as a factory that generates standardized products—"infects everything with sameness."[109] One of the consequences of this infection is that cultural producers and consumers get attached to images and sounds that are familiar and comforting; inversely, they are disciplined to ignore, or not detect, that which is dissonant and unsettling. The culture industry acts like a Kantian schema, insofar as it determines the relationship between thought and affect; it structures our perceptions and regulates how we experience the world. What troubles Adorno is how cultural media converts antagonism into harmony, suffering into simple enjoyment, in a manner that subordinates consumers to the triumph of capital and the general status quo. Thinking about the enjoyment that is derived from conventional formulas and genres, he writes, "To be entertained is to be in agreement. . . . Amusement means putting things out of mind, forgetting suffering, even when it is on display."[110] (This would seem to provide an appropriate critique of hip hop, insofar as popular tracks seem to desensitize us to the sounds and depictions of violence, misogyny, and vulnerability to death within these songs.)

For Adorno, certain works of art refuse the general thrust toward harmony and prompt us to experience the violent antagonisms that structure the world.

According to Adorno, art incorporates the world's fractured quality, a process that is expressed in the form and style of an artwork.[111] Here we might think about how dissonance, cutting, layering, and sampling in hip hop's visual and sonic practices act as stylistic counterparts to the tensions and fragments of the social world, one that mutilates certain kinds of subjects/objects and (non) beings. As Rose points out, we might think of the DJ's *cut*, the emcee's vocal *rupture*, the dancer's *break*, or the graffiti artist's *bombing* of a train as a reexpression of the violent conditions that brought hip hop into existence. Thinking with Adorno and Rose, the important point is that music is not a simple reflection of the social world. It is more like a refraction, since it places existing relationships and conditions into modified configurations, interactions, and sounds in a manner that enables us to experience differently the world's cuts, wounds, and alternative possibilities. If the "non-existing in artworks is a constellation of the existing,"[112] then art is both a product of the social world and an indication of an excess with respect to the protocols and rules of this world. While this excess or "More" is a signal that things might be otherwise, this lambent possibility is tethered to art's capacity to figuratively wound and interrupt the listening and viewing subject. As Adorno puts it, "The socially critical zones of artworks are those where it hurts; where in their expression, historically determined, the untruth of the social situation comes to light."[113] This sense of hurt and dissonance is for Adorno intertwined with other affects and responses— shuddering, trembling, energy, excitement, and wounded pleasure. The artwork for Adorno can provide the experience of being overwhelmed by the Other, irrupted by the "touch of the Other."[114] For Adorno, art moves within the logistics of capital and power to occasionally disappoint our inclinations toward control, self-possession, and indifference in the face of suffering, death, and ephemeral prospects for something different. Art can be an expression of the opaque sacred that, as a substitute for the traditional god, can make us shake, tremble, and become more open to the imperceptible.

What is crucial for my study is Adorno's insistence that art and music are both determined by the logic of capital (commodification, exchange, profit) and reminders of something more that cannot be completely regulated by this logic. Art simultaneously reflects and exceeds the grips of capital (how this interaction between reflection and excess plays out depends on a variety of factors). As Adorno writes, "There is no system without its residue."[115] Adorno's formulations resonate with Fred Moten's claim, in the context of black aesthetics, that objects cry and protest against the conditions of objectification. Or as Moten puts it, "The history of blackness is testament to the fact that objects can and do resist."[116] Alluding to Frederick Douglass's description of his Aunt Hester's terrifying beating and his related homage to slave spirituals, Moten takes seriously qualities and expressions of the commodified body that cannot be reduced to the structures of exchange—the sound of the cry, the intensity of the scream, the unsettling character of the shriek, the materiality of the voice. As he describes, there is something internal to the cry of the enslaved body that "disrupts and resists certain formations of identity and interpretation by challenging the reducibility of phonic matter to verbal meaning or conventional musical form."[117] Because the cry of the enslaved body—in response to everyday torture and sexual violence—cannot be reduced to musical form, it cannot be exhausted by the "protocols of [capitalist] exchange."[118] While Moten's understanding, or hearing, of the residue that eludes the system of exchange focuses on jazz and blues, this study extends Moten's insightful analysis into the realm of hip hop. Such an extension enables us to acknowledge that hip hop has increasingly become a lucrative commodity (but what isn't infected by capital?), without preventing us from hearing and being touched by the cries, refusals, and cuts made by black subjects responding to, and reenacting, deeply entrenched racial and gendered antagonisms. The question isn't so much if there is a cry that remains; the issue is whether we are able to hear, feel, contemplate, and be moved by the cry and other dissonant moments. This would involve, for instance, hearing pain, vulnerability, and anguish in lyrics that appear to be expressions of mastery and invincibility. Inversely, this might require hearing joy and laughter in moments that seem to be exclusively an articulation of agony. This could entail being more attentive to the sound and grain of an artist's voice; to the divergences between the sound and affective mood of a song's production and the taken-for-granted meanings in the lyrics of a composition. It might mean paying more attention to how the female and femme body is positioned within hip hop culture, looking for signs of irony, sarcasm, and refusal as she is ordered to "work" for the sake of heterosexual male fantasies. It could entail detecting how hip hop's heteronormative order is undercut by homosocial intimacy, cross-dressing, and anxieties about sounding queer—when rappers say "no homo" or "pause" after uttering something that sounds suspicious, there is an implicit acknowledgment, and immediate denial, of a moment of identity with queerness and the queer Other. Or as Moya Bailey puts it, "The repetitive use of the phrase 'no homo' signals an anxiety around the fragility of straightness."[119] As consumers and critical readers of hip hop, we participate in revealing the excess, or residue, that haunts the regulations of capital and concomitant modes of power and normalization.

This residue is often experienced in the contradictions, incongruities, and misfirings of hip hop projects, in addition to the pauses and hesitations.

And yet the language of misfiring, or the divergence between intention and effect, must be held in tension with Frank Wilderson's claim that black people are those that magnetize bullets.[120] To put it differently, if listening to hip hop as an expression of the black sacred gets at an unassimilable exorbitance, then it also registers the excessive violence (physical, symbolic, visual, discursive) directed at blackened subjects. It similarly gets at the excitement toward and fascination with black flesh, desire, sexuality, and drama, a libidinal attachment that is never separable from fear and repulsion, as well as indifference to suffering. If the left-hand sacred is an indication of what cannot be instrumentalized into an object, then it is also a reminder of the relentless energy exerted to contain, suppress, and objectify those that have the burden of giving a corporal form to blackness, the void, and so forth. The magnetic power of blackness, its tendency to attract forces of obliteration, is often rearticulated in hip hop as an intramural hostility, to riff on Spillers. This hostility is felt the most intensely in rap music when directed toward black women, the figure of the black queer, and gang adversaries or opps/opposition. To broach this intramural violence is risky in light of the tendency to pathologize black-on-black violence or to separate what Spillers calls the intramural, or that which resides within the walls of black sociality, from exterior modalities of power and regulation to which black people are subjected. But alongside pathology and omission lies what Christina Sharpe calls wake work or care for the dead, the living dead, or those that have been positioned to secure the boundary between life and death.[121] While the wake includes a celebratory moment, it is a celebration that is always attached to, and occasioned by, death, mourning, anguish, sorrow, and disturbing flows (precipitated by the ship's movement across water). In what follows, I do my best to practice this wake-inflected care.

Itinerary

The Disturbing Profane examines hip hop at the intersection of black studies and critical religious thought in the attempt to trace the volatile sounds, images, and energies of hip hop rituals and practices. Focusing on hip hop's poetic, sonic, and visual dimensions, this study contends that hip hop's sacred quality lies in its enduring capacity to interrupt, disturb, haunt, and thwart yearnings for purity and coherence. The volatile sacred in hip hop forms an intimate connection with blackness, which Moten defines as those drives and energies that confound strategies of containment and the general insistence on transparency—an insistence that results in a refusal to experience and encounter the complexities and densities of hip hop. As described above, blackness is not reducible to black people or racial identity, even if black persons exhibit a vital relationship to blackness. Blackness, on this reading, necessarily takes shape through gender, class, and sexuality and the nonnormative, dangerous (yet attractive) subjects/objects subordinated by these categories and positionings. To study the volatile and opaque features of hip hop, *The Disturbing Profane* foregrounds themes like sorrow, opacity, (social) death, rupture, excess, monstrosity, contradiction, laughter, and intimacy through cuts and wounds. At the same time, this study explores the interplay between scenes of exuberance and moments of quiet, subtlety, and absence within black expression, performance, and writing. My reading does not involve denying or downplaying how hip hop participates in and rearticulates prevailing social conventions and power relationships. In addition, my reading does not assume that hip hop exclusively or even most of the time enacts a dark, left-hand religiosity. Rather, it entails an investigation of a certain tendency—how the flows, images, and wordplay of rap music operate within the ordering of things while simultaneously disappointing general attachments to order, coherence, and stability. Hip hop's troubling presence can be felt in moments when artists refuse tendencies to locate causes of violence and death outside the United States; moments when artists demonstrate how redemptive narratives of wealth and success acquisition founder and break down; instances when black female artists reveal how hip hop's self-preservation, like that of the broader social world, relies on the sacrifice of black feminine flesh; occasions when the contradictions in hip hop cannot easily be managed and harnessed for conventional political projects and aspirations. In this study, I contend that hip hop's dark sacred quality is inseparable from how it performs, reenacts, and depicts the (anti-black and racially gendered) violence that organizes the world; in this reexpression, hip hop opens up space for us to experience, contemplate, and relate to this violence in alternative and yet-to-be-discovered ways.

Each chapter in *The Disturbing Profane* explores themes in hip hop culture that invite us to listen to and interact with hip hop's volatile religiosity. Each meditation relies on an understanding of hip hop as "more than bars and hooks," a phrase I sample from Mark Anthony Neal. Part of this "more" includes the conversations and discussions that have emerged about hip hop and religion discussed above; this "more" also encompasses literary, aesthetic, and religious traditions that rap culture draws from and remixes—signifying, poetry, call and response, spirituals, jazz, blues, funk, disco, cinema, and so forth.[122] As I take it, Neal's pithy phrase is a reminder that hip hop generates aesthetic styles and modes of being in the world that exceed the more demonstrable elements of rap music. One of these aesthetic styles, one way that hip hop relates to the world, is through what Rose calls layering and what Adorno and Benjamin call a constellation. A constellation is a construction, or arrangement, of disparate images, concepts, sounds, and elements; in the construction, the sense of coherence does not diminish the dissonance and tension-filled quality of the interactions among the elements that make up the configuration. In what follows, I mimic hip hop aesthetics by creating constellations in my endeavor to flesh out the unsettling sacred. Each chapter juxtaposes artists, songs, and images with authors and discourses that may not seem to be immediately relevant to hip hop culture. In addition, this layered approach pairs "old school" tracks with more contemporary songs in a manner that reveals both discontinuity and continuity across time. Yet this pairing also unravels linear, straightforward notions of time and experience and reminds us that reaching back is an occasion to listen to and experience the obsolete in unanticipated ways. Finally, this constellational approach thinks at the intersection of sound and image, which enables us to see and hear the occasional discrepancies and gaps between the acoustic aspects of a song and its visual/video counterpart.

My hope is that this approach of going back and forth and from side to side, which entails gathering fragments and repeating the cuts and breaks, will reach and contact readers with different levels of familiarity with hip hop, in addition to black studies and religious theory. Similarly, I hope to persuade those who continue to maintain a division, and prohibition, between *high* theory and *low* popular culture that the crossing and blurring of that enduring line of demarcation has always been in effect. Furthermore, this study finds resonance with recent scholarship by colleagues, such as J. Kameron Carter, Biko Gray, Josef Sorett, An Yountae, Cecilio Cooper, and Amaryah Armstrong, who are thinking with black studies to reconceive the sacred, profanation, and black religious practice and thought. Or to put it differently, I am galvanized by the recent endeavors to show how black studies exposes the theological and religious underpinnings of antiblackness while offering alternative, heretical, and unruly conceptions of sacrality, profanation, and the religious. I elaborate on these possibilities in the conclusion, but for now I invite the reader to think of the conjunction of hip hop and religion, or hip hop, black studies, and the dark, volatile sacred, as another way to examine the religiosity of blackness, as well as black thought and aesthetics. Following Long's notion of the extra-church, or that which exceeds established religious institutions and doctrines, this religiosity, which entails an expression of the sacred as a kind of opening toward death, anguish, opacity, and dissolution of our attachments to coherence, is found in desires, cries, echoes, rhythms, and moments of silence that defy capture but can still be felt, encountered, and contemplated.

Chapter 1, "Sorrow/Death," takes seriously themes of death, loss, and anguish as they circulate in hip hop and rap music. To track these themes, I broach Du Bois's reading of sorrow songs in *The Souls of Black Folk*. Reflecting on the significance of the spirituals for captive, enslaved communities, Du Bois links sorrow to unacknowledged black death and disappointment as well as exaltation, joy, and striving. While desire for liberation in these rhythmic cries frequently includes commitment to a traditional deity, Du Bois also suggests that there is a kind of liberation in the event of death, in escaping the terror of social death. Underscoring the opacity of sorrow—how it collapses but retains a dissonance between certain affective contrasts such as anguish and enjoyment—I offer a reading and hearing of a series of rap songs, including compositions by Grandmaster Flash and the Furious Five, Arrested Development, and Lauryn Hill. Through this reading, I compare tracks that appeal to a divine power that identifies with suffering, but often remains silent, to works by artists like Biggie Smalls that locate a form of liberation in death, but a death that is not opposed to a different way of inhabiting a violent world. Part of my analysis will examine the connections between the readiness to die heard in Biggie's first album and the dynamics of black masculinity, especially as expressed and consumed within the precincts of the rap industry. In the conclusion of the chapter, I revisit Nas's "Hip Hop Is Dead," a pronouncement that invokes Friedrich Nietzsche's madman, a figure who proclaimed that "God is dead." By comparing Nas and Nietzsche, I suggest that we can read Nas's controversial utterance as an Eliade-like yearning for pure beginnings or as an implicit rejection, or dissolution, of the very pursuit of purity.

Chapter 2, "Redemption/Rupture," interrogates the theme of redemption, including the idea of hip hop being a salvific power, one that can rescue black subjects from a life of social death, impoverishment, and terror. While there is a strong tendency within hip hop (and the broader Christian-structured world) to conceive of redemption as being rescued from an undesirable predicament and recovering a sense of wholeness or fulfillment, I listen for other possibilities alongside this familiar rehearsal of the concept. Drawing on the work of black studies (especially Saidiya Hartman and Frank Wilderson) and critical theory (Walter Benjamin and Theodor Adorno), I trace a shared notion of weak or blackened redemption where the term looks less like fulfillment and more like a rupture into narratives and grammars of fulfillment and arrival. Similarly, through these authors, I think of redemption as the retrieval of the ruin more than the recovery of plenitude or wholeness. In this chapter, I offer a reading of Lupe Fiasco's 2006 song "American Terrorist," in which I focus on the pairing of America and terror. This conjunction, I argue, exposes how US exceptionalism is predicated on a denial of the terror that is internal to settler colonial formations, Western imperial sovereignty, and antiblack racism. To put it differently, Lupe compels the listener to hear the violence, through a cut into ascendant narratives and temporalities, that is necessary for the protection of an idealized image of America, one that relies on attaching gratuitous violence and fear elsewhere, including Muslim countries and regions. To accomplish this, Lupe rescues images of terror and anguish, including slavery, the Middle Passage, and native genocide, to cut against the self-redeeming logic of US exceptionalism. I conclude the chapter by engaging Kendrick Lamar's first studio album, *Section.80*, showing how it strains against the compulsion to look backward for a time of plenitude, exemplified by the rehabilitation of the Ronald Reagan era, sovereign time, et cetera. By refusing to separate the sovereign, the president, or the Reagan era from conditions and qualities that get affixed to pathologized black places, Kendrick draws attention to desires to restore and make whole through a disavowal of structuring forms of violence. I end the chapter by examining how Kendrick's own attempts to make and be made complete, by folding black female characters into his narratives, founders and breaks down.

Chapter 3, "Monster/Monstrous," ventures into the realm of the monstrous. In this chapter, I show how the figure of the monster that circulates within hip hop draws together, and introduces tensions, between two strands of thought. One strand is exemplified by the work of Georges Bataille, whose understanding of the left-hand sacred arrives at the monstrous or those experiences and facets of being that ruin an attachment to form and coherence. The other strand includes black studies and black feminism, authors such as Hortense Spillers, Frantz Fanon, Christina Sharpe, and Zakiyyah Jackson, who describe in different ways how blackness has been configured as monstrous, between the animal and human, within the paradigm of Western imperial Man. Thinking between the volatile sacred and black (gender), I offer a reading of "Monster" performed by Kanye West, Nicki Minaj, Jay-Z, and Rick Ross. I underscore how the enactment of the monstrous can be an occasion to parody imperial modes of sovereignty and power and a way to visualize racial/gendered/sexual contradictions, wounds, and fantasies that are part of a monstrous formation, a horrifying visual and libidinal economy, that gets unduly affixed to and located in black flesh. I end the chapter by reading Minaj's "Anaconda" alongside Spillers's call for black women to reclaim, and rework, the monstrosity that has been imposed on them by a racist/sexist world.

In the conclusion, I situate my project within the broader discourse on black religion and black studies, particularly on the ambiguity of the sacred. I underscore my claim about hip hop being a disturbing presence that exposes us, in particular ways, to a constitutive wound and a terrestrial anguish that cannot be wished away.

Sorrow/Death

While Wu-Tang Clan's debut 1993 album *Enter the Wu-Tang (36 Chambers)* contains a variety of memorable songs and skits—tracks that are violent, nostalgic, vulnerable, discordant, self-aggrandizing, torturous, comical, and pensive—one song that particularly stands out is "Tearz." In the first verse, group member RZA tells a story that culminates with his younger brother being murdered. This verse actually elaborates on the opening scene, in which we initially hear RZA depicting an assailant (the Wu-Tang artist commands someone to relinquish their possessions and reiterates that he is going to "blast" his adversary). This assertive, imposing sound and posture abruptly turns into a cry of shock and dismay as RZA realizes that his brother has been shot. The high-pitched quality of his opening exclamations—"Oh no," "Don't touch him," and "Call an ambulance"—reverberates throughout the first verse as his voice constantly drifts toward a shout or scream in the retelling of his brother's murder. In the second verse, Ghostface Killah offers a narrative about a "promiscuous" friend named Big Moe who contracts HIV. The penultimate line—"No life to live, doc says two more years"—suggests a preparation for or anticipation of death, as if mourning can be directed forward as well as backward. In addition, this fragment reminds us that HIV has promised premature death for certain kinds of subjects, those (indigent, queer, black) who are positioned at the edge of social life/death. The hook that gets repeated in the song is a sample from Wendy Rene's 1964 soul ballad "After Laughter Comes Tears," reminding the listener that the song is about intimacy, love, friendship, and reminiscence as much as death and sorrow. In fact, the preposition *after* could be replaced with "alongside," since the laugh and the cry are often inseparable. The *tear* indicates a kind of *tear* or rip in experience. Sorrow, pleasure, and longing form a tension-filled assemblage in hip hop as in the spirituals, blues, and related genres. In fact, Ghostface Killah's 1996 track "Motherless Child" directly enacts this connection between hip hop and the spirituals, as the Wu-Tang artist samples the inherited slave song to capture experiences of anguish, alienation, and survival in black urban terrains.[1]

It should not be surprising that a group like Wu-Tang Clan regularly samples and rearticulates other genres, other forms of music that according to Baldwin have enabled black people to tell their stories, narratives that express the unsaid and the "dangerous and reverberating silence" within everyday speech.[2] As hip hop studies scholars have pointed out, hip hop is best understood as an extension, and reinterpretation, of black aesthetic and cultural traditions. To understand the significance of hip hop, one must examine how artists sample and cut from a rich tapestry of black musical expression (that includes jazz, soul, reggae, funk, disco, house, and rock 'n' roll) in the process of creating something new and different. Tricia Rose, for instance, notes that there is a "necessary tension between the historical specificity of hip hop's emergence and the points of continuity between hip hop and several Afrodiasporic forms, traditions, and practices."[3] Although Rose underscores the postindustrial forces that render hip hop somewhat discontinuous with previous articulations of black culture, she rightly insists that "hip hop is propelled by Afrodiasporic traditions."[4] The new is often enabled and made possible by the reexpression of, and cut into, what already exists, circulates, and waits to be supplemented.

While Rose contends that hip hop incorporates the improvisational and experimental qualities of jazz, blues, and rock, this chapter examines traces of what W. E. B. Du Bois calls the sorrow song in hip hop culture, which can be heard in Wu-Tang Clan's musical corpus.[5] A variant of black spirituals, the sorrow song is the object of tribute in Du Bois's classic text *The Souls of Black Folk*. Du Bois hears sorrow songs like "Motherless Child" or "My Way's Cloudy" as acoustic stories that register forms of anguish and death conditioned by white supremacist regimes and arrangements. At the same time, there is a duplicity in his notion of sorrow, an opaque quality, insofar as the extended cry of sorrow songs contains what we usually define as the opposite of sorrow—hope, confidence, ecstasy, and celebration. Sorrow, in other words, exists at the fraught conjuncture of anguish and exaltation, loss and survival, death and life. In what follows, I contend that Du Bois's redefinition of sorrow encourages us to listen to key themes and patterns within hip hop, most notably: the experience and anguish of being thrown into a world that places indigent blackness at the lowest frequencies of (human) being; a readiness and preparation for death, which is always internal to life; relationships with the divine marked by presence and absence, intimacy and alienation; and perennial concerns about the demise of hip hop under the sway of commercialization and rap's increasing popularity. I listen for sorrow in artists like Grandmaster Flash and the Furious Five, Arrested Development, Lauryn Hill, Mary J. Blige, and Notorious B.I.G. as a way to foreground and elicit reflection, introspection, vulnerability, care, and the wound. This is my attempt to expose and depart from enduring tendencies to treat black people as more tolerant of pain and less capable of internal anguish.

Du Bois, Doubleness, and the Opacity of Sorrow

In Du Bois's thought, there is an indirect connection between the sorrow-filled holler of the slave—a holler that gets passed on to successive generations—and what he calls double-consciousness, a term that continues to inform interpretations of black existence and experience.[6] Du Bois's idea, for instance, is used by Imani Perry in her magisterial text *Prophets of the Hood* to make sense of hip hop's ambivalent relationship to the United States. According to Perry, contemporary black American culture often expresses this duplicity, which explains why there are moments of strong identification with America in US-based hip hop music and other moments marked by alienation and renunciation.[7] For Du Bois, double-consciousness signifies the social predicament of black Americans, who generally experience a conflict or tension between their black and American identities. This sense of "twoness" for Du Bois is partly a result of social arrangements that depend on black people's labor, coercively incorporating them into the American project but preventing them from participating in and enjoying vital social goods and resources. It is also the alienating result of being measured by and subordinated to ideals that subordinate and spurn black subjects. For Du Bois, this experience of double-consciousness, of being in but not of America, is both debilitating and enabling. Although Du Bois hopes that this broken predicament will be reconciled once blacks are permitted to share their gifts and become "co-workers in the kingdom of culture,"[8] he also suggests that double-consciousness offers black people a second sight, a double vision, or an alternative way of seeing and diagnosing the world they inhabit. For Du Bois, this second sight has something to do with witnessing and contemplating racial/colonial terror while also envisioning, and enacting a witness to, a better future, a more just and liberated world. To be sure, Du Bois's formulation should initially be interpreted within its early twentieth-century context (where blackness meant, among other things, riding in a Jim Crow train car). At the same time, Perry's use of Du Bois's concept to frame her discussion of the dissonant relationship between hip hop culture and the United States shows how ideas can travel beyond their immediate context. In addition, it signals the continuation of conditions, operations, logics, and investments that asymmetrically imperil black people and keep black life under duress.[9]

To understand how this tornness of black subjectivity relates to sorrow, we must linger a bit in Du Bois's description of this predicament, one initiated by the violent confrontation between the Euro-American world and Africa, the kidnapping and forced servitude of black bodies, and the lingering effects of slavery. According to Du Bois, the antagonistic relationship between blackness and Americanness, or the condition of being a problem for the social order, renders the black subject a "stranger in [her] own house." It produces a peculiar and queer feeling of being an outcast within a world that feeds on black labor and culture but treats blackness as a tertium quid, an indefinite space between the human and animal. According to Du Bois, "It is a peculiar sensation, this double-consciousness, this sense of always looking at one's self through the eyes of others, of measuring one's soul by the tape of the world that looks on in amused contempt and pity."[10] Not unlike Georg Wilhelm Friedrich Hegel's conception of subject formation, Du Bois's formulation indicates that the self is defined in relationship to the Other; the self's coherence is made possible by recognition, language, and shared social norms. Yet for Du Bois, the self/Other relationship is distorted when the Other is a black person, when the Other is positioned as not quite Other or below the level of normal alterity.[11] Consequently, when black people desire recognition from a world that is antiblack, that defines itself against blackness, they tend to find a fragmented image of themselves within that social world. Frantz Fanon might add that the contemptuous gaze of whites (think here of the child that stares at him, afraid that Fanon is going to eat him, a scene I analyze in the third chapter) can figuratively cut the black body into pieces insofar as the gaze, especially when internalized, ridicules and censures those qualities associated with blackness.[12] But we must be careful not to reduce Du Bois's image of doubling to a wound or a painful cut. Because double-consciousness is also associated with the gift of a second sight, with the possibility of seeing otherwise or imagining something *else* through the veil, we might say that the "double" and the gift indicate a surplus or excess as much as a wound/lack. In line with Nahum Chandler's study of Du Bois, the doubling of blackness, a process that involves the conjunction, alteration, and transformation of both Africanness and American identity, is a site of "exorbitance" that erodes stable identities and neat distinctions.[13] The double, in other words, indicates a painful cut as well as a multiplication that cannot be easily managed or grasped by thought. This sense of a cut/multiplication also alludes to the internal differentiation and dissonance within blackness, the wound that precludes any unified notion of black peoplehood.

Anne Cheng helps us think about sorrow as a response to conditions that have placed black people at the edges of the human in her classic formulation of the conjunction of race and melancholia. According to Cheng, the "melancholy of race" involves a distinction between grievance and grief, the former alluding to an injustice or wrong that can be measured and redressed and the latter referring to injuries that cannot be easily defined or translated into political grammars.[14] For Cheng, there are several ways that racial melancholy operates in the US context as an indicator of intractable grief. Following Sigmund Freud's famous description of this psychic state, Cheng describes melancholy as the simultaneous exclusion and retention of black people within the dominant imaginary. In the same way that the melancholic individual responds to loss by paradoxically incorporating and rejecting the lost object, the racial order assimilates black people while denying them access to certain ideals, rights, and social goods. The black person in this drama is both the lost object and the subject of loss; as subject, the black individual is both enticed and mutilated by ideals like freedom and equality, which have been constructed over and against the slave, nature, and those populations that serve as stand-ins and extensions of nature. Since the black subject is excluded from, yet retained by, the social order (which rewards her as she distances herself from the denigrated qualities of blackness), one effect of this process is an ongoing trauma and wound—not unlike Du Bois's description of double-consciousness. Yet Cheng, like Du Bois, refuses to exclusively associate melancholy with dejection and loss. She also hears in the melancholic drama of race practices of resistance, survival, and beleaguered sociality. Cheng writes, "Racial melancholia . . . has always existed for raced subjects both as a sign of rejection and as a psychic *strategy* in response to that rejection. Black cultural forms have hosted and even cultivated dynamic rapport with the presence of death and suffering."[15] Alluding specifically to Du Bois's account of the sorrow songs, Cheng contends that sorrow and melancholy within black culture and art are not mere "expressions of sadness," but attempts to "wrestle with meaning and freedom" in a world organized against black people. In other words, Cheng suggests that racial melancholy is generative even as it testifies to a heritage of violation; as much as it registers a legacy of dispossession, erasure, and violent assimilation/exclusion, melancholy also gets taken up by black subjects as an aesthetic practice and a mode of endurance in a world that feeds on black life and death.[16] And yet, as Sharpe suggests, there might be something about melancholy, as a way of describing, framing, and responding to black loss, that is inadequate to the "interminable event," to the structure of slavery and its afterlives that "are unfolding still."[17] To put it another way, if the language of loss assumes a prior possession that has been taken away, then melancholy might be insufficient to capture how prevailing conceptions of human life position black people as always already barred from the potential of accessing that domain.

Cheng's reflections encourage us to hear the sorrow songs, and contemplate the very notion of sorrow, as an aesthetic rearticulation of conditions that have systemically placed black people closer to death and its intimations. She encourages us to revisit the final chapter of *The Souls of Black Folk*, where Du Bois gives a kind of shout-out to the rhythmic cries of the slave, which have been passed down (in a scattered manner and through "eloquent omissions") and remixed in slavery's aftermath. One thing that immediately stands out is Du Bois's description of the spirituals as weird, strange, and haunting. For instance, he confesses, "Ever since I was a child these songs have *stirred me strangely*."[18] To be stirred, whether by a sound, vocal expression, or instrument, is to undergo a combination of stimulation, arousal, and disturbance. It means to experience an altered state, to lose one's sense of coherence. A stirring indicates a capacity to move and be moved, to be subjected to a figurative twisting. (Here we might think of the artist Rakim's claim that to him, MC means "move the crowd,"[19] a movement that goes both ways, an affectability that is reversible.) The adverb "strangely" accentuates the disturbance and introduces uncanniness into the forms of agitation that sorrow songs prompt. Perhaps because of Du Bois's upbringing in the austere, stilted Great Barrington, Massachusetts, community, these songs oscillated from sounding unfamiliar to feeling close and at home. This strange stirring is not too far from what Du Bois calls the "frenzy" in his description of black religious practice.[20] This frenzy alludes to church gatherings and music-inflected rituals that entail shouting, shrieking, murmuring, stomping, waving, weeping, and laughing. Similar to Durkheim's understanding of the "effervescent" quality of sacred festivals, the frenzy connotes a moment of being beside and outside oneself, an ecstatic event that blurs the very distinction between interior and exterior. It is a way of a catching or being caught by the spirit. And even though Du Bois and Durkheim focus on the outward expressions of the "wild and demonic" state, I am also interested in the ways these strange stirrings and the frenzy relate to internal thoughts and reflections; how sorrow reconfigures how we might discuss and experience the interactions between thought and affect, the conceptual and the emotional, and the contemplative and physical activity. Finally, the stirrings induced by the sorrow songs and this emphasis on affectability refuses what Denise Ferreira da Silva calls the transparent I, the image of the self-contained European subject that defines itself through its opposition to affectable, racialized Others.[21]

For Du Bois, the sorrow song upsets prevailing early twentieth-century accounts of the complacency and happiness of the enslaved. In opposition to those who would "tell us that life was joyous to the black slave, careless and happy," Du Bois contends that spirituals tell another, more complicated and terrifying story.[22] They "are the music of an unhappy people, of the children of disappointment; they tell of death and suffering and unvoiced longing toward a truer world, of misty wanderings and hidden ways."[23] Sorrow, or the extended black cry, tells us something about death and anguish under the regime of slavery. This genre is a witness to the violent foundations of colonial modernity and the US settler nation-state; sorrow gives a voice/sound to, and retains the painful details of, these projects, even as it registers omissions, absences, and lacunae (the motherless child). This unhappy music, in response to kidnapping, war, forced labor, torture, sexual violence, and separation from kin, disappoints the kinds of narratives that would retrospectively diminish or explain away the anguish and protest of enslaved black people. By underscoring death, suffering, and discontent, Du Bois creates what Sara Ahmed calls an "unhappy archive."[24] For Ahmed, happiness, among other things, is "a form of world making [that] makes the world cohere around" proper objects, ideas, and values.[25] This form of world-making treats happiness as the end or telos of the good life and treats unhappiness as an obstacle, as what "gets in the way" of a fulfilled life.[26] We might say that this form of world-making can be directed toward the past and the future. In Du Bois's context, the discourse of the complacent and careless slave is part of a project that attempts to fasten subjects to happy and affirmative narratives about freedom, progress, and civilization.

It would be shortsighted to only focus on sorrow as an aesthetic reexpression of death and disappointment. As the above quote indicates, Du Bois also describes the sorrow song in terms of "unvoiced longing," hidden modes of being, and wandering in an unanticipatable manner. Here we might think of the concealed practices and rituals that enabled the slave's endurance—stealing away, surreptitiously gathering, using code words and secret language to plan an escape, and general forms of dissimulation under systems of surveillance and confinement. At the same time, the notion of wandering, as Sarah Cervenak points out, can refer to fantasies, daydreams, meditations, and forms of actual and imaginary roaming that appear wayward to the Master, the self-contained subject, the will to keep things in line.[27] These qualities of sorrow that are not reducible to death and suffering lead to Du Bois's claim that "through all the Sorrow Songs there breathes a hope—a faith in the ultimate justice of things. The minor cadences of despair change often to triumph and calm confidence."[28] Du Bois claims that he often hears in spirituals a "transition" from despair to triumph and confidence. This transition could signify or anticipate a complete shift from anguish, or what Bataille calls a "rupture . . . that leaves one at the limit of tears,"[29] to a state of composure and stability. It could, in other words, sound like a movement from pain and burden to the appearance and performance of wholeness and self-possession, a desired passage that would have significant implications for hip hop, which can serve as a staging for triumphant fantasies and expressions. Yet one might also read the term *change* as an in-between state, a suspension, a fraught interval and interplay between anguish and exaltation even as the cadences of victory can make the enduring pain difficult to register.

Du Bois suggests by his use of the preposition *through* that hope is not acquired easily or unequivocally. Sorrow requires one to make a passage through the moan and the violent conditions and arrangements that the cry reexpresses. A strange sense of possibility is made available by being worked on by the cry; the breath of hope is a kind of aspiration that is ensconced in the sigh, the choke, and the gasp.[30] According to Du Bois, this aspiration/hope is split and takes different directions. As he puts it, "Sometimes it is a faith in life, sometimes a faith in death, sometimes assurance of boundless justice in some fair world beyond."[31] The allusion to a fair world beyond points to black people's commitment to a "god of right"; to the Exodus narrative and the image of Jordan as both an earthly and divine space that exists on the other side of enslavement and torment. As Eddie Glaude points out, the Hebrew Bible's account of a god identifying with the suffering of the Israelites and rescuing them from their tyranny under Pharaoh was taken up by antebellum black people, allowing them to inscribe themselves into a metastory of deliverance and redemption. For Glaude, Exodus created a sense of commonality and shared obligations among nineteenth-century black folk; it similarly provided a grammar to make sense of present injustices and give shape to future aspirations for freedom.[32] But this is not all it did. The Exodus paradigm, as Sylvester Johnson points out, also annexed black people to settler colonial projects, the justification of the ongoing displacement and removal of indigenous peoples, and imperial pursuits of war and expansion.[33] For Johnson, similar to Edward Said, there is no Promised Land without the displacement and destruction of those who occupy the space of the Canaanites. Consequently, as William R. Jones warns, it is not always clear if the biblical god is on the side of the oppressed, as the textual and historical evidence indicates that god often demands, sanctions, or shows indifference to the suffering of various groups.[34]

In addition to "boundless justice," Du Bois claims that spirituals also attach hope to life and death, as if life and death are interrelated sources of inspiration apart from "some fair world beyond." Here Du Bois prompts the reader to think through the fraught intimacy between life and death, especially for black slaves and their descendants. The *life* and preservation of the racial-capitalist order, for instance, relies on black *death* and suffering, on rendering black people more vulnerable to violence, state surveillance, indigence, and imprisonment. In response to life being a social death sentence for the slave, Du Bois points to a legacy of considering death as a kind of liberation from this predicament, one that includes kidnapped Africans "flying home" from slave ships or captive mothers killing children to rescue them from a life of gratuitous violence. While flying home or infanticide accomplishes liberation from social death—or the death that defines black life, the condition of being the living dead—slave songs and spirituals suggest that there is a life that exceeds, while being traversed by, death. More specifically, sorrow songs give a sound to, keep alive, and reexpress experiences of torment and loss; through dance, song, and surreptitious gatherings, slaves did not necessarily surmount a series of ruptures, dislocations, and losses. As Hartman points out, slaves performed and rearticulated these ruptures in spaces and meeting places characterized by ecstasy and danger, transcendence and potential punishment.[35] In other words, the life that remains and survives in black spiritual practices, including slave gatherings and bush arbor meetings, is h(a)unted and beleaguered.

ANTHONY PINN UNDERSCORES this "remainder" motif in his discussion of the connections between spirituals and hip hop music. He writes, "Perhaps the sounds and sights of [the Middle Passage] *remained* alive in the new rhythms of [the enslaved's] new world musical expression, first presented through the spirituals."[36] The spirituals, according to Pinn, are the cries of those who survived what Glissant would call the "terrifying abyss" of the belly of the slave ship and the depths of the ocean;[37] they bear witness to those bodies that perished during the brutal passages across the Atlantic. By bearing witness, by mourning those at the bottom of the ocean, the spirituals refuse a system that treats black flesh as relatively ungrievable and unworthy of care, compassion, and lament. Consequently, slave songs for Pinn "humanize a dehumanizing environment"[38] and confer sense to senseless violence and torture. Here we should not think of the spirituals as the simple fabrication of legible meaning or as aesthetic pathways to the sphere of the recognizable human. Rather, we should hear sorrow at the edge of sense and nonsense, at the intersection of meaning and absurdity, and perhaps at the brink of the human and animal cry. Du Bois gestures toward these intersections when he reminds the reader that "before each thought I have written in [*The Souls of Black Folk*] I have set a phrase, a haunting echo of these weird old songs."[39] Du Bois underscores how each chapter in his classic text begins with a succession of musical notes; a trace of the spiritual forms the epigraph of each essay. In other words, an echo of the cry precedes, haunts, and accompanies the procession of arguments. Du Bois's thoughts and reflections are prompted by weird, strange, and dark vibrations that cannot be captured by ordinary language and frameworks of meaning. The material sound of anguish both propels and exceeds black thought and writing. Therefore sorrow, as both Du Bois and Pinn indicate, should be heard as the volatile interaction between death and survival, loss and remains, and sense and non-sense. And as Pinn argues, the spirituality in hip hop has something to do with how it remixes these qualities and motifs in a postindustrial, late capitalist world.

The use of the term *sorrow* to describe the slave song and its afterlife can seem reductive and misleading. Zora Neale Hurston famously disagreed with the tendency of race leaders like Du Bois to conflate the spirituals with sorrow, thereby narrowly portraying black people as sad and unfortunate. In response to this predicament, Hurston writes, "So the same old theme [suffering and sorrow], the same old phrases get done again to the detriment of art. To [the race leader] no Negro exists as an individual—he exists only as another tragic unit of the Race. This in spite of the fact that Negroes love and hate and fight and play and strive and travel and have a thousand and one interests in life."[40] In this passage, Hurston suggests that politics and the politicization of black culture require the black leader to downplay individuality and complexity for the sake of uplifting the race as a whole. She describes how the painful experience of being a black body in predominately white institutions—the source of the race leader's double-consciousness—is projected onto black people in toto, making the race wo/man the spokesperson for the race. In the process, the multiple and dispersive interests, desires, passions, and activities of black people get interpreted through a framework of tragedy and suffering. For Hurston, black music and vernacular are just as much the occasions for laughter, joy, creativity, intimacy, and play as they are the expression of pain and suffering. While it is clear that Du Bois is one target of Hurston's critique, it is not clear that Du Bois operates with a simple notion of black sorrow that Hurston rightly disputes. As described above, Du Bois's hearing and reading of spirituals prompts him to reimagine sorrow as inflected by hope, confidence, ecstasy, meandering, and opacity. Since he associates sorrow songs with "misty wanderings and hidden ways," Du Bois indicates that the sounds and meanings of these musical cries cannot be reduced to a clear, unified theme or emotion. Sorrow cannot be confined to a fixed point. While he focuses on "death and disappointment" in the final essay of The Souls of Black Folk, this is a strategy responding to accounts that depict the regime of slavery as idyllic and benevolent, and as if it were not structured by torment, torture, and the perpetual threat of violation. On the flip side, Hurston questions the centrality of the tragedy/suffering motif in opposition to ongoing endeavors to politicize black cultural and spiritual energies in a narrow manner, a project that flattens the complexities of black people's lives. She reminds us that the relationship between art, politics, and representation is never simple, direct, or transparent. Furthermore, as Lindsey Stewart argues in her work on Hurston, we can acknowledge that black joy has been used to "justify enslavement" while also being wary of the "danger in confining our stories to racial sorrow" without making a space for joy, laughter, and the erotic.[41] In my understanding of sorrow, taken and revised from the spirituals, I am interested in what Frederick Douglass calls a convergence of the "highest joy and the deepest sadness."[42] It is this "meeting of extremes" that I attempt to trace in hip hop, a conjunction that can sound like dissonance, blending, or something that cannot quite be put in words.[43]

In the final chapter of The Souls of Black Folk, Du Bois also expresses his own lament about the misuse of sorrow songs in US popular culture. Alluding to nineteenth-century minstrel shows and coon songs, Du Bois makes a distinction between those "debasements, imitations, and caricatures" and the "quaint beauty" of songs delivered from the "hearts of the Negro people."[44] In other words, Du Bois separates the true expression of the Negro's soul and spirit (found for instance in the Fisk Jubilee Singers) from those simulacra that parody and demean black people. Something authentic gets corrupted and devalued in the move from the plantation field to the gospel choir to the minstrel stage. Something is lost or taken away when the cry is disconnected from the internal life of black people.[45] There is so much that could be unpacked in response to Du Bois's concerns. Yet in preparation for the transition to hip hop, I highlight some key points. First, when discussing the debasements and misappropriations of blackness, one has to be careful about how this kind of lament can assume and stumble into romantic conceptions of blackness that advance circumscribed conceptions of peoplehood, community, and propriety. In other words, well-deserved concerns about the appropriation and commodification of black aesthetics, as a kind of repetition of the condition of being property under slavery, tend to rely on assumptions about the *proper* place of black expression (the heart and soul of the Negro). But if we think of blackness, in line with Moten, as that which interrupts the rules of property, perhaps we might arrive at a vantage point that refuses *both* the history of enjoying and being amused by black people while absconding from the slot of blackness *and* responses to this predicament that hinge on replicating a proprietorial idea of blackness. This might be an impossibility, considering how the second tendency has been a protective strategy against the many versions and variations of treating black people as objects of "amused contempt."

Du Bois's lament about popular performances of black sorrow, expressions that imitate and debase the true songs sung from the hearts of black people, bespeaks a desire to preserve something sacred, to protect certain elements of black culture from theft, misappropriation, distortion, and further loss. This sentiment raises a series of questions. How does one preserve a sequence of rhythmic cries, hollers, and cuts that have always been birthed and passed on within a constitutive wound, an indescribable loss? Furthermore, what does it mean to protect a space for sorrow, anguish, opacity, and frenzy, those qualities that overflow the kinds of boundaries associated with protection and property? What does it mean for a people who have been hailed as intrinsically corrupt to be invested in spaces, gatherings, and performances that are free from certain kinds of corruption? These questions haunt my reading of sorrow within hip hop, including perennial concerns about the demise, and renewal, of authentic hip hop culture and rap music.

Of Contemporary Sorrow Songs and Divine Shadows

If Du Bois claims that the sorrow songs have been sent down through generations (with fissures and cuts), then I suggest that we continue to discover echoes of these rhythmic cries in hip hop music. Imani Perry points out that hip hop's investment in the practice of call and response often manifests itself in a dialogue and "conversation with the black musical tradition."[46] As rap artists and producers sample, revise, and resignify tracks from previous generations and historical contexts, they respond to the calls and wails of ancestors while at the same time prompting us to hear these calls differently. In other words, there is a recursive relationship between the call and the response; while the call spurs and occasions a response, the response modifies and alters how one hears the call, not to mention what the proverbial call silenced or omitted. This call-and-response relationship between hip hop and sorrow songs can be heard in tracks like Ghostface Killah's 1996 track "Motherless Child," Kanye West's 2004 "Spaceship," or Pharoahe Monch's ironic "Let My People Go," released in 2011. While I am interested in these more overt allusions to the spirituals in hip hop, I am also committed to tracing and listening to the more general, and occasionally less detectable, Du Bois–inspired trope of sorrow within rap music. As described above, sorrow is an attitude, mode of being, and sound that exists at the conjunction of melancholy and exaltation, life and death, sense and nonsense, frenzy and stillness, escape and confinement, and divine presence and abandonment. Hartman would say that the opaque quality of sorrow blurs or smears the lines that we usually imagine separating, for instance, melancholy from exaltation or life from death. Consequently, in what follows, I read a series of rap compositions through the opacity of sorrow.

Consider, for instance, "The Message," a 1982 track performed by Grandmaster Flash and the Furious Five. Hailed as a classic by many hip hop pundits, "The Message" reexpresses the severe economic and social conditions in post–civil rights urban America, conditions out of which hip hop emerged and conditions that disproportionately beleaguered black and Latinx communities, especially in places like New York City. This classic song corroborates Rose's claim that "life on the margins of postindustrial urban America is inscribed in hip hop style, sound, lyrics, and thematics."[47] As Rose further points out, the style of hip hop is enacted through naming, titling, and taking on new identities and personas.[48] This is relevant considering how the prominent DJ's name brings together mastery with an instantaneous eruption . . . and disappearance. In addition, the adjective "furious" anticipates a gathering defined by intense energy, outrage, and being beside oneself. Melle Mel, one of the members of the Furious Five, begins his verse, "Broken glass everywhere, people pissin' on the stairs, you know they just don't care."[49] At the same time that Melle Mel's voice is introduced, a glass shattering can be heard in the background. The broken glass most likely refers to discarded bottles and the glass from abandoned buildings. At the same time, it points to a more general sense, and sound, of the break, or the ruin. In other words, the brokenness that the artist makes audible is everywhere, a ubiquity that precludes the desire to imagine oneself separate from the conditions that the group is about to expose and protest. As Walter Benjamin puts it, "In the ruin, history has physically merged into the setting."[50] In other words, the setting portrayed by Melle Mel is a physical sign of historical arrangements and forces that have devastated certain kinds of spaces and topographies. Think here of patterns of divestment or urban planning projects that displaced residents in working-class neighborhoods while obliterating and disappearing infrastructure; think of the fires that destroyed buildings in the Bronx in the 1970s and 1980s, some of which were initiated by landlords attempting to collect insurance. The allusion to urine elicits the notion of waste, as if urban spaces had become the repository for the discarded and disposable. It also signifies excess, spilling over, and flow that cannot be held or contained. The conditions in these spaces, according to Melle Mel, produce subjects who "just don't care," who lack a sense of concern for the neighborhoods and terrains they inhabit. But the referent of "they" is ambiguous here, and those who do not care extends beyond the immediate referents and includes a broader social world that routinely draws lines between those who are worthy of care and attention and those toward whom indifference and neglect are socially acceptable. This biopolitical and racial division regarding care, concern, and attunement gets internalized by those of us who make up "they," a predicament Melle Mel attempts to refuse.

In the tradition of the sorrow songs, "The Message" gives a voice and consideration to discordant dimensions of the social and political order—drug addiction, poverty, homelessness, prostitution, labor strikes, police harassment, incarceration, suicide, and low-quality education. Melle Mel and Duke Bootee, the two emcees on the track, express a desire to escape these circumstances, to break from these social realities, even as this desire runs up against socioeconomic constraints—"Got no money to move out, I guess I got no choice. . . . I tried to get away, but I couldn't get far cuz a man with a tow truck repossessed my car." As the lyrics suggest, the capacity to move and pursue options is largely determined by access to wealth and capital, to possessions that can be taken away. And yet the track indicates that there might be other kinds of movements and modes of stillness that hang alongside the unfulfilled desire to break free from the unfreedom that capital imposes. Consequently, if a constraint can denote a limit, then "The Message" plays with the notion of a limit or edge. The hook for the song reads, "Don't push me cuz I'm close to the edge. I'm trying not to lose my head. It's like a jungle sometimes, it makes me wonder how I keep from going under." Here the edge or limit connotes being on the verge of insanity, collapse, depression, or even death. La Marr Bruce might describe this as a moment of becoming mad while trying not to lose one's mind. As Bruce points out, within the protocols of enlightened reason and its anti-black formulations, blackness has been "framed . . . as always already wild, subrational, pathological, mentally unsound, mad."[51] Blackness exists at the edges of the proper human, maintaining the precarious line between human and animal. And insofar as "it's like a jungle sometimes," the group suggests that the human-animal boundary is traversable, even as certain kinds of subjects are routinely associated with animality, allowing this unstable relationship to appear secure. And yet, perhaps residing on the general edge or limit also enables one to hear possibilities, to discover new ways of being in the world that lie beyond imposed limits and boundaries. Perhaps going/falling under, "swinging low," or encountering the underside of the social world is necessary for radical change and transformation.

The content of the hook indicates that whatever prevents the members of the group from *completely going under* is an occasion for awe and wonder. Here I want to suggest that one of the things that prevents such collapse is laughter, but a distorted kind of laughter. Interspersed throughout the hook is the famous chant, "Uh huh huh huh," which almost sounds like a laugh that is tinged with irony and sarcasm.[52] This distorted laughter, which can also be heard as an exaggerated breath due to exhaustion, becomes more striking when juxtaposed to the line, "Cuz it's all about money, ain't a damn thing funny." The twisted laughter therefore registers, on the one hand, the seriousness and gravity of the themes that are being voiced. There is nothing funny, for instance, about the final verse, in which Melle Mel tells the story of a child who grows into a life of crime and eventually commits suicide in prison. The final verse concludes, "It was plain to see that your life was lost, you was cold and your body swung back and forth. But now your eyes sing the sad, sad song of how you lived so fast and died so young."[53] Even in this untimely death, the eyes of the suicide victim cry out and signify sorrow and loss, as if the cold, twisting body becomes a trace of a life lived in excess of regular rhythms and tempos. This is reminiscent of the rapper Scarface's confession that he could "never see a man cry 'til I seen that man die."[54] Death in these cases becomes a kind of inescapable recognition of our exposure to an outside, while the tear is a trace and enactment of that exposure. Scarface seems himself in the Other's death, and the man could be an impersonal reference to himself. At the same time, the "uh huh huh huh," refrain, read as a kind of twisted laughter, reminds us of how important laughter can be for those who regularly confront pain. As the narrator in Toni Morrison's novel *Jazz* points out, "Laughter is serious. More complicated and more serious than tears."[55] As intimated above, laughter, like a cry, can be a response to painful incongruities and tensions in one's life; laughter doesn't necessarily resolve these tensions, but it can enable us to reimagine our relationship to them, to face life's discordant notes with vibrancy and buoyancy or a willingness to surrender. When rap artist Q-Tip claimed, "I laugh to keep from crying," in response to "so much going on, people killing, people dying,"[56] he seems to be affirming the triumph of laughter over tears. Yet, insofar as laughter is a substitute for tears, Q-Tip also implies the presence of ongoing conditions that tempt him to weep and collapse. The distorted, sarcastic laughter in "The Message," I argue, is inflected with traces of sorrow, vestiges of the cry.

Melle Mel suggests that this dynamic between twisted laughter and tears, or pleasure and sorrow, reflects God's relationship to humanity. Referring to a child being born "with no state of mind" (the child whose end is the rope in prison), he raps, "God is smiling on you, but he's frowning, too, cuz only God knows what you go through."[57] In this line, the "you" is an ambivalent signifier with an uncertain referent, a technique that is prevalent in hip hop music. The "you" may refer to the fictional child in Melle Mel's story, the next blackened subject that seems fated toward prison, the listener, the viewer, et cetera. In this verse, we get a sense that God is affected or moved by human stories, decisions, and actions. According to Melle Mel, God has an intimate and unique understanding of what we "go through." The simultaneous smile and frown suggests that God identifies with the human tendency to oscillate between and across feelings of pleasure and pain, joy and sadness, satisfaction and anger. (And yet the image of God smiling and frowning on subjects can also be interpreted as vertical distance, separation, and spectatorship from above.) Recall that the Exodus narrative was popular in slave communities, in part, because it depicted a god who identified with their condition. Whether the notion of the Promised Land referred to escaping to the North, repatriation to Africa, or crossing an earthly Jordan to heaven, within antebellum black communities this idea carried a set of connotations that overlapped with and diverged from Puritan-inspired allusions to America as the new Jerusalem, a land of abundant opportunity and prosperity. This different relationship to America's promise is reiterated in one of the lines in "The Message"—"You got to have a con in the land of milk and honey." To survive in this contemporary Promised Land, according to the group, one often must subscribe to forms of deception, chicanery, and theft because the "abundant" resources and opportunities in this country are distributed unequally, a predicament sustained by the operations of racial capitalism. The language of "conning" also points to how the very idea and imaginary of America as the Promised Land is always entangled with dispossession, theft, and justifications of settler violence.

In the video component to "The Message," we see members of the Furious Five congregating on stoops and sidewalks, posing and styling on street corners, and rapping alongside dilapidated New York City tenements. The documentary-style footage oscillates between long shots of the group members against the environmental background and close-up shots of black men talking, walking, posing, gesticulating, greeting each other, carrying a boombox, and so forth. This reminds the listener and viewer that black masculine forms of intimacy, play, and sociality occur under regimes of exploitation and violence. These images that focus on the members of the group are intercut with shots of everyday movement in the broader New York cityscape, the movement of automobiles and people that is interrupted by visions of the ostensibly unhoused sitting and lying on the sidewalk. There is a complex interaction between Melle Mel and Duke Bootee, on the one hand, and some of the characters incorporated into their narrative or message. There are moments when a sense of proximity or sharedness with others is in tension with a separation from, for instance, the "crazy lady" who eats out of garbage cans and "used to be a fag hag." In other words, the emcees' narrative authority relies on a distance from the crazy and queer subject, even as madness, or a loss of coherence, is inscribed in the hook and pathos of the song. At the end of the video, the viewer sees and hears group members talking about a friend's mother who just underwent a robbery while a police car arrives on the scene. The group is accused, or misrecognized, by the officers of being a gang, and they are thrown into the police car. Consequently, this concluding scene reveals a connection, an affinity, between the group members and the child in the final verse whose life culminates in prison. There is a tinge of irony, since Melle Mel complained earlier of not being able to escape his confining predicament due to his car being repossessed. As the members are taken away by state authorities, we are reminded of how black life and sociality, especially in working-class and indigent spaces, are consistently under duress and surveillance. The viewer witnesses the criminalization of black bodies just hanging out, loitering, or congregating in spaces without a determinate aim or purpose. Riffing on the work of Ruth Gilmore, this last scene exemplifies how mass incarceration in the era of late capitalism is motivated by the need to turn surplus populations, or those subjects who bear the burden of excess, into something productive, even if this demand for productivity requires excessive violence and strategies of detainment.[58]

There is an incongruous interaction between these images, the lyrics, and the general sound/beat that drives "The Message." According to Dan Cairns, "Where [the song] was inarguably innovative, was in slowing the beat right down, and opening up space in the instrumentation—the music isn't so much hip hop as noirish, nightmarish slow funk, stifling and claustrophobic, with electro, dub, and disco jostling for room in the genre mix."[59] There is much to unpack in Cairns's description of the track's sonic innovation. For one, while he makes a contrast between hip hop and genres like funk, electro, and disco, Cairns also recalls how hip hop samples and blends multiple forms and sounds, in a manner that resembles bricolage. As Shanté Smalls argues, in opposition to one-dimensional narratives about hip hop's beginnings, what we experience in hip hop is a queer aesthetic defined by "performativity, bricolage, and pastiche."[60] While "The Message" exemplifies this incorporation and reexpression of multiple forms, Cairns also draws attention to the slowing of the beat (which allows for the lyrics to come through, for the listener to hear the message) and the haunting, overwhelming quality of this slowness. There is a ponderous and stifling quality to the beat, which is articulated through an echoing, or a repetition that fades in and out. And yet this reexpression of conditions that strangle and smother is supplemented by an allusion to disco, the club, dance, and the party. The festive is not easily separable from the "nightmarish." Even the term *funk* brings together multiple connotations, moods, and dispositions, exhibiting a cut in the genre. While associated with grooving, enjoyment, "super-freaky" desires, and ascension/escape, funk also signifies odor, smell, and the emissions of the body. In addition, to be in a funk means to experience sadness, to feel the downbeat, to be temporarily depressed.[61] Through the sampling of funk and disco, tracks like "The Message" keep alive and rearticulate an opaque cut, a dissonant interaction across various elements such as the groove, the unsanitized, and the expression of sorrow.

One feature of "The Message" that deserves further inquiry is the allusion to a divine power that is affected by suffering (smiles and frowns) while being ostensibly powerless, or unwilling, to intervene in the life of a black child fated toward prison and a twisted rope. While Melle Mel briefly invokes god, subsequent songs assume the form of a prayer or a protracted conversation between the artist and the divine. Think, for instance, of Arrested Development's "Tennessee," released in 1992. An alternative to the popularity of gangsta rap in the early 1990s, Arrested Development celebrated rural, southern black life and adopted an Afrocentric sound and look not unlike Jungle Brothers. "Tennessee," the first single from the group's debut album, is a prayer, a mourning song, and a dreamscape in response to personal and social loss. Listening to the first verse, we find out that the lead vocalist, Speech, has recently lost his grandmother and brother.[62] His recent grief becomes the occasion for a series of rhythmic petitions and confessions.

The listener is invited to hear, and participate in, the song as a journey from death to life, from exile to home, from darkness to enlightenment, a passage made possible by the "obvious relationship" and friendship between Speech and God. In the first verse, Speech reveals, "Lord, I've really been real stressed, down and out, losing ground." The prayer therefore begins with a crisis, a shattering, a sense that one's foundation has been taken away. Speech admits that he has become pessimistic as a result of the recent deaths in his life in addition to "brothers and sisters messin' up." In other words, his momentary pessimism derives from loss within his immediate family and a concern that his extended black family—his brothers and sisters—is a mess, in a state of confusion, a predicament of structural loss/death. This situation prompts Speech to ask for guidance, a desperate cry that for some "strange reason" leads him to Tennessee. In the second verse, one notices that returning to Tennessee is a signifier for working through the past, connecting with ancestors, and dealing with specters—childhood memories that remain with him and collective traumas that continue to haunt southern spaces and black communities ("Walk the roads my forefathers walked, climbed the trees my forefathers hung from"). It is important that Speech connects family lineages and names with physical spaces and objects such as roads and trees. The artist suggests that being in touch with the past, reaching back toward the ancestors, requires intimacy with the land and its ecology. One experiences the disjointed presence of the past, the spirits that inhabit the earth even in death, by walking and climbing and through song, dance, and contemplation. In the final verse, Speech suggests that his knowledge of history gives him a greater understanding of black people's general predicament, one that he still describes as a mess. He even questions God about the gap between his personal enlightenment and the perceived darkness in which his people are stuck. Here we could read the final verse as an expression of reconciliation and victory. In line with the kinds of shifts that Du Bois hears in the sorrow song, Speech has moved from confusion and incoherence to a position of fullness and assurance, a transition that enables him to look with pity and scorn at "brothers on the corner playing ghetto games." But this reading is complicated by Speech's admission to God and the listener that his thirst has not been quenched, that his desires have not been satisfied. While the Lord gives him more to consume and contemplate, Speech acknowledges a gap between aspiration and actuality, a result of the instability inherent in that dynamic. This gap means that his search for some ultimate truth "in front of him" will be "blurry." The blurring quality renders untenable any stable distinction between the enlightened (Speech) and the benighted (his people).

One theme that reverberates through "Tennessee" is the idea and sound of home. Throughout the track, the word *home* is exclaimed intermittently; in addition, toward the end of the song, group member Dionne Farris wails, "Take me home," several times, each time increasing the intensity. According to Farrah Jasmine Griffin, "With the word home, Farris's voice rises several octaves, making that portion of the song a space of transcendence."[63] Another way to put this is that home and flight (flying home) become inseparable in Farris's vocal ascension. In contrast to Speech's masculine vocals, her female voice/cry becomes an ecstatic opening, taking the listener to another space and time. As in the spirituals, the term *home* has different connotations in "Tennessee." On the one hand, home is associated with the rural South. While the urban North was imagined in slave narratives and the early twentieth century as a promising site of freedom and opportunity, Arrested Development conjures an enduring legacy within black culture of claiming the South as home, source, and origin. But home also has a less determinate referent in the song—another place, a now/here that is devoid of the remembrance of pain and hurt. Speech associates this other place with a dream, as if he knows that prayer and song operate at the intersection of "real" life and fantasy. Finally, home is linked to death, a funeral for Speech's grandmother, which confirms Karla Holloway's claim that "in African America the cultural tradition of *going home for a funeral* [is] strong and seriously attended to."[64] In the video, the complexities internal to home are visualized. We see members dancing, singing, and painting in open fields and wooded areas, images that contrast with the kind of urban topography depicted in "The Message." Visions of desolate space are juxtaposed with images of bodies moving across and congregating against the rural landscape in a manner that suggests a fraught relationship between emptiness, loneliness, and intimacy. The video's black-and-white stock invokes yearning for the southern past, a yearning that is interrupted by an image of hands in chains and portraits of lynched black bodies—flesh hanging from ropes, similar to the child in the final verse of "The Message." Through these images, the conventional understanding of home as a place, and existential state, of comfort and stability undergoes a tearing and reconfiguration.[65]

Even though Speech and God have a relationship that is cultivated through prayer and conversation, this relationship is fraught with pain, doubt, and occasional estrangement. These qualities are similarly voiced and moaned in Ghostface Killah and Ox's 2007 song "The Prayer," an extended cry in the form of call and response between the two artists. In this prayer, Ox sings a mournful prayer to the sound of a finger snap, suggesting that this kind of communication does not need the assistance of external instruments. Or this is a reminder of the ways that the body becomes an instrument of pleasure and connection. In addition to the accompanying finger snap, we hear Ghostface Killah responding to and encouraging Ox's emotional expression. It stands out that two black men, with names associated with violence and animality, perform a particular homosocial vulnerability and intimacy throughout the prayer. Listening to the protracted moan, we hear an ongoing tension between sorrow and hope, gratitude and doubt. Ox proclaims, "Life is so painful, yet I'm so thankful."[66] Although life is marked by pain and hardship, Ox expresses a sense of gratitude for the life that has been bestowed. One is tempted to think that, for Ox, there is an excessive quality to life that always includes and exceeds the pain that comes with it. At the same time, Ox repeatedly wonders whether God is responding to his mournful call: "Sometimes I feel like he don't hear me. Sometimes I wonder, do he love me?" Here the use of the third-person pronoun—*he* instead of the more interpersonal *you*—indicates a moment of alienation or separation as well as an attempt to draw the listener into the suspended cry. Therefore, when Ox sings, "I keep reminiscing on my loved ones that are gone," this loss is intensified by a fissure in the divine/human connection, an occasional lack or abyss that constantly thwarts this relationship. And yet Ox's cry, fueled by memories and morning, becomes the occasion for what remains, for an absent presence that both propels and unsettles.

The concern about God's potential absence or neglect resonates with 50 Cent's confessions in "Many Men (Wish Death)," a song released in 2003 that reenacts a near-death experience in which the Queens, New York, native was shot nine times. In reexpressing this traumatic event to a haunting piano melody, 50 Cent reveals, "Every night I talk to God, but he don't say nothing back. I know he protecting me, but I still stay with my gat."[67] Like Ox, 50 suggests that he must confront the absence, or silence, of God as part of his earthly experience, his endurance through life. This means that 50 cannot feel too secure; the gat is a kind of phallic replacement for God's protection (which 50 simultaneously affirms and doubts). While 50 claims that he does not cry anymore or look to the sky, one can hear "Many Men" as a cry in response to those who have "wished death" on him, a prayer in protest against the violent, worldly conditions that produce antagonistic interactions among black men who have been trained to survive in the streets. The allusion in the hook to "blood in my eye" refers to the traumatic event that 50 is reenacting, while also signifying troubled vision. We might also wonder if the allusion to blood in the eye is a substitute for the tears that he supposedly no longer sheds. While there is a melancholic undertone and downbeat to "Many Men," 50 Cent claims, "Joy wouldn't feel so good, if it wasn't for pain." In other words, joy always bears the trace of the anguish that makes moments of exaltation necessary. Immediately after making the joy-pain connection, 50 raps that death "gotta be easy cuz life is hard, it'll leave you physically, mentally, and emotionally scarred." According to 50, death might be a liberation, or moment of relaxation, from a life that scars and wounds both physically and emotionally. In other words, death is a release from, but remains in continuity with, the modes of violence and anguish that permeate life and the psyche.

In addition to the sharp piano sound that brings to mind a ponderous teardrop, the hook looms large and draws attention. There is a peculiar relationship between the "many, many, many men" and the death wish or drive that 50 voices (as he transitions from rapping softly to singing the hook). According to Freud, the death drive is a general compulsion toward destruction and aggression that can be directed internally or externally. More generally, it is a compulsion to return to an inorganic state. While the death drive is usually opposed to the erotic impulse to create and preserve unities, Freud contends that the death drive "can be pressed into the service of Eros."[68] Among other consequences, this means that aggressive desires and attachments can be organized and directed toward certain kinds of animate and inanimate beings for the sake of preserving prevailing modes of social life and attachment. 50 Cent's participation in the constancy of the death drive is complicated. On the one hand, there are people in his immediate environment who wish to obliterate him. Conversely, he warns that he will "put a hole in a nigga" for messing with him. This puncturing, directed toward others, is of course something the artist has experienced and the song is reenacting. And yet this back-and-forth hostility circulates within a broader world that sustains and reproduces social life by disproportionately positioning certain subjects, especially poor black people, closer to death, desperation, and loss. 50 expresses an implicit understanding of this predicament when he takes a moment in his second verse to recognize his friends/niggas serving life behind bars, those whose lives have been condemned to a death sentence. The "many men," a *many*, a countlessness that seems in the hook as if it could be iterated infinitely, points to an abundance of people and arrangements that sustain a particular direction and circulation of the death drive toward 50, black masculinity, and blackness more generally. Even the title of the album, *Get Rich or Die Tryin'*, indicates how the pursuit of wealth is intertwined with the risk of death, death that can be assumed by the self or directed toward others within the matrix of capital. Like most gods and sacred economies, capital demands its sacrifices and offerings.[69] Consequently, as some commentators have mentioned, 50 Cent's album and his subsequent ventures (including the self-help book *The 50th Law* with Robert Greene) align nicely with late capitalist reasoning, even as the trace of death and murder punctuates any casual account of capital and what it demands from its subjects to acquire wealth.[70]

Artists like Ox and 50 Cent gesture toward a fissure between God and the black male subject. As Ebony Utley powerfully argues, this fraught gap resonates differently in cases where black women desire fulfillment from a divine power that, especially in dominant Christian traditions, is figured as a paternal sovereign. Drawing on bell hooks's "doin for daddy" motif, Utley shows how female artists often imagine God as a father or lover, and in some cases both. She indirectly combines the insights of Ludwig Feuerbach (God as projection of human attributes) and Sigmund Freud (God as the symbolic father writ large) by claiming that women rappers often depict God in terms of an ideal, protective father (sometimes a substitution for an absent biological father) or the imperfect lover who too often takes advantage of the unequal power relations between men and women. As Utley succinctly puts it, "Female rappers' relationships with God reflect their relationships with men."[71] In her astute reading of Lauryn Hill and Mary J. Blige's classic duet, "I Used to Love Him," which appears on Hill's 1998 album *The Miseducation of Lauryn Hill*, Utley claims that Hill and Blige strive to overcome oppressive romantic relationships by uncritically submitting to the divine father, a substitution that still keeps them subordinated to a patrimonial order. While relationships with men are described as "addictions" and women playing the sand to the male lover's ocean, Utley questions whether this unhealthy relationship changes structurally when the beloved object becomes the transcendent "father." To be sure, Utley acknowledges that reliance on a divine father occasionally provides women with a sense of self-esteem and power in a male-dominated industry with rigid gender norms and expectations. Yet ultimately she contends that "doin' it for daddy is problematic because it demands domination and [female] submission."[72] Blige and Hill's duet represents a tendency within black female strategies to turn to daddy with the hope of being rescued from loss, trauma, violence, and betrayal. This reliance on a sovereign father as a replacement for pernicious, hierarchical relationships with men is for Utley a rearticulation of black female submission and sacrifice. The result is that black women bear the onus of performing self-renunciation, or self-dissolution, for the sake of maintaining the fantasy of patriarchal order and plenitude.[73] While Utley focuses on the displacement of gendered hierarchies in a track like "I Used to Love

Him," she also directs our attention to the immanent back and forth between Blige and Hill, an exchange of cries that can sound like competition, fusion and separation, as well as shared vulnerability. We could call it a black feminine practice of anguished intimacy, of communicating through cuts and wounds.[74]

Throughout "I Used to Love Him," one hears a sample from Raekwon's "Ice Cream" percolate into the foreground of the track. On this song from Raekwon's debut 1995 purple tape album, *Only Built 4 Cuban Linx . . .*, he and other members of Wu-Tang speak about the different flavors of women that can get "touched" and sexually "torn up." The comparison of women of different racial and ethnic identities to various flavors of ice cream connotes a relationship between (heterosexual male) erotic desire, consumption, and the association of female bodies with sugar and sweetness. As the Raekwon sample cuts into Hill and Blige's vocal expressions, a juxtaposition emerges, a connection between androcentric fantasies of consuming (black and brown) women and a particular black feminine experience of being "torn and confused, wasted and used."[75] The sample and call and response is an occasion to reflect differently on the routine ways that black women undergo and refuse subordination, consumption, and disposability within hip hop's androcentric economy, one that mimics the law of the father but that also (as I will discuss in chapter 3) overflows and undermines conventional sex/gender logics, norms, and patterns of performance. The track by Hill and Blige is also an occasion to reflect on how love is inseparable from relations of power, discordance, and anguish. Love and death form a tortuous pairing.

And this pairing can be heard throughout both *The Miseducation of Lauryn Hill* and her broader musical corpus. Think, for instance, of the introduction to the album, which depicts a classroom attendance call. When other children's names are called, there is a silent response of "Here!" but when Lauryn Hill's name is called and repeated, there is a glaring silence, an absence. The album begins with Hill's subtraction from a particular kind of pedagogical subject formation, a classroom discussion (dispersed and continued across the album) about love and relationships led by Ras Baraka.[76] The introduction fades into the first song, "Lost Ones," which, among other things, alludes to the frictions between Hill and other members of her group, Fugees. There is a "you" that has just lost "one" or a sense of oneness and wholeness; Hill introduces a cut into the very notion of the one, the unified, or some coherent sense of relationality. The articulation of loss, or being lost, is accompanied by a fierce drumbeat and Jamaican patois; it elicits dance and bodily movement while discussing a defeat, a break, a breakdown between the you and the one. Consequently, loss does not exclusively lead to sorrow, or a limited notion of sorrow equated with sadness. On another release, Hill sings, "How sad, how sad that all things come to an end,"[77] while reminiscing about the sweetest Thing she has ever known. Here notice the doubling of the "how sad" (which is intensified by Hill ad-libbing the words alongside the singing). This sadness, attached to the evanescence of things, is juxtaposed to the sweetness of the Thing (in an indirect tribute to Chaka Khan and Rufus), an enjoyment that is necessarily fleeting and subject to change and inversion. Perhaps the Thing is impossible to grasp and keep; perhaps the Thing will always be the occasion for a kind of ambivalence regarding desire and affect—think of Hill singing "When it hurt so bad, why's it feel so good?"[78] Or maybe Hill's claim that everything comes to an end is a difficult embrace of the nothing that subtends things. In her duet with D' Angelo, "Nothing Even Matters," one wonders where the stress should be placed—is it that *nothing* at all matters or has meaning, or should we think about the ways that nothing, that which cannot be thingified, still indicates a kind of matter and mattering, producing senses and meanings that cannot be captured or quantified.[79] While I won't pretend to resolve this doubleness in the relationship between nothing and matter, it does underscore how a sense of the evanescence of things can be an occasion for sadness and anguish as well as a kind of intimacy with a void at the heart of (black) existence.

And if this void upsets a commitment to oneness and unity, perhaps Queen Latifah's 1993 song "U.N.I.T.Y." resonates with this dynamic. On this track, Latifah provides various accounts of how the word *bitch* gets used to "make a sista feel low,"[80] to embolden intimate partner abuse, and to justify undesired touches and grabs. Even as Latifah says that there are exceptions to the rule (the B-word is permissible in moments of play), she articulates a predicament in which naming, or interpellation, can be fatal (especially when the name, the moniker, is part of a racialized and gendered American grammar that positions black women as available objects and flesh). As Spillers points out, this kind of "naming and evaluation" demonstrates that "sticks and bricks might break our bones, but words will most certainly kill us."[81] While Latifah is getting at something like intramural violence, the hook combines love, blackness, and infinity. There is a sense that "loving a black wo/man from infinity to infinity" might be the vehicle to black unity and solidity. And yet the appearance of the song title introduces ambiguity. The punctuation between the letters suggests that the title is an acronym, a name for something else that is never defined. In addition, the marks in between the letters draw attention to the gaps between letters and words as if there is an abyss subtending language and speech. By spelling out *unity* on the hook, by breaking the title down into its components, one is left with a reminder that the coherence of black unity as concept, desire, and practice is punctured and punctuated by the tear, the breaking down of meaning. Sorrow points to a void in meaning and the unified, even when these qualities are secured by appeals to a divine presence/absence.

Preparing for Death, Hearing the Life After

As Du Bois points out, and as intimated in previously discussed tracks and artists, the sorrow song does not only direct hopes and desires toward a divine entity. The cry from the blackened subject occasionally treats life and death as "standalone" sources of hope and liberation. As described above, there is a discordant interplay between life and death, especially in the context of black strivings. Social life defines itself against the death that black flesh signifies; death for the kidnapped African was a twisted sort of liberation from the anguish of earthly existence; through practices of remembrance, mourning, and conjuring, black people find ways to speak with the dead, to inhabit the infinitesimal gap between life and death. How does hip hop imagine and dwell in this liminal space? Within all the gratuitous violence in hip hop, can one hear rap artists self-identifying as subjects and objects of cruelty and anguish? Does a readiness to die connote an intimacy with death, loss, and abjection? Or does it become an occasion for self-aggrandizing violence and cruelty toward other bodies associated with nonbeing? What is the relationship between a readiness to die and a readiness to kill?

These questions haunt any listening of *Ready to Die*, the debut album from Notorious B.I.G. (aka Biggie Smalls). As Joan Morgan points out, below and alongside the all too familiar machismo in these songs, one can also hear "guilt, regret, and depression."[82] And, as described by Aimé J. Ellis, this album is part of an aesthetic tradition, which includes Richard Wright's *Native Son*, in which artists, writers, and musicians respond to the "a deathly history of racial terror and state violence" that has shaped black masculinity by defining freedom in terms of the prevalence of death and the impulse to overcome fear.[83] Biggie's classic 1994 album was released in the aftermath of the popularity of Dr. Dre's *The Chronic* in addition to transitions within New York City–based hip hop toward stark street narratives, themes associated with drug culture, gritty lyrics, and increasing fascination with mafia icons, both fictional and historical. The very name "Biggie Smalls" derives from a gangster character in Sidney Poitier's 1975 film *Let's Do It Again*. Biggie also assumed the name Frank White, the fictional drug lord in Abel Ferrara's 1990 film *King of New York*, to indicate his drug-dealing past and to crown himself as the best, most dominant rapper in New York City. Grandmaster Flash and the Furious Five's "The Message" was released in the

Reagan era of supply-side economics and severe government retrenchment, while Biggie's album was born into a Clinton administration that in many ways extended the neoliberal policies (reduction and redistribution of welfare and state assistance, tough-on-crime legislation, antilabor policies) that connect Republicans and Democrats. When Biggie claims in "Everyday Struggle" that "Mayor Giuliani ain't tryin' to see no black man turn into John Gotti," he alludes to the ways the New York mayor's crime prevention policy in the 1990s disproportionately surveilled and punished indigent and working-class blacks. This line also reveals how mafia figures are touted as symbols of wealth, power, and success within certain hip hop imaginaries, even as there is something about black maleness that cannot reach the level of even a criminalized white subjectivity.[84] Or to put it slightly differently, in those instances where Biggie alludes to himself as "the Teflon Don,"[85] he reminds us of how Italian Americanness has historically inhabited, shared, and been separable from the slot of blackness.[86] Finally, as we saw in "The Message," the enduring conjunctions and attractions between hip hop and the mafia demonstrate how the American Dream and fantasy of becoming a complete subject through economic mobility is never far from crime, criminality, and violence (and the pleasures that accompany representing and consuming images of these conditions).

Perhaps what initially strikes one about *Ready to Die* is the album cover. Against an all-white background, we see an image of a black child that is supposed to represent Biggie as an infant. The juxtaposition of the child, whiteness (usually a signifier for innocence or purity), and the theme of anticipating death generates tensions and queries. Here we might think of queer theorist Lee Edelman's engagement with the figure of the Child, a figure that represents cultural and political investments in futurity, the fulfillment of meaning, and the reproduction of order. As he puts it, "The Child remains the perpetual horizon of every acknowledged politics, the fantasmatic beneficiary of every political intervention."[87] In other words, the figure of the Child is an emblem of collective fantasies for some future wholeness, a repository for our hopeful commitment to a future in which the fissures and breaks that mark the social world will be sutured. For Edelman, queerness—not unlike blackness for Moten—is associated with the death drive that unravels our identification with "governing fictions" and solid identities: "Where futurism [the figure of the Child] always anticipates . . . a realization of meaning that will suture identity by closing the gap, queerness undoes the identities through which we experience ourselves as subjects."[88] As José Esteban Muñoz points out, Edelman's powerful analysis of the function of the Child in *No Future* leaves out a discussion of race and antiblackness. This omission prevents him from engaging the different ways that black people have imagined, constructed, and deconstructed futurity and the accompanying figure of the Child.[89] The album cover for *Ready to Die*, like the final verse to "The Message," suggests that the future for the black child has often been marked by death, rather than being an occasion for the reproduction and affirmation of social order. Or, to put it differently, futurity, or the extension of the order of things, means the reproduction, and anticipation, of untimely death for black subjects. Death and futurity are intertwined in an antiblack and exploitative capitalist world; Biggie makes this imbrication audible on his debut album.[90]

Listening to the album, one constantly experiences the tangency between life and death, a proximity that is associated with birth and the black mother's womb. Consider the introduction, for instance, an intro that offers a musical biography of Biggie's life up until that point.[91] The album begins with an ominous sound that emerges slowly from silence; then we hear a pulsating heartbeat intertwined with the voice the album's executive producer Sean "Puffy" Combs saying "Come on, push," as he encourages the woman in the scene (depicting Biggie's mother), who is on the verge of giving birth.[92] We hear several cries, including one that was clearly a mother in pain and another that was less clear whether it was the mother or child. When the cry of the newborn becomes more legible, it is heard against the backdrop of Curtis Mayfield's song "Superfly," which points to a film about a drug *pusher*. By juxtaposing the mother's push with drug pushing, the introduction suggests that Biggie's life is always already entangled with forms of social death—violent conditions that involve the wide distribution and consumption of illegal drugs, while placing the burden of blame and criminality on indigent black communities. The allusion to the 1972 Blaxploitation film *Superfly* brings to mind the cinematic roots of hip hop as well as an enduring legacy of commodifying the allure and appeal of black masculine cool. The subsequent scenes in the introduction—an argument between Biggie's parents, an unsuccessful train robbery, Biggie's release from prison—all include diegetic fragments of classic hip hop songs such as "Rapper's Delight" and "Top Billin'." Consequently, Biggie's birth/life becomes coextensive with the emergence and development of hip hop.

In the introduction, Biggie traces the origins of *Ready to Die* from black female labor and his own birth; on "Respect," he even goes so far as to imagine what it was like being in the womb. Biggie talks about the womb as a place from which he wants to escape, suggesting that it is a kind of prison or space of confinement. He raps, "Umbilical cord's wrapped around my neck, I'm seeing my death and I ain't even took my first step." Here Biggie suggests that his inauguration into the world is preceded by an anticipation of death. Echoing Martin

Heidegger, Biggie describes himself as a being toward death, one whose very life begins with the presentiment of self-loss and erasure. We should linger a bit on the fact that his "mother's gut" becomes the occasion for these reflections on the interplay between life and death. As Victor Turner points out, the maternal womb has traditionally been imagined as a site of liminality, or a space that is betwixt and between two determinate positions. As the opposite of structure and stability, liminality connotes a state of ambiguity. Turner writes, "This liminality is frequently likened to death, to being in the womb, to invisibility, to darkness, to bisexuality, to the wilderness, and to the eclipse of the sun and the moon."[93] The chord that links the womb to liminality, and the black mother to the son, generates several questions. How does the son's formation and deformation in the world (going from "ashy to classy")[94] depend on his separation from the mother, his disavowal of the womb? In other words, does the desire for recognition, transparency, and self-possession require Biggie to deny the qualities associated with the womb, femininity, black motherhood, et cetera? Does this denial contribute to his violent depictions and relationships with women, as heard in songs such as "Get Money" or "Just Playing (Dreams)"? Here it is important to underscore an ambivalence in Biggie's relationship to the womb from which he retrospectively speaks. On the one hand, he seems to desire liberation from the black mother's body, even as in other contexts he speaks vividly about sucking on his mother's breast, indicating an ongoing dependency and attachment. At the same time, the intimacy with death, the sonic interplay between life and death, the openness to that which social life excludes and denigrates, is made possible by painfully embracing those qualities—opacity, liminality, wild(er)ness—associated with the black mother's womb. In addition, Judith Butler would remind us that the fact that he can retrospectively use the pronoun *I* when speaking about his experience inside his mother is a necessary disavowal, and slight acknowledgment, of a moment when this separable I could not exist, when the child is completely dependent on the mother.[95] Or, as Spillers might put it, the moment indicates how Biggie is forever touched by the black mother, even if he occasionally feels alienated from her.[96]

Throughout *Ready to Die*, Biggie articulates an intimate relationship with death and violence. Often, he is self-depicted as the agent of violence ("Gimme the Loot"), while at other times he expresses susceptibility to being the object of envy and potential theft, as we hear in "Warning." While Biggie adopts the proverbial pimp or Big Poppa persona, he also expresses vulnerability, lament, and tears in a song/narrative where his girlfriend is murdered. And even though Biggie generally takes on a self-aggrandizing posture, he also becomes the target of deprecating humor in a sex scene/skit in which his female partner's arousal is intensified by poking fun at Biggie's blackness and obesity. As Mecca Sullivan points out, Biggie's fatness gets mobilized on the album in ways that consolidate conventional masculinity and enable nonnormative sexual desires and fantasies.[97] When, for instance, Biggie admits on "Me and My Bitch" that "you looked so good, I suck on your daddy's dick," he is relying on queer desire, as excess and shock, to express the intensity of his heteroerotic attraction (he is also riffing on a comedy skit by Richard Pryor). In "Everyday Struggle," we hear the refrain, "I don't want to live no mo, sometimes I hear death knockin' at my front do." On this track, Biggie associates everydayness with a succession of images and experiences: drug dealing, hustling, a friend being murdered, crack smoke that "makes his brain feel so strange," syringes in the veins, waking up stressed, "broken" pockets, et cetera. One is prompted to think about how these kinds of harrowing conditions have become so mundane, so second nature, and perhaps too familiar for the casual listener. When Biggie claims to "hear death knockin'" at his front door, he suggests a familiarity with, and proximity to, death, while repeating the home/death connection heard in Arrested Development's "Tennessee." This line also invites consumers to "hear death," to be attuned to the losses, vulnerabilities, and general condition of precarity that sometimes go undetected when listening to an album like *Ready to Die*. This may be due to the ways black men are disciplined to appear and perform within hip hop, or the related ways we are framed to see and not see the complexities of black male subjectivity, all within the context of systemic violence that conditions this subjectivity. Paying attention to this complexity means hearing moments in "Everyday Struggle" when Biggie reminisces about another time and place when he/you didn't have to live "so devilish." This pleasant, nostalgic memory resembles the wistful verses in "Things Done Changed," where he invokes family cookouts, childhood games, and amiable relationships before things in his community took a turn for the worse. Perhaps we can reject the rigid distinction between "back in the day" and the petrifying present and instead acknowledge that alternative practices and modes of sociality are always being fabricated and remembered amid situations that are cruel and frightening. For Biggie, recollection of another mode of being is linked to a wish, a fantasy, or a dream with no determinate content. The wish is simply defined as a momentary departure from/within the violent predicament into which he has been thrown.

The notion of departure takes on a serious note in "Suicidal Thoughts," the album's final track, in which Biggie confesses a yearning to "leave." In addition to the eerie, ominous beat that accompanies a voice that sounds heavier and more depressed than in previous songs, there are several aspects that painfully stand out. For one, "Suicidal Thoughts" begins with the sound of phone numbers being dialed. There is an attempt to reach someone, to be heard by another person, in this case Combs. In light of the fact that Biggie reveals how alienated he feels from the women in his life (both his mother and his baby's mother), the disjointed conversation between Biggie and Puffy demonstrates the desire for homosocial intimacy, even as one prepares to undergo self-inflicted death. In addition to the yearning for connection with another, Biggie begins his verse by rejecting a religious imaginary that links the achievement of salvation and immortality with the rejection of blackness and what Cecilio Cooper calls "chthonic underworlds."[98] Not only does he confess a desire to go to hell, but he suggests that he would not be accepted in heaven by the "goodie-goodies dressed in all white." By affirming his attachment to "black Timbs and black hoodies," Biggie indicates how the typical imagination of heaven, an extension of the will to purity, cannot assimilate signifiers of blackness, opacity, and abjection. Because God is often depicted as a sovereign lawgiver "on some strict shit," Biggie protests that this picture of the divine contributes to the denigration of erotic pleasure and indolence—activities that are seen as excessive and unproductive. While Biggie can be read as stereotypically associating blackness with gambling and carrying guns, we might also read him as refusing to desire a purified domain that would require him to reject those bodies, desires, and qualities that the compulsion toward purity defines itself over and against. It is important that Biggie compare himself to Pookie, the crack addict who is killed in the 1991 film *New Jack City*, and Ramo, the graffiti artist in the 1984 film *Beat Street*, who is electrocuted on the subway's third rail while fighting an adversary. Here we are given a slightly different understanding of a suicidal thought. Perhaps this term alludes to a way of thinking with the unrecognized—those who have been erased under the sway of cruel paradigms, those who do not survive the unfolding of prevailing narratives. In other words, to think with, alongside, and in intimacy with the dead entails a kind of death to the self, or the very notion of a coherent self. As Albert Camus points out, in his discussion of the relationship between thought and suicide, "Beginning to think is beginning to be undermined."[99] But this is a death that is not necessarily discontinuous with life or a different way of living.

The song, and album, ends with the piercing sound of a gunshot, followed by Puffy crying out several times, "Ay yo, Big." Puffy's frantic voice fades into the sound of a heartbeat, indicating a sort of circularity with respect to the opening birth scene. In this instance, the heartbeat gets increasingly slower and eventually fades into silence, as the album reaches a denouement. We know that Biggie's second album, released in 1997, is called *Life After Death* and begins where the first album ends. We also know that the album was released two weeks after Biggie was gunned down in Los Angeles. The final song on the album, "You're Nobody ('til Somebody Kills You)," which riffs on Dean Martin's "Nobody 'til Somebody Loves You," replaces *love* with *death*, as if death converts you into a body, a coherent identity, a corpse.[100] Death is the horizon and end of becoming; for those who have been relegated to the realm of nothing and no-bodiness, death, as physical demise, is kind of a telos or culmination of the death lived within life. And yet, what are we to make of the life after, the life that exceeds death but is always already haunted and permeated by the actual possibility of erasure, violence, and obliteration? How does the listener participate in this "after" that grammatically resides between (Biggie's) life and death? What kind of listening practice would enable us to acknowledge the simultaneous enjoyments and frustrations involved in reexperiencing *Ready to Die*? When we listen to this album, how does the violence that punctures and shapes the subjectivity of black men—and which is often reenacted and redirected toward other black men, black women, and queer individuals within hip hop's masculine performance—affect, interrupt, and destabilize us? Is there a way to better hear the forms of social death that are always knocking, calling, enticing, and repelling us, while also cultivating forms of intimacy and sociality with those who "all of their lives have been considered the worst"?[101] More generally, how might we listen differently to the forms of sorrow and mourning within hip hop—pouring out liquor in remembrance of the dead, calling out a deceased friend or family member, shouting out loved ones who have been imprisoned, reenacting the death of those no longer present, telling stories that involve depression, disappointment, and alienation—that punctuate fantasies of triumph and invincibility? Furthermore, how does one attend to the unmourned and ungrievable within rap performance and practice?

Lamenting the Death of Hip Hop

Recall that in his tribute to the sorrow song genre, Du Bois laments the misappropriation of authentic spirituals by the minstrel shows. He makes a distinction between real spirituals that emanate from the heart and soul of the Negro and those that are debased imitations used for crude entertainment. Therefore, while Du Bois touts the Fisk Jubilee Singers as the inheritors of the sorrow song tradition, he also indicates a concern about the potential death or loss of authentic spirituals. This understandable anxiety, which acknowledges how antiblackness operates through cultural theft and caricature, resonates with enduring concerns about hip hop's state, predicament, and decline. Think, for instance, of when Nas shook up the hip hop world in 2006 with his "Hip Hop Is Dead," a pronouncement that, as Monica Miller points out, is analogous to Nietzsche's madman who proclaims the death of god.[102] Whether in agreement or disagreement with this bold claim, many took Nas to be saying that hip hop has become too mainstream, a development that has undermined the quality, value, and vitality of the genre. Back in the day, according to this interpretation, hip hop artists were motivated by the desire to create and innovate, to delineate politically relevant hardships and difficulties faced by black people, and to demonstrate skills in accordance with the internal goods and standards of the art form. Now that the production of hip hop is almost entirely regulated by the profit motive, "real" hip hop is dead or dying quickly. Similar to Du Bois on the sorrow songs, those who agree with Nas worry that hip hop has been tainted and corrupted by the entertainment industry, which increasingly presents exaggerated and one-dimensional depictions of urban life, black culture, black people, and so forth. If this formulation conjures up the caricatures of black life involved in minstrelsy, recall that Spike Lee made connections between the hip hop industry and the tradition of blackface in his 2000 film *Bamboozled*. Artists like Lupe Fiasco, in his 2012 song and video "Bitch Bad," and Little Brother, whose 2005 album is called the *Minstrel Show*, have also made this comparison. For many people, Nas's performative utterance is clear: Hip hop is no longer what it once was. It lacks the quality and depth it once had, and this is partly because it has lost its rootedness in the local communities and venues that originally nurtured the genre. For many celebrants of East Coast hip hop, this simply means that New York City is no longer the epicenter.

Nas's lament/eulogy might seem outdated, considering his own career revival in the last decade and the sense that his recent albums are part of a wave of artists bringing that "old feeling back." Yet I am interested in a particular logic of declension that Nas's speech act articulates, which continues to be expressed and contested through various channels such as music, websites, social media, and informal gatherings and debates. The lyrics to "Hip Hop Is Dead" seem to convey this narrative of decline. Nas suggests that commercialization has taken something vital out of hip hop: "Everybody sound the same, commercialize the game. Reminiscing when it wasn't all business. It forgot where it all started. So we gather here for the dearly departed. . . . Went from turntables to MP3s, from *Beat Street* to commercials on Mickey D's, from gold cables to Jacobs, from plain facials to Botox and face lifts."[103] Here Nas notes that the mainstreaming of hip hop has led to monotony and repetition. His critical stance resonates with Adorno and Horkheimer's concerns about the culture industry and its tendency to diminish creativity and individuality.[104] Nas, however, does not fall into the trap of thinking that hip hop used to be completely unfettered by market forces. Rather, he reminisces about a time when these forces were not the *central factors* determining the production and consumption of hip hop culture. This wistful evocation of a time when turntables, *Beat Street*, and gold cables defined hip hop is a response to a culture of forgetfulness, a contemporary youth culture that has neglected hip hop's origins. There seems to be a contestable assumption that "where it all started" is a place and time that is more authentic, meaningful, and creative than the present state. And the reference to Botox and facelifts, in contrast to plain facials, is an allusion to the overly fabricated quality of hip hop and its move away from authenticity, as evidenced by its flawless, blemish-free appearance.

Although the title of this song indicates that the death of hip hop has already occurred, it is not always clear that Nas endorses this position. As Miller contends, Nas's prophetic statement is not necessarily anticipating the "ontological death of hip hop" but making a call for renewal and reinvigoration.[105] Think, for instance, of the hook that reverberates throughout the track—"If hip hop should die before I wake, I'll put an extended clip and body 'em all day. Roll to every station, wreck the DJ." Although we hear in the background that "hip hop just died this morning," the hook indicates that there are still signs of life in this cultural legacy, that the death of hip hop has not occurred just yet. The hook also suggests that Nas will not allow the DJs to murder hip hop without some kind of retributive justice. He seems to be sending out a warning to those DJs who are contributing to hip hop's demise. The fact that Nas even wrote this song suggests that he, like other artists, is fighting to keep the legacy of hip hop alive. But we must remember that hip hop, for Nas, is not some cultural object separate from the people who embody and live it. He raps, "If hip hop should die, we die together. Bodies in the morgue, lie together." Insofar as hip hop has shaped and formed Nas, he cannot divorce his own life/death from that of hip hop.

There are at least two ways to think about the broader implications of Nas's contestable proclamation. One way, as intimated above, is to interpret Nas as saying that hip hop has simply fallen from its original state. As Eliade points out, the general commitment to golden-era tropes shows how mythic narratives continue to operate in a supposedly secular world. For him, myth entails a story about the beginnings and origins of some phenomenon, a story that tends to include gods and divine beings but generally gives an account of the original moment when that phenomenon was the most real and meaningful.[106] According to Eliade, "It is difficult to imagine a radical outmoding of mythological thought as long as the prestige of 'origins' remains intact."[107] Here my point is not to reject or celebrate the permanence of myth. I simply want to highlight how the investment in origins, founding figures, and the accompanying golden-era motif demonstrates an investment in mythic narrative. One problem with this particular veneration of origins is that it expresses a will to purity that divests the past (and present) of its discordance and opacity. Critics of contemporary hip hop culture often employ the golden era—the 1980s and early 1990s—as a standard for measuring and evaluating current styles, performances, and modes of being. In light of the industry's predicament— repetition, uniformity, commodification of racialized violence and sexuality— there is a temptation to look backward, to reminisce about when things were different, even if this difference is not as pronounced as many pundits suggest.

The dichotomy between the idealized past and the impure present accompanies a disposition toward time when the main alternative to the present is the past, which needs to be purified (or imagined as more pure) to serve as that substitute. To be sure, this diachronic contrast has always been accompanied by a synchronic distinction between the real and fake, the underground and mainstream, the originators and imitators. Earlier hip hop artists and consumers also imagined and regulated a boundary between the pure and impure, the authentic and inauthentic. Consequently, the term *crossover* has been attributed to groups or individuals who endanger hip hop by dragging it across this boundary to cater to the mainstream. In addition, prior to Nas's pronouncement, other rap artists have advertised the impending "death" of hip hop, often as a hyperbolic admonition and call for revival. Common's 1994 tracks "Resurrection" and "I Used to Love H.E.R." both reflect this all too familiar tendency. In the latter track, Common tells the story of a girl who used to be "original, untampered, and pure" but is now corrupted by money and commercialization.[108] She acts as a metaphor for hip hop, which is feminized to underscore paternalist concerns about manipulation and exploitation and hold onto dreams of purity/virginity. As Common demonstrates, perennial worries and anxieties about the death of hip hop or the loss of its authentic quality are tied to a sex/gender politics that imagines hip hop as a woman who has lost her way. Here Hill and Blige's "I Used to Love Him" could be seen as a response to this inclination to imagine hip hop in the feminine to fit within (black) masculine expectations and anxieties. Or consider Joan Morgan's depiction of hip hop as an abusive partner, a metaphor that indicates a love/hate relationship and a picture that underscores the "gray" area between enjoying rap music and refusing the violent masculinist desires and depictions that circulate throughout it.[109] Morgan's notion of "messing with the grays,"[110] or those ambiguities and opaque zones, departs from the will to purity that shapes certain narratives of "where it all started."

Yet there is another way to think about the implications of Nas's speech act. Nas himself has suggested that his critique of the current state of hip hop is also a critique of America. In an MTV interview, Nas claims, "When I say hip hop is dead, basically America is dead. There is no political voice. Music is dead. . . . Our way of thinking is dead. Everything in this society has been done."[111] Here Nas suggests that there is a pervasive decadence in American culture. (He even claims that if we don't change, we will fall like Rome.) American culture, in other words, lacks life and creativity. Yet if this indictment is correct, then the nostalgia for a golden hip hop past contributes to our culture's inability to create new ideas, styles, and practices. If we are constantly looking toward some age of plenitude, then we miss possibilities in the here and now, which are partially facilitated by thinking about and relating to time in unconventional ways. Nietzsche's critique of antiquarian history is helpful here. According to him, the antiquarian stance "belongs . . . to him who preserves and reveres—to him who looks back to whence he has come, to where he came into being, with love and loyalty."[112] For Nietzsche, the desire to preserve valuable elements of the past for future generations can be healthy. Yet it becomes unhealthy when we venerate the past and reject possibilities for change and transformation in the present. The antiquarian attitude "knows only to preserve life, not to engender it."[113] If Nas suggests that there is no life in hip hop and American culture, then the pervasive tendency to look backward and idealize the beginnings of hip hop reinforces this predicament by preventing us from engendering, hearing, and experiencing novel forms and styles. Therefore, we are invited to reinterpret Nas's pronouncement and think beyond the standard narrative of pristine beginnings and gradual decline.

Nietzsche's critique of antiquarian history is predicated on the assumption that the past should be used to enhance or create life in the present. Whereas nostalgia for a pure past is intertwined with a pessimistic attitude toward the present, he argues that the past should be used to inspire hope for a different kind of present and future. In addition, yearnings for a pure and coherent past, especially in the context of black strivings, ignore the break, the rupture, the wound that defines time and history. The Eliadean search for a time of abundance disavows and displaces the unruly and opaque aspects of history that origin stories always have trouble making sense of and incorporating. In a culture that can be enamored with the newness and the ever-fleeting present, critics are also right to remind people of a rich legacy of emcees, DJs, producers, and artists who tend to be forgotten. Yet, while critics often become captivated by an idealized past, I am suggesting that the difficult legacy of hip hop might be used and reinterpreted to imagine novel possibilities and trajectories; it also might precipitate a hearing of the continuities and repetitions between now and then regarding, among other staples, queerphobia and misogynoir. As Walter Benjamin claims, images from the past can disrupt the prevailing logics of the present and destabilize the current state of things, including the conceptions of time and temporality that secure the status quo.[114] An image, idea, or sound from the past can form what Benjamin calls a "constellation" with the present, potentially opening up unprecedented ways of seeing, hearing, and being attuned to our contemporary social worlds. (I elaborate on the constellational approach in the next chapter.) These possibilities are not opened up by venerating the past, but by taking neglected/forgotten dimensions of the recent past and creating a dissonant relationship with the present. This is done in the hope of rupturing the occasional monotony of the present and instead engaging the unnoticed qualities of the past and present (or noticing those qualities differently). The practice of retrieving and reassembling fragments from the past has always been a part of hip hop, exemplified in the art of sampling.

But the creative and poetic dimension is not easily separable from imposition, destruction, and erasure. Even the language of creating something out of nothing carries a danger, since certain bodies and beings stand in for the nothing that makes creation and creativity possible. Consequently, the creative use of fragments and cuts should involve cultivating sounds and images that reflect on the multiple ways hip hop encounters death, becomes death, and is conjoined with death. Insofar as hip hop is one site where blackness is performed, it is an arena where the conjunction of blackness and death is re-sounded, displaced, and commodified. I am not making death an exclusive preoccupation, nor am I suggesting that a preoccupation with death is somehow not concerned about life and living, particularly given the intractable shadow of violence that unduly targets black flesh. I am simply offering a slightly different way of thinking and hearing the conjunction between hip hop and death. Similar to Nietzsche's concerns about cultural decadence in nineteenth-century Europe,[115] Nas's "Death of Hip Hop" is affixed to a claim about American decadence and the need for renewal. But since renewal and new life, especially life that is tethered to the image of America, is predicated on death and its disavowal, we might embrace, examine, and lean toward the attachment of death and hip hop while taking this pairing in directions that Nas's utterance and song did not intend (even if his musical corpus gestures toward them).

While a certain yearning for the past in response to the so-called death of authentic hip hop represents one pattern of thinking, there are other ways of thinking about hip hop's development and current state—alternatives that even Nas has adopted since his controversial pronouncement. As many commentators have reminded us, hip hop is not only motivated by appeals to authenticity and origins; it is also infatuated with flow, rupture, and unstable movements.[116] Consequently, the hip hop root is rhizomatic, impure, and heterogeneous. Any stable image or conception of hip hop is always subject to a kind of death, undoing, and refabrication. In response to standard narratives, this approach would position the Bronx, in particular, or New York City as a whole as one site where hip hop begins or takes shape; and this taking shape was made possible by diasporic dislocations and movements from other places and regions, such as Jamaica, Barbados, and Puerto Rico. Hip hop moves and is itself derivative of dispersive and coalescing motions; it entails lines of flight and death.[117] Along these lines, Eliade's notion of the eternal recurrence, where the original disclosure of the divine is repeated through myth and ritual, becomes something like the repeat at the break or groove, a kind of rupture that is its own beginning and principle of unruly movement. Following Shanté Smalls, this redescription that highlights internal differentiation and movement prompts a "heretical" stance toward standard narratives of hip hop's origins, stories that rely on narrow and straightforward conceptions of blackness and black authenticity.[118] (Thinking with Smalls's shift toward the queer beginnings of hip hop, we might relisten to an album like Azealia Banks's *1991*, released in 2012, as a yearning backward that honors house, disco, dance, nonnormative intimacies, and other elements that cut against straight, heteronormative time and modes of remembrance.)

Even as we should cultivate an openness to hip hop's internal instability and flow, we should also identify inveterate patterns and structures that contribute to its current manifestations. These include state violence against black people, the simultaneous fascination with and aversion to black flesh, the enduring profitability of this ambivalence, the framing of (black) women as sexually available objects, the tendency to portray violent conditions in a manner that mitigates anguish and torment, the positioning of hip hop celebrities as emblems of US exceptionalism and the advantages of late capitalism, and the unequal distribution of grief and grievability within blackness and across gender and sexuality. Because of these intractable realities, I contend that sorrow is an attitude and mode of being that we might deploy and look for when listening to hip hop and engaging in cultural practices in which scripted displays of triumph and assurance often betray—that is, both conceal and reveal—black anguish, vulnerability, and intimacy with death.

Redemption/Rupture

Lupe Fiasco's "Hip-Hop Saved My Life," a song featuring Nikki Jean from his second album, *The Cool*, warrants careful listening. On the track, Lupe tells a story (as a third-person narrator) about an underground rapper who dreams about acquiring success and recognition. Hip hop, the semifictional artist imagines, will enable him to escape poverty, the block, drug dealing, and limited options more generally. Consequently, the underground rapper's grind is inspired by the cry of his child (who needs diapers and food), his mother's exploitative, slave-like job at the Minute Maid beverage production company, family members and friends who are dead or in prison, and the desire for a Cadillac. The latter object of desire exemplifies Paul Gilroy's critical observations about contemporary black culture, particularly how commodities and luxury objects, such as the automobile, have become symbols of individual freedom.[1] In the video's opening shot, the camera zooms in briefly on a sign that reads, "Welcome to Fifth Ward," letting the viewer know that the story takes place in a primarily black and brown and economically impoverished section of Houston. Underneath the welcoming phrase, there is a line that reads, "Established in 1865," which brings to mind the end of the Civil War and the aftermath of racial slavery. Throughout the video, we see cameos of well-known Houston rappers such as Willie D, Slim Thug, Paul Wall, and Bun B, as if the video is reminding us of historical and sonic connections between Chicago (Lupe's hometown) and Houston, or the Midwest and the South.[2] There is a moment in the track when the description of a song is chopped and screwed, or the voice is mutated and slowed, in the tradition of Houston's DJ Screw, who died in 2000. The video portrays the black male protagonist engaging in a range of activities, from selling drugs on the corner to writing rhymes and performing at local clubs, as well as showing him caressing his partner and their child. These scenes are interspersed with images of Lupe rhyming in a gateway or a passage located in the middle of a barred fence. The gateway is almost like a threshold, an opening that accentuates a general condition of being barred and confined. Nikki Jean is positioned on a porch behind a fence; toward the end of the video, Lupe joins her. As Trudier Harris points out, the porch, especially in black southern traditions, is that "liminal space between private and public," or interior and exterior.[3] It is a gathering space that comprises many activities and interactions, including conversation, games, storytelling, political organizing, and the gaze (i.e., watching and being watched). There is something about the threshold and the porch that encapsulates the song's desire to break free from confining conditions, to be released to an outside, even if staying in that threshold, or gathering on the porch, carries its own possibilities and forms of relation.

The hook introduces a tension regarding the temporality of the track. Nikki Jean sings, "Hip-hop, you saved me. . . . Hip-hop, you saved my life," as if the act of being rescued from an earlier state and position has already occurred. And yet the video primarily depicts the protagonist trying to make a transition—by pushing harder and grinding—from inhabiting the proverbial streets to being heard and recognized as a rap artist. Even though the final verse includes images of transformation, including the protagonist getting his "momma out the 'hood" and showing his friends an alternative to "flippin' yay," the penultimate shot shows the protagonist returning to the block with his peoples, his coconspirators. He looks toward the camera with an expression that combines melancholy, sternness, and uncertainty. Even as the track addresses and exhibits gratitude to hip hop in a personal, I/thou manner, for rescuing the emcee from harsh, economically insecure conditions, the video leaves us with a gap between an individual rescue/escape narrative and the enduring conditions that make "flippin' yay" appear as a tenable choice among limited options. (This replicates the gap between Lupe / Nikki Jean's position and that of the fictional protagonist in the video.) The other young black men on the corner, dressed in dark clothing, come into view before the aforementioned shot, in which the protagonist's facial expression is isolated. We see the aspiring artist give one of his friends dap, an embrace, a hug. This is not a glorification of the "streets" but a visual strategy that prevents the viewer from being untouched by those who are left unredeemed by prevailing narratives and aspirations.[4]

Lupe and Nikki Jean's track demonstrates that the relationship between hip hop and redemption is a two-way street—if artists have suggested at certain moments that hip hop needs to be saved, then hip hop has also been honored as a redemptive and rescuing force. As Miller points out, this song demonstrates how "artists of hip hop culture explicitly make known through their rap their perspectives on the longevity, power, and [im]mortality of hip hop culture."[5] But this particular track also shows how hip hop interrogates and cuts into redemptive narratives and trajectories, even as it tends to mimic and reenact some of these prevailing frameworks—"Started from the bottom, now we're here."[6] Consequently, in this chapter I draw closer attention to the general idea of, and desire for, redemption, especially as it gets performed and reworked by artists like Lupe Fiasco and Kendrick Lamar. Acknowledging that redemption has different connotations and different religious and secular expressions, this chapter pinpoints the will to make whole and the desire to rescue or be rescued from a wounded, divided condition. If the last chapter on sorrow and death broached the theme of redemption (think of Biggie's life after death or Du Bois's emphasis on the transition within the sorrow song), this chapter foregrounds how certain hip hop artists approach the notion of being rescued from an undesirable predicament; how they respond to various instantiations of the promise of making human subjects whole and protected from fracturing. There is a kind of twisting and reworking of the concept as artists like Lupe and Kendrick retrieve images and sounds of catastrophe and black anguish from narratives and mechanisms—progress, sovereignty, imperialism, the idea of America, the war on terror, self-actualization—that promise future coherence through justifications of the violence that upholds these mechanisms. In the tracks I select by Lupe and Kendrick, redemption is more of a rupture than a drive toward completion or fulfillment.

To flesh out this uncanny notion of redemption, I juxtapose Lupe and Kendrick with authors in black studies (Hartman and Wilderson) and critical theory (Benjamin and Adorno). These figures offer ways to think about retrieving the irretrievable in the face of secular redemptive paradigms like progress or humanism, narratives that erase or incorporate legacies of suffering and anguish in the name of betterment and advancement, especially models of betterment that have propelled and justified colonial and imperial agendas. After working through the insights of black studies and critical theory on the complexities of redemption, I concentrate on Lupe's "American Terrorist" as an indictment of US exceptionalism, a disciplinary mechanism that, among other things, affixes terror to an elsewhere and denies the terror intrinsic to (US) nation-building. I conclude the chapter by reading aspects of Kendrick's early albums against the grain of the conventional Christian themes in his music. This perspective allows me to hear and elaborate on moments when Kendrick constructs and retrieves images of the past and passing present that mess with and dislodge desires to make, and be made, whole at the expense of the unredeemed and irreparable conditions.[7]

The Wound of (Secular) Redemption

Redemption is a promiscuous concept that has taken on a multitude of forms and shapes. Within a social world that bears the heavy imprint of Western Protestantism, the will to redemption demonstrates a significant overlap between the religious and the secular, as well as the theological and the political. Even if one does not fully accept Carl Schmitt's claim that "all significant concepts of the modern state are secularized theological concepts," the enduring commitment to redemption prevents any simple separation between the religious and the political.[8] In fact, one difference may be that redemptive logics are less explicit, and more insidious, within secular paradigms than in self-described religious imaginaries. For instance, according to Karen Bray, neoliberalism, which establishes economic principles and rationalities as the ultimate horizon of human desire and striving, operates as a soteriological framework. Along this line, neoliberalism "demands that we be productive, efficient, happy, and flexible in order to be of worth and therefore get saved out of the wretched experience of having been marked as worthless."[9] As Bray argues in her work, neoliberalism promises to save and safeguard those who are capable of falling in line with the demands of capital, accumulation, and productivity. Those who are unable, and those who are associated with negative and backward affects like depression or exhaustion, are deemed unworthy for life. While there are myriad differences between Christian notions of salvation through Christ and the soteriological thrust of neoliberalism, what connects them is a redemptive framework that offers the potential of transcending a wretched condition and becoming whole, undivided, and optimal (through the requisite practices, disciplines, sacrifices, and so forth).

If the distinction between religious and secular redemption tends to break down, then George Shulman introduces another distinction between re-demption *of* and redemption *from* some predicament. In his thoughtful book on the more progressive instantiations of American prophecy in figures like Toni Morrison and James Baldwin, he contends that the prophetic stance car-ries with it both a mournful tone toward current injustices and a redemptive promise, the latter involving deliverance from exploitation and the formation of less destructive relationships.[10] And yet the author underscores the dan-gers internal to the language of redemption, especially when the weight is on redemption from a condition. As he puts it, deliverance from an undesirable predicament anticipates recovering a "prior condition of freedom, purity, or wholeness," whereas the idiom of redemption of history "means to endow [suffer-ing] with meaning, to atone for it or heal it, to make it justified, worthwhile, of value."[11] Shulman understands that there are shared problems with both idioms of redemption. The first produces hierarchical distinctions between the saved and unsaved, distinctions that have legitimated the violence directed at "the pa-gans and racialized others who embody unredeemed life."[12] The second form of redemption seems more innocuous, since finding some way to make sense of suffering, including giving an account of the causes of anguish, is necessary to overcome or alleviate it. Nevertheless, Shulman draws from Nietzsche to broach the dangers that occur when meaning is called on to impose order on life's messy and tragic character, or when life and death are subordinated to unifying narratives and forms of meaning-making. In many cases, the will to impose meaning on life's unwieldy features is animated by a desire to be deliv-ered from and elevated above the impure, the contaminating, and that which thwarts efforts of redress and making amends. And yet, as Shulman suggests, aren't human subjects, especially those who have been systemically oppressed, condemned to something like redemption, narrative, meaning, and endeavors to make life worthwhile?[13]

The twentieth-century German Jewish thinker Walter Benjamin has some-thing to say about the simultaneous peril and necessity of redemption, even as he reconceives the relationship between redemption and making whole.[14] His writings handle these matters in a way that accentuates form, presentation, and composition, which, as I show below, makes for some interesting affin-ities with the poetics of rap. In "On the Concept of History," an aphoristic 1940 essay written in exile, in response to the German-Soviet Pact (a moment of overlap between communism and fascism), Benjamin confronts the cata-strophic quality of the idea and machinery of progress. As Preciosa de Joya points out, Benjamin's essay is a rejoinder to the ways progress operates as a mode of "secularized redemption," a rearticulation of Christian eschatology in which "the end of time awaits the promise of restored harmony, of total freedom and happiness."[15] The idea of progress has gone through various permutations and interpretations. In its stronger expressions, this idea claims that humanity (through the development of reason, science, technology, and liberal democracy) is advancing, ascending, and growing toward a more complete and harmonious state. In its less pronounced iterations, it assumes that the ideas, norms, and practices necessary for perpetual advancement are latent within the prevailing institutional arrangements and just need to be actualized more fully. The imago of progress is usually accompanied by a division between those who are positioned as the embodiments and agents of progress and those that need to be folded into the movement of civilization and human advancement. Progress determines who and what has worth and value, which beings are grievable and worthy of recognition and compassion. In the last five or six centuries, the idea of progress has facilitated and justified the subordination of non-European peoples to what Sylvia Wynter might call Western imperial Man.[16] In addition, as a redemptive mechanism, the notion of progress works to compensate, ascribe meaning to, and rationalize the violence that is both necessary for, and mollified by, progress and its concomitant ideas and arrangements—civilization, freedom, democracy, and so forth.[17]

In "On the Concept of History," Benjamin juxtaposes the idea of progress with a different kind of redemptive power, a weak redemptive capacity. This juxtaposition occurs in an aphorism in which Benjamin gives an interpretation of Paul Klee's *Angelus Novus* painting. As Benjamin describes, the angel is pictured staring at something that he also wants to move away from; his eyes are wide and mouth is agape, as if shocked and startled by what both fascinates and repels him. The angel's face, according to Benjamin, is turned toward the past, even as a storm "drives him irresistibly into the future."[18] Whereas progress teaches us to see a chain of events (leading toward some fulfilled state), the angel "sees one single catastrophe, which keeps piling wreckage upon wreckage."[19] This pile of wreckage, the ongoing catastrophe, is what the storm of progress produces. And while the angel would like to stay with the vanquished, resurrect the dead, and "make whole what has been smashed,"[20] the storm of progress inserts a separation between the angel and those who have been crushed and excised by history. Perhaps there is something about the force of progress—the need to minimally go with the grain, the pressure to conform to the sway of history, and the injunction to move on—that places constraints on the desire to stay with and defend those that progress could only incorporate through death and erasure. Perhaps mourning and what Sharpe calls wake work can only happen as an immanent break within the regime of progress, an interruption or halt that would itself expose progress as a perpetual form of legitimated destruction and wrecking. This is why Benjamin writes elsewhere that a revolution is not necessarily tantamount to locomotion, but rather entails "activating the emergency brake" (i.e., break).[21]

Even though the angel in Benjamin's aphorism cannot convert the ruins of history into something whole, one gets the sense that he is called to be a perpetual witness to the casualties of progress. This responsibility enjoins a certain relationship to the past and present (and temporality more generally). For Benjamin, history is not simply an objective account of things. It is more like a struggle to seize memories as they "flash up in a moment of danger."[22] The language of flashing, as discussed in the chapter 1 with Grandmaster Flash, indicates a sudden irruption and interruption, something that appears briefly but can disappear or be taken away immediately. Alongside this quality of the flash, one danger for Benjamin is that images of the past will become a "tool of the ruling classes" and utilized to consolidate the order of things. Think, for instance, of how legacies of struggle and resistance against imperialism, sexism, or heteronormativity get utilized and celebrated to shore up and cultivate collective assent to US dominance. Consequently, for Benjamin the dead are not even protected from the clutches of power and conformity, since they can be put to work, instrumentalized for the very mechanisms of domination that crushed them. On this reading, progress threatens to kill repeatedly. Not only does it rank-order populations and facilitate domination in the name of advancement and improvement. It also relegates dissonant memories of anguish and diminishes the severity of violence by incorporating experiences of suffering into unifying, conciliatory narratives. Progress can acknowledge the wound, but only by subordinating it to the desire to win, triumph, and reach a fulfilled state.

In response to the catastrophe that is progress, Benjamin writes, "There is no document of culture [civilization] which is not at the same time a document of barbarism."[23] What does this mean? On the one hand, Benjamin is anticipating the arguments in Adorno and Horkheimer's *Dialectic of Enlightenment*, in which the authors give an account of how humans' attempts to free themselves from nature have resulted in new forms of dominance over nature and those who are deemed closely associated with it, including those not considered fully human.[24] But Benjamin is also making a more comprehensive claim regarding the transmission and preservation of culture, knowledge, and tradition. As Shoshana Felman points out in her interpretation of Benjamin, history is told, written, and authorized by those who survive, those who have escaped death.[25] And that which survives necessarily relies on mechanisms that engender and demand modes of silence and "speechlessness that remain out of the record."[26] If official history tells the story from the perspective of a certain kind of victory, then this history is also a transmission of a certain disavowal of loss, silence, death, and the unincorporated.[27] How does one keep alive or retrieve what eludes conventional discourse, speech, and intelligibility? How does one retrieve the ruin, fragment, and that which flashes and interrupts from narratives that promise fulfillment while leaving wreckage? What I am after here is a conception of weak redemption that must take on the paradox of retrieving the irretrievable, or recovering and staying with a wound that history produces and claims to suture. The grammar of ruin, wreckage, and interruption indicates that this weak redemptive relationship to time and history will not only involve contemplating the content of events and experiences. It will also involve thinking about form, style, genre, and composition. Along this line, a song tells a story differently, using different accoutrements, than an official history or a novel. A genre such as rap, which is explicitly based on spoken words and rhyme patterns, mobilizes and arranges content differently from other genres. Generally, it is important to think about the organization of a story or song, how the form of the composition refracts and expresses the content. In the context of hip hop and rap, this concern draws attention to how the construction of words, beats, sounds, silences, and pauses might capture, among other factors, the wounds, fractures, and im/possibilities that blackness and black people have been burdened to assume.

It is well known that Benjamin experimented with different styles of writing and ways of presenting ideas and images—aphorism, essay, montage, fragment, and constellation.[28] Among other possibilities, these compositional styles typify and enact a certain deviation from the whole, the systematic, and the centripetal. They defy a general will to unity and coherence without abandoning the importance of configuring relations, interactions, and dissonant connections. In addition, the form of the aphorism or the fragment bears the imprint of the break, the effect of the catastrophic. The form undergoes a deformation so to speak; in the process, the writer and reader must experience the trace of anguish in the collected ruins, an anguish that is not necessarily incompatible with intimacy, utopian desires, pleasure-filled memories, and an openness to the not-yet.[29] We might say that the unconventional mode of constructing ideas and images is a way to rescue the ruin from erasure or incorporation into progress, expansion, and the drive to totality. The constellational approach, as Adorno points out, constructs concepts and combines them (not unlike the emcee) in a manner that points to a "more" or excess that eludes identity thinking and the desire to make things fit together neatly.[30] This more is not simply quantitative; it also registers a qualitative excess. In other words, the "more" encapsulated by the constellation also refers to qualities, characteristics, and modalities that exceed endeavors to grasp, subsume, and integrate into a prefabricated form. For authors like Adorno and Benjamin, experimenting with alternative types of writing and construction potentially allows one to address "[that] which fell by the wayside [of history] . . . the waste products . . . the cross-grained, opaque, unassimilated material."[31] The decisive challenge for a weak redemptive capacity is to stay with the opaque and unassimilated without acceding to the demand to make, and be made, transparent and productive for the order of things.

This relationship between the unassimilated, the opaque, and the will to redemption is taken up by thinkers within black studies, most notably Saidiya Hartman and Frank Wilderson. As authors like Benjamin and Adorno refuse strategies to "talk us out of suffering,"[32] Hartman and Wilderson think about this strategy in the context of legacies of antiblack violence and terror. While Benjamin suggests a general ruin within time and human existence, these authors within black studies suggest that the imaginary suturing of this wound accompanies an aspiration toward wholeness and completion that relies on an opposition to blackness and black people. Hartman and Wilderson's respective projects share a concern about how blackness has been both a stumbling block for prevailing conceptions of freedom, democracy, and humanism and an opportunity to reaffirm and consolidate these frameworks. In "The Position of the Unthought," an interview and conversation between Hartman and Wilderson, this concern comes to the foreground. The discussion revolves around Hartman's groundbreaking 1997 text *Scenes of Subjection*, which begins with the premise that "the slave is the foundation of the national order, and . . . the slave occupies the position of the unthought."[33] The kidnapping of Africans and coerced slave labor, in addition to the genocide of indigenous peoples, formed what Karl Marx called the primitive accumulation of capital; in addition, the position of the slave negatively defined republican notions of freedom as nondomination. Furthermore, there is something about the unthought position (and the mundane terror that slaves were subjected to) that refuses the transparency of categories like agency, consent, and hegemony. How does an enslaved black woman consent to the sexual desires of the master if the master has complete legal control over her? How does one pinpoint the agency of the enslaved when that agency was often coerced for the "instrumental amusements of the plantation" or ascribed to slaves to license punishment when they violated laws and codes?[34] These questions in many ways riff on the interrogative tendencies in Hartman's text, a device that prompts reflection, patience, and a willingness to sit with unresolved, and perhaps irresolvable, tensions and conundrums.

For Hartman and Wilderson, the desire to comprehend slavery through familiar political categories dovetails with a tendency to integrate black strivings into a nationalist project that, "when . . . in crisis . . . black people are called upon to affirm."[35] Affirmation is the key term and concept here. The authors are alluding to how a certain kind of tension, contradiction, or negativity is resolved or explained away by corralling the anguish-filled experiences, desires, and refusals of the very people who have been positioned as embodiments of negation. Along this line, Wilderson laments that so much scholarship about black people, especially in the United States, "consciously or unconsciously peels away from strength and the terror of their evidence in order to propose some kind of coherent, hopeful solution of things."[36] Notice that Wilderson's qualm is directed at the quality of the proposals usually put forth by black scholarship. He is underscoring the pressure to offer something coherent and positive in a manner that diminishes the severity of the terror of antiblackness. Or as Hartman puts it, there is something "obscene" about the "attempt to make the narrative of defeat into an opportunity for celebration, the desire to look at the ravages and brutality of the last few centuries, but still find a way to feel good about ourselves."[37] There is a certain "metanarrative thrust" that these authors are getting at—a compulsion to turn violence and terror into an occasion to affirm and celebrate the narratives and grammars that facilitate this violence. They suggest that the redemptive impulse toward black anguish is just as much about making ourselves feel comfortable as it is about doing justice to the past, the vanquished, and the dead and dying. In other words, the will to convert the terror of history into a general affirmation is motivated by affective attachments, desires to feel positive, whole, and content in the face of relentless violence. As Amaryah Armstrong claims, there is an "antagonism between a redemptionist political theological imagination and black freedom."[38]

And yet one can find traces of weak, or blackened, redemption in both of these authors' accounts of black life and death, even as Hartman and Wilderson refuse the all too familiar recourse to progress, humanism, and integration, which might be called secularized sources of redemption and fulfillment. Think, for instance, of Hartman's notion of the "afterlife of slavery." For Hartman, this alludes to "the fact that black lives are still imperiled and devalued by a racial calculus and a political arithmetic that were entrenched centuries ago. This is the afterlife of slavery—skewed life chances, limited access to health and education, premature death, incarceration, and impoverishment."[39] The language of afterlife suggests that something about racial slavery lives on, even after its legal elimination. Like a ghost or a specter, there is a racial arithmetic inaugurated during slavery that continues to haunt, disturb, and disconcert. The afterlife of social death does not deny change and shifts in the racial order; rather, it makes "emancipation appear less the grand event of liberation than a point of transition between modes of servitude and racial subjection."[40] (Hip hop artists know a bit about this afterlife of slavery—think here of Meshell Ndegeocello's 1993 album *Plantation Lullabies* or Showbiz and AG's 1992 album *Runaway Slave*. Also think of KRS-One's track "Sound of da Police," on which he makes a theoretical and phonetic connection between officer and overseer.[41] And then there is the idiom of "the trap" so popularized by southern rap, which alludes not only to criminalized drug activity but also to capture, confinement, and enclosure.) Hartman therefore resists the conflation of emancipation and liberation. She rejects the idea that liberal democracy and the sphere of the human can somehow repair the fracture that is slavery and its aftermath. And yet her work, especially after her essay "Venus in Two Acts," wrestles with the im/possibility of retrieving stories and experiences of the enslaved that remain dormant and silent in historical archives.[42] In this essay, Hartman responds to an ethical call to attend to those black female subjects for whom the archive is a "death sentence, a tomb, a display of the violated body."[43] Like Benjamin's angel, she knows she cannot "recover the lives of the enslaved or redeem the dead," but she is called to put together narratives that transgress the constraints and erasures of the archive while acknowledging the limits of any form of narration regarding those who barely leave traces of existence.[44] Broaching this paradox of representing the unrepresentable, or retrieving the irretrievable, indicates a cut, or a tear, in the very idea of recovery. In the process, one must be prepared to replicate the violence that one wants to overcome, hoping that with the repetition comes a difference.

Wilderson's writings and reflections on the antagonistic relationship between blackness and the sphere of the human are also informed by an aversion to a particular kind of redemptive logic. His understanding of Afropessimism, at its most basic, refutes the aspirational idea that black people can eventually be recognized and folded into the category of the human, a domain that positions blackness as its constitutive Other. Humanism, in its liberal or Marxist forms, cannot make black people integrated because violence against black people is necessary for the idea of the human to retain its coherence. As Wilderson puts it, "Redemption, as a narrative mode, is a parasite that feeds upon me for its coherence."[45] In other words, for humans to acquire or restore a sense of plenitude and fulfillment, they will have to align themselves with a "regime of violence that bars Black people from the narrative of redemption."[46] Wilderson is associating redemption with the fantasy of coherence and fullness, one that needs black people as props for its perdurance. Even though he rejects the possibility of black redemption within a world organized by antiblackness, he does introduce an apocalyptic line of flight. He writes, for instance, "Afropessimism is . . . critique without redemption or a vision of redress except the 'end of the world.'"[47] The "except" here opens a space for thinking beyond some binary—redemption or no redemption. It also prompts a thinking beyond worldness, which according to an author like Eliade is associated with settlement, established boundaries, and the imposition of form and order onto embodiments of the wild and opaque. Wilderson does not tell us what this end looks like or what might be on the other side of this world. He does not give a positive proposal. Instead, he stays with the negative, with the disruptive, and a spirit of openness to what might appear but what cannot yet be articulated.

Wilderson is therefore reticent about making positive and normative claims about what another world, or what life on the other side of the human, would look like. He remains apophatic because that other world, that other of the world, can barely be envisioned or only limned via the negative. In an interview with Percy Howard, Wilderson responds to a question about the movement for reparations with the following: "I support the movement [for reparations] because I know it is a movement toward the end of the world; a movement toward a catastrophe in epistemological coherence and institutional integrity—I support the movement aspect of it because I know that repair is impossible. [I support] a movement toward something so blindingly new that it cannot be imagined. This is the only thing that will save us."[48] Notice here that the Afropessimist author underscores motion or a drive toward incoherence, toward a disorder that an antiblack world both creates and contains. This movement is directed toward the impossible, toward a dazzling, form-dissolving novelty that cannot be imagined or articulated within existing language and grammar. Furthermore, consider how Wilderson introduces the language of salvation, locating the potential for being saved in this drive toward the incoherent, the unimaginable, and the impossible, rather than in a wish for repair. For Wilderson, the only redemption available to us is in the end of a governing principle, the world, that relies on and coheres around antiblackness. Wilderson is not necessarily saying that this will lead to something better; his refusal to affirm a something better tethers redemption to the undecidable and to movements and flows that are form-shattering.

By thinking alongside Benjamin, Hartman, and Wilderson, I have attempted to flesh out the repetitive terror of redemptive narratives while gesturing toward a blackened redemptive possibility. Here I use the term "blackened" as a qualifier to introduce a rupture into the ordinary conception of redemption as rescue and recovery, a cut that makes redemption look like a retrieval of the ruin(s) from the clutches of progress and humanism. The will to redemption, understood as the drive to make, and be made, whole and complete, undergirds and secretly propels many of the narratives, symbols, and mechanisms of domination that constitute and maintain the violent ordering of the planet. Among other things, this framework creates divisions between peoples, beings, and regions that approximate completeness and those that can only be converted into livable subjects through the machinations of the civilized, of those who represent proper Man. In addition, the redemptive impulse converts the ruins that it produces into an opportunity for affirmation, an occasion to celebrate the social arrangements that rely on death, war, and disavowed terror. At the same time, a basic attachment to redemption—redress, justice, liberation from white supremacy, a new world being possible—has also been indispensable for groups and peoples that have inhabited the underside of the political and racial order. Black people, for instance, have imagined, longed for, and practiced redemption from the effects of slavery and coloniality through religious practices, political movements, working-class struggles, art and music, cultural and physical repatriation to Africa, and so forth.[49] In fact, these practices and traditions demonstrate that blackness and black people are not reducible to the white supremacist and colonial operations that converted Africans into property, subhumans, and the world's defect. Within the world of hip hop, these restorative strategies and commitments have been remixed, rearticulated, contested, and debated. (Here I think of the debates in the early 1990s on wax between KRS-One and X Clan over whether humanism or Afrocentric cultural nationalism is the best framework for black healing and liberation.)[50]

As discussed at the beginning of the chapter, hip hop itself has been held out by many artists as a redemptive matrix. According to Pinn, hip hop can be viewed as a mode of wrestling with, and finding meaning in, suffering, evil, and prospects for transformation.[51] Or it can be interpreted in a more specific manner such that hip hop is praised for its capacity to help emcees escape harsh economic circumstances and provide financial comfort for these artists and their loved ones. To bring together the insights of Lester Spence and Karen Bray, it could be that hip hop's salvific power is enabled by its increasing alignment with neoliberal sensibilities, where economic freedom and productivity has become a fundamental horizon of subjectivity, desire, and aspiration. Wealth accumulation and financial security, according to the religion of late capital, will make you whole. While attentive to these concerns, I want to pursue a "what else," an "alongside" to the prevailing, or at least more popular and visible, trends within hip hop and rap music. In line with the insights of black studies and critical theory, I am after a strange and paradoxical form of redemption, one that brings together retrieval and ruin, possibility and rupture, without a facile resolution. By turning attention to Lupe Fiasco, especially his track "American Terrorist," I reflect on the way he conjures and constructs images and memories to accentuate the terror internal to US nation-building. This tactic works against redemptive US exceptionalist frameworks that exonerate the violence of US imperialism by locating terror elsewhere (apart from the image of America) and affixing it primarily to Islam. I then turn to Kendrick Lamar's *Section.80*, showing how this debut album refuses an antiblack longing to restore the Reagan era, or a particular iteration of sovereign time. I also examine how his own attempt to recover the stories and make sense of the experiences of black female subjects falters and breaks down.

Cutting Constellations: Lupe, Blackened Islam, and the Terror of US Exceptionalism

Lupe Fiasco's debut 2006 album, *Food and Liquor*, is aptly described by music critic Nathan Rabin as an achievement that "masterfully melds his peerless story-telling gifts with his idiosyncratic passion for skateboarding ['Kick, Push'], fantasy ['Daydreamin''], and incisive sociopolitical commentary ['American Terrorist']."[52] The album cover shows Lupe floating in dark space (blackness, stars, rays of laser-like lights) among scattered objects, not unlike Klee and Benjamin's angel of history.[53] The name "Fiasco" similarly indicates that the artist has incorporated into this moniker the catastrophic, whether this is a reference to life and existence or what he brings competitively to other emcees. (This latter possibility aligns with the Spanish etymology of the name *Guadelupe*, which brings together the image of the wolf and the flow of the river.) In the introduction to the album, we initially hear the voice of Lupe's sister, Ayesha, as she offers a poetic description of various places, intersections, and activities in Chicago (such as eating at Harold's Chicken Shack, rockin' braids and Timberland boots, and the violence that keeps funeral homes in business and hospitals full). There is a moment in the poem when Ayesha articulates a longing for the days of Martin and Malcolm; or better yet, these days "have ended. Our hope has descended and off to the side. Waiting for the reinstallment of the revolution."[54] The poem exists at the nexus of loss and anticipation, grieving missed possibilities for black liberation and waiting for a return. The poem is also heard against the backdrop of neighborhood voices, conversations, and chatter; it is almost as if Ayesha's desire to be set apart from the noise is in tension with an intimacy, a connection and contact with these background voices, persons, and relationships. Her poem blends into Lupe reciting in Arabic the bismallah prayer, expressing his devotion to Allah (and immediately after that, a dedication to his grandmother). We soon find out that the food portion of the album title symbolizes goodness, while liquor represents evil. While this can sound like a strong contrast, and a preparation for Lupe to turn the "fiasco into good," he introduces the conjunction, the "and" between good and evil, food and liquor, as a mix or a (musical) blend. What becomes clear throughout the album, and his career more generally, is that Lupe is adept at creating dissonant juxtapositions and tangencies, a skill that will be exemplified in "American Terrorist."

Lupe Fiasco, whose given name is Wasalu Muhammad Jaco, released this album in the midst of the Bush regime's war on terror, a campaign that relied on an enduring tendency to imagine Islam as a signifier for despotic violence and antithetical to Western democratic modes of life.[55] The invidious and all too familiar contrasts between Islam and the West, among other problems, downplays the long presence of Muslims in the Americas, including African Muslims who accompanied Columbus as crew persons and were converted to Christianity by force.[56] The connection between blackness and Islam has been prominent in rap music and hip hop grammars, especially as this relationship was remade by twentieth-century movements like the Nation of Islam and the Nation of Gods and Earths. These religious organizations have reinterpreted the tenets and practices of traditional Islam in response to white supremacy and antiblack racism. As Juan Floyd-Thomas points out, the "synergy of African American Islam and hip hop" has gone through various shifts and transitions.[57] In the 1980s and 1990s, much of East Coast–based rap, including groups like Brand Nubian, Poor Righteous Teachers, and Wu-Tang Clan, was influenced by the Five-Percenters—those who call black men gods and refer to black women as (fertile and subordinate) earths; follow Clarence 13X's split from the Nation of Islam; created their own numerology, alphabet, and daily lessons; and tend to associate whiteness with evil and trickery.[58] With artists like Mos Def and Lupe, according to Floyd-Thomas, we hear a shift to more conventional expressions of Sunni Islam, which resonates with Malcolm X's spiritual journey and broader transformations within black Muslim communities. Alongside these changes within hip hop, what remains consistent is a commitment to verbal jihad, a contemplative and discursive way of striving against racial injustice, the denigration of blackness, and Western imperial modes of being.[59]

While Floyd-Thomas describes how various iterations of black Islam have influenced hip hop, Su'ad Abdul Khabeer introduces the image/sound of the loop to discuss how Islam's influence on hip hop gets returned and repeated as hip hop and blackness shape and inform the experiences of young black and nonblack US Muslims in the twenty-first century. As Khabeer points out, the loop, which is a "hip hop sampling technique in which a selected piece of music is played over and over as part of the creation of a new piece of music," can be taken up as a metaphor for the "linkages between Islam, hip hop, and Blackness."[60] Here linkage includes repetition, expansion and return, and an interplay between continuity and variation. One of these linkages involves Arab and South Asian US American Muslims "establishing connections to specific notions of blackness" to "configure a sense of US Muslim identity that stands as a counterpoint to hegemonic norms of whiteness."[61] And these connections, according to Khabeer, occur in a twenty-first-century context in which blackness is constantly being co-opted by narratives of multiculturalism and American exceptionalism.[62] Think of how Barack Obama's first presidential campaign did its best to distance him from Islam (or his middle name, Hussein) in response to those who challenged Obama's citizenship. Think of how antiblack racism can get displaced and rearticulated through anti-Muslim and anti-Arab racialization and animosity. In this case, post-racial progress and the solidification of the idea of an exceptionalist America relies on ideas and justifications that have made Muslim populations the targets of US imperial/capitalist agendas. Or consider how a certain kind of Muslim is treated like the external (religious, political, and sexual) Other of America, while blackness is figured as a form of internal alterity and excess. This internal alterity can be taken as a danger and threat, or as an expedient to dream about a fulfilled and more complete democracy. As I take it, Khabeer broaches the looping trope to not only think about the back-and-forth influence between hip hop and Islam; she also intends to draw attention to a series of dissonant interactions, linkages, and imbrications. Lupe Fiasco's work is situated within an assemblage that includes blackness, Islam, hip hop, and US imperialism.

Lupe's music also emerges at a moment when there is another shift within hip hop, alongside the one that Floyd-Thomas delineates concerning Islam. According to Josef Sorett, while hip hop has been a site of noninstitutional religious plurality and bricolage, there has been a noticeable "shifting of allegiances from Islam to Christianity" within twenty-first-century rap music.[63] Here Sorett is thinking about lyrical content, album titles, and album iconography that mark this transition toward Christianity—Remy Ma's *Shesus Khryst* mixtape, Nas's *God's Son* album, and KRS-One's turn to evangelical Christianity. The Nas example stands out considering that on his debut musical appearance, Main Source's "Live at the Barbeque," Nas boasts, "When I was twelve, I went to hell for snuffin' Jesus."[64] Sorett also has in mind the ideological convergences between bling-era rap artists and prosperity gospel preachers such as Creflo Dollar, alignments that demonstrate again a conjunction between religiosity and neoliberalism (or the redemptive function attached to wealth accumulation, material prosperity, and victory).[65] While there are strands of Christianity that stress identification with the poor and oppressed, Protestant Christianity in the United States is primarily a symbol of power, legibility, and acceptability, which helps explain why "in [hip hop's] move towards the mainstream Christianity became more central."[66] In other words, Christian images, tropes, and themes facilitate hip hop's uneasy inclusion in the mainstream. Christianity is a form of cultural capital; it produces value, worth, and intelligibility. It makes hip hop, or blackness and hip hop, appear and sound more in line with a particular idea of America, the human, and the possibility of becoming whole and complete.

As Sorett points out, Lupe draws on this Christian cultural capital on his 2006 track "Muhammad Walks," a rejoinder to and riff on Kanye West's popular song "Jesus Walks," which was released two years earlier. On this track, Lupe seems to make Islam more acceptable to American listeners, a strategy that involves extricating Islam from "Osama and Saddam" and underscoring how, beneath the divergent beliefs, Christians, Muslims, and Jews worship the same god. In addition to stressing commonality among difference, Lupe "articulates his faith in relationship to Christian figures [like Creflo Dollar and Yolanda Adams] who have achieved celebrity status in the American religious landscape."[67] One might conclude that by making connections with mainstream Christianity, Lupe is merely trying to render the prophet Muhammad and the Koran more palatable and less threatening, in response to widespread misconceptions about Muslims and ignorance about the textual and historical continuities between Christianity and Islam. Moreover, his lyrics express a desire for recognition and inclusion, envisioning Muhammad sitting alongside Jesus in the American religious pantheon. And yet things are not so simple. When Lupe replaces Jesus with Muhammad and then stresses a logic of sameness, or identity, between the Muslim and Christian object of devotion, something important happens. While Emmanuel Levinas rightly argues that the paradigm of the same does a certain violence to the Other, there are other moments when this very logic creates a contact that upsets desires for separation from an undesirable object, idea, or group.[68] (Think, for instance, of the 2015 decision by Wheaton College, an evangelical Christian institution, to suspend Professor Larycia Hawkins for claiming that Christians and Muslims worship the same god.)[69]

In addition to making Muhammad walk alongside Jesus, in a manner that both relies on and contests US Christian hegemony, Lupe begins "Muhammad Walks" by dedicating the song to "all my brothers and sisters who died in Iraq, Israel, Afghanistan, and right here in America."[70] In this opening line, Lupe exposes the limits (and the potential of crossing the limits) of grievability in the context of empire, war, and conquest. In other words, this line compels one to reconsider to whom and where grief, lament, and concern should be directed; what persons and regions of the world are worthy of life and recognition after death; whose life and death should I see myself accountable to and intertwined with.[71] Lupe introduces an ethos of concern and care that includes an interplay between here and there, the United States and other countries/places that are connected by political, economic, and military projects, refusing the stark contrasts and partitions that regulate how people are disciplined to think about the distribution of violence, death, and vulnerability. The language of brothers and sisters, which might allude to fellow Muslims in countries under military occupation, to US soldiers trained to kill and die for the sovereign state, and to Arab Muslims and Jews in Israel, points to forms of alliance and intimacy that exceed the horizon of the nation-state. On this track, Lupe begins to undo a pervasive tendency to place a premium on American life, which is enabled by locating the sources of death and terror elsewhere, including peoples and histories within and at the borders of the United States that present a problem for the idealized image of America. But his song "American Terrorist" goes even further in transgressing the sacrality of that image.

Before delving into the dynamics of the track, it is important to pause and reflect on what the initial juxtaposition of *America* and *terror* accomplishes. On the one hand, the title reminds the listener of what Erica Edwards calls "the long war on terror" or the "multi-pronged campaign" of defense and protection during the Cold War against groups deemed to be domestic threats like the Black Panthers.[72] In this case, "terror" is an internal threat to and aberration from the coherence and perdurance of a nation-state project that defines itself as the democratic opposite of terrorism and terrifying violence.[73] Inversely, the juxtaposition prepares one to confront modes of terror that Americans cannot easily separate themselves from, forms of violence and erasure that the imago of America relies on but disavows. In other words, the terror beside and internal to this collective self-image collides with US exceptionalist attachments that convert the violence internal to nation-building into a grammar of defense, security, operation freedom, and so forth. As Jasbir Puar notes, there is a duplicitous aspect of exceptionalism, since it connotes both superiority and exteriority, or "a departure from yet mastery of linear teleologies of progress."[74] As I take it, this doubleness within the notion and practice of US exceptionalism treats America as the highest ideal and benchmark for freedom and democracy while enabling the US nation-state to violate international laws in the name of protecting those sacred values and ideals. In fact, violation in the name of protection and preservation becomes the law itself. This operation renders America (and its transatlantic allies) synonymous with life, health, and wholeness; this exceptionalism replicates and normalizes contrasts between civilized and uncivilized violence, actions that make the world safe for democracy and actions that are a threat to peace, law, and order. US exceptionalism, which consists of discourses, narratives, symbols, political rituals, assumptive logics, and forms of regulation, works to protect those attached to the idea of America from the racial violence and settler colonial terror that has been essential to the formation and solidification of the US nation-state. In the process, the dead, as Benjamin points out, are in danger of being killed repetitively (through erasure, tidy accounts of history, grammars of affirmation) for the sake of keeping the idea of America whole, coherent, and solid. US exceptionalism is a redemptive and terrifying paradigm.

The images and memories that are invoked and assembled in the opening verse of "American Terrorist" begin to desediment conventional understandings of terror. Lupe raps, with a cadence that includes pauses and fluidity, "We came through the storm, nooses on our necks, and a smallpox blanket to keep us warm, on a 747 on the Pentagon lawn, wake up, the alarm clock is connected to a bomb." Introducing a nebulous *we* or collective subject, born within the storm of progress, Lupe creates a constellation that includes images of the Middle Passage, lynching rituals, native and indigenous genocide, and the al-Qaeda attacks against the United States on 9/11. As Benjamin put it, "Ideas are to objects as constellations are to stars."[75] At its most basic, this cryptic statement gestures toward a different way of thinking about the interactions among ideas, images, and objects that departs from the subject/object model or the picture of a concept subsuming the nonconceptual. In other words, the constellation draws attention to relationships, connections, tensions, as well as continuities and discontinuities. It underscores how meanings and affective intensities can change and shift depending on what ideas and images are being juxtaposed and brought together. The constellation also refuses linear ways of thinking about time and history; instead, it prompts us to think in terms of juxtapositions and tangencies, proximities and distances, repetitions and ruptures. This strategy refuses to turn the past into a moment within the fulfillment of progress, history, and proper humanity. For Lupe, this constellational style enables him to gather, rearticulate, and stay with fractured images of the past in a manner that enacts an immanent break from the regime of progress, especially as it operates through American exceptionalism.

By placing verbal images of slavery (Africans kidnapped and brought through the storm of the Atlantic, the Middle Passage, the violent hold of the ship, the storm of progress) and settler colonial violence next to more conventional examples of terror (an alarm clock connected to a bomb), Lupe augments and reconfigures our understanding of terror. Rather than reducing it to an event, his lyrics suggest that, especially in regard to black and native peoples, terror is more like a structure, paradigm, or condition of possibility for the development of US sovereignty. Along this line, at the end of the first verse Lupe brings together a picture of the fire department using hoses to quell civil rights protests with the burning and destruction of teepees. Not only does this moment compel the listener to think about the interplay between fire and water (both can be destructive and cleansing), it also visualizes a legacy of state-sponsored repression and containment. Immediately following this pairing, Lupe ends the first verse with "and move"—in a vocal tone that is pronounced but then trails off and disappears before and into the hook. I am prompted to think about a host of possibilities: the police officer instructing the protester to move along, the forced displacement of indigenous peoples, and the firebombing of the anarchist Philadelphia MOVE community by police helicopters in 1985. In addition, the listener might hear this "and move" as a call to put into motion various thoughts, memories, affects, and modes of reflection. Consequently, the call to move is not incompatible with the need to pause, slow down, and contemplate.

This pairing of settler colonial violence (smallpox, the destruction of teepees) and antiblack terror (Middle Passage, lynching, an allusion in the second verse to the Ku Klux Klan) brings to mind Wilderson's understanding of the racial antagonisms that organize and haunt American civil society.[76] For Wilderson, as indicated above, there is a structure of violence and terror that defines the relationship between the proper human on the one hand and blacks and indigenous peoples on the other. This is a structural violence that cannot be redressed or redeemed by a paradigm (liberalism, humanism, US democracy) that relies on the confiscation and occupation of indigenous lands, the elimination of indigenous peoples, and the positioning of black people as the slaves of the social world.[77] Similarly, Lupe's constellational style, and the earlier allusion to "coming through the storm," brings to mind what Tiffany King refers to as the shoal, or that liminal space between the water and land, where legacies and discourses of slavery and settler colonialism collide and interact. Among other things, the shoal functions to halt and impede navigation and movement; the metaphor prompts a slowing down and interrupts the ways discourses about settler colonialism turn conquest, murder, rape, and genocide into euphemisms about removal and displacement. In other words, King underscores how liberal humanist narratives "invoke settlement, land, clearing and territory [in a manner that] effaces the violence of conquest."[78] Even when we talk about the terrifying, we can be under the compulsion to convert that terror into something palatable and recuperable. In the process, terror is excised from the idea/essence of America, the proper human, and nation-state sovereignty.

Whereas terror is often aligned with the spectacular, there is also a way that structural terror operates at the nexus of the spectacular and the mundane. Here I am reminded of Saidiya Hartman's reluctance about reiterating the "terrible spectacles" of slavery, exemplified by Frederick Douglass's account of seeing his Aunt Hester beaten and ravaged. Concerned about the casual and nonchalant ways that these lurid exhibitions are narrated and passed down, Hartman redirects attention to "those scenes in which terror can hardly be discerned, . . . the terror of the mundane and quotidian."[79] Here she is thinking about moments when slaves were forced to amuse the master and his guests; or those regular episodes when slaves were instructed to look happy and content on the auction block. For Anthony Pinn, the auction block, and the later emergence of postbellum lynching to contain and keep in place black subjects, are best described as "rituals of reference," or "repeated, systematic activity . . . intended to reinforce the enslaved's status as object."[80] According to Pinn, the conversion of Africans into things involved dread-filled rituals and ceremonies (exchange, humiliation, torture, natal separation) that helped solidify the subordination of black people to white people. For authors like Hartman and Pinn, terror has been a formative part of nation-building, a constitutive element in the containment and disciplining of black flesh. These thinkers also remind us that violence is never outside the law; rather, it gets internalized and legitimized through statutes, customs, and prevailing sociopolitical arrangements. Moreover, it gets entrenched and normalized in socioeconomic inequities and devastations, qualities that seem to always have an unbalanced impact on black, brown, and indigenous peoples. Consider when Lupe utters, "Rich must be blind cuz they ain't see the poor there" and then "Need to open up a park, just close ten schools, we don't need 'em." In this fragment, the artist compels the listener to think and feel the dominion of capital (and the policies and decisions routinely made to uphold wealth, property, and leisure at the expense of those deprived of basic resources) alongside more stereotypical images of unacceptable violence, such as a "Muslim woman strapped with a bomb on a bus." There is something about not seeing, or even rendering invisible, what is in plain sight that keeps in place a system based on hunger, exploitation, and economic precarity. Similar to Hartman and Pinn, Lupe draws attention to both the mundaneness of violence and the violence of the ordinary.

Another aspect of "American Terrorist" that stands out is the hook, performed by Matthew Santos. Here we should consider the multiple connotations of *the hook*, a term associated with catching, hanging, striking, and cutting. It is usually some kind of repeated phrase or sound, a refrain. It is also a kind of flight from the main verses and lyrics of a rap song, especially when the hook involves a different vocal expression. On this track, Santos's voice fills the hook with a combination of sounds—high notes, raspy utterances, and at times an extended cry. There are moments when Santos utters *American* and *terrorist* in a manner that accentuates the syllables in both words. As the song nears its conclusion, he utters these words in a prolonged cry that resembles the scatting of a jazz singer, causing the two terms to merge together seamlessly. Among other possibilities, this vocal and sonic strategy underscores a refusal to separate the idea of America from the significations and affects affixed to terror. More generally, there is also something about the protracted cry that makes audible, for a moment, the exorbitance of violence and suffering in the world. But it also evokes the beautiful, the moving, that which is both haunting and enjoyable; it is an expression of the ecstatic. This is a moment when ordinary grammar and expression breaks down. Besides the aforementioned features of the hook, we hear the refrain of "The more money they make" and "Whatever they want to take." The reiteration and aligning of *making* and *taking* indicates that, especially under the regime of capital and Western imperialism, the accumulation of wealth and power relies on theft, confiscation, and expropriation of land, resources, and bodies. And the power that accrues from wealth turns theft into a recursive process. To be sure, the pronoun *they* is indeterminate and unstable; as hip hop has shown, this *they* that makes and takes can maneuver to include subjects who previously inhabited the underside of capital and its accumulative logic.

The interplay between making and taking in the hook anticipates the back and forth between gift and death in the concluding segment of the track. Lupe raps, "Don't give black man food, give red man liquor . . . give yellow man tool, make him railroad builder . . . give black man crack, Glocks, and things, give the red man craps, slot machines." Here Lupe is alluding to a host of historical realities—from Chinese immigrants building railroads in the nineteenth century under deadly conditions, to reservation systems that cannot substitute for the devastating endurance of settler colonialism, to the ways weapons manufacturing relies on, and creates surplus value from, violence and death. While some of the images might strike the listener as trite, I take it that Lupe is sounding out a general association between giving and taking, or donation and death, within Western/US imperial projects. Earlier on in the track, he makes a satirical reference to "break 'em off a little democracy," which suggests that the gift of democracy is intertwined with a history of breaks and tears. Or more specifically, we can only think of democracy (even its more radical versions) as a fractured legacy, a splintered form of life and death. While the work of Jacques Derrida certainly comes to mind here (*The Gift of Death*), I also think about Du Bois's claim that the gift of civilization, for those peoples deemed uncivilized and in need of redemption, has meant "war, murder, slavery, extermination, and debauchery."[81] Immediately after this repetitive pairing of gift and destruction, Lupe says, "Bring it back," several times before his voice fades into the final iteration of the hook. The "bring it back" might be an antiphonal prompt for Santos. It might be a call to return to the beginning of the song, where Lupe asks the listener to close their eyes and make an internal journey. The "bring it back" might allude to recovering what has been taken from exploited peoples, especially the darker denizens of colonial modernity. Or the "it" that gets returned and reenacted could be a history marked by terrifying episodes and experiences that render impossible something like repair. Perhaps in the sonic reiteration, retrieval, and assemblage (or what Khabeer calls looping), we might experience a kind of halt in response to narratives and practices predicated on death and its denial. We might even hear and experience differently the mundaneness of death. The cut might touch us in an unexpected manner. To put it another way, the song brings back a sound and image of the fracture caused by attempts to recover that which promises to make history and existence complete and coherent. In the process, Lupe's track resists the tendency to deny and diminish the terror inherent in the formation of US sovereignty. This strategy reinforces a strong separation between America and terror, which in turn justifies imperial state repression against subjects and regions that are designated as the primary embodiments of gratuitous violence.

Kendrick Lamar and the Long, Fractured 1980s: The Gendered Limits of Storytelling

In hip hop, there's often a cut or break that reminds us of a DJ's techniques and also disrupts the typical notions of coherence, wholeness, and fulfillment. While artists like Lupe yearn for these qualities and find them in conventional places (religion, uplift), I am interested in exploring other moments when redemption looks more like retrieving a wound from efforts to turn the wreckage of history into fodder for progress, settler time, or longings to recover some previous plenitude.[82] This wound is both a marker of hurt and anguish as well as an opening, an exposure, a marking that occasions various sorts of relations and intimacies. While Lupe Fiasco performs this uncanny redemption in a certain manner, Kendrick Lamar's musical corpus, especially his debut album *Section.80*, does as well.[83] Like other commentators, I underscore how Kendrick's 2011 album conjures the Reagan era, or a particular iteration of sovereign time, to sound out the pernicious effects of the administration's economic policies, especially on impoverished black communities.[84] At the same time, I want to push further and pursue how this album gestures toward a conception of time as the repetition (with differentiation) of a fracturing, of which the time of Reagan is one significant section or piece. In the process, the album refuses tendencies to rehabilitate Reagan and the office of the presidency more generally. It works against the urge to disentangle Reagan/sovereignty/whiteness from economic devastation, crack, neurodevelopmental disorders, gang violence in Compton, and a general sense of the nihilistic or "I don't give a fuck" disposition toward the world. In what follows, I attempt to stay with the break heard in Kendrick's music, despite fantasies of making, and being made, whole and complete.

It could be argued that Kendrick's music typifies what Sorett describes as a transition within mainstream hip hop from Islam to Christianity as the primary religious muse. As Floyd-Thomas points out, "Lamar [generally] invokes the issue of sin derived by traditional church theology."[85] He often contemplates and interprets his life and his relationship to Compton, home, and the world through sin, evil, individual vices, redemption, and so forth. His second album, *good kid, m.A.A.d city*, begins with the Sinner's prayer, and this is repeated later on the album by the late poet Maya Angelou. And yet Kendrick recently has identified with the Black Israelites, a group that, among other beliefs, "considers black, brown, and Native peoples as the original tribes of Israel."[86] And then there are moments when Kendrick's aesthetic expressions can be considered part of a general African-Atlantic religious piety that involves honoring ancestors or becoming a vessel for one's "dead homies."[87] According to Bettina Love, Kendrick's music resembles what Kevin Quashie calls quiet, a set of interior dispositions that, for Love, include self-reflection, questioning, doubt, and existential struggle.[88] I take it that all these religious and spiritual descriptions are part of Kendrick's aesthetic practice and arsenal. Like many rap artists, Kendrick is a sort of bricoleur, drawing from the fragments/sections of different traditions and practices. I also maintain that there are moments in his musical corpus when he is confronting themes like death, black gender, redemption, and beauty in a manner that cannot be fully encompassed by discrete, recognizable religious traditions, practices, or doctrines. He reminds us that hip hop has its own ways of decomposing and reassembling religious practices and beliefs. At times, this process includes generating sounds, rhythms, and images of the volatile and unsettling sacred.

What does Kendrick's *Section.80* unsettle and cut against? Even as the album rehearses many conventional narratives and tropes (gender, black pathology, natural beauty, etc.), how does it also refuse prevailing conceptions of sacrality, redemption, and becoming whole? How does the album do this by reconfiguring how we think about politics, temporality, and the relationship between sovereign/political violence and the violence that gets unduly located in, and deposited on, impoverished black spaces like Compton, California? One place to begin responding to these questions is the album cover and title. On the cover, we see a Bible with marijuana ashes on it; we also notice prescription pills, condoms, ammunition, cash, lipstick, and other sundry objects. As Margarita Guillory argues, this clustering of items, including the Bible and the marijuana, "blurs rigid lines of demarcations between the sacred and profane."[89] By working against a particular procedure of separation, the album cover compels one to ponder the inseparability between the holy and the accursed, sacredness and sexual desire, and durability and scattering. The grouping of these images also elicits the historical connections between the sacred text and ammunition, spreading the good news to those deemed in need of redemption and the violent conditions and machinations that have enabled that dissemination, such as war and conquest. But it might also remind the viewer that the Bible has been a spiritual weapon of the exploited. In the case of black religious practices and rituals, it has been reinterpreted and resignified in a manner that has provided relief, hope, and inspiration for forms of resistance against white supremacist regimes (even as the sacred text has helped to establish internal antagonisms within blackness toward, for instance, women and the figure of the queer).

In addition to the images on the cover of *Section.80*, I draw attention to the title itself. The name blends Section 8 housing and the 1980s, the presumed era of Ronald Reagan. This blending is noticeable because under the Reagan administration, government aid for low-income housing (along with food stamps and child welfare services) was drastically reduced.[90] Inversely, the Reagan regime augmented funds and resources to escalate Nixon's war on drugs, which, for Tupac, really translated into a continuation of state and militarized police repression of (poor) black people.[91] But something else is going on with the name, concerning the inscription of "section" and the decimal or punctuation in front of the 80. It could be that the album is introducing us to a musical project that is less than (and in excess of) one, the whole, the integer, and the integrated. The fraction, in this reading, is unwhole, incomplete, and indicative of a cut that deviates from desires to be singular and indivisible.[92] It could be that making a correlation between the 1980s and the present, between the Reagan era and the effects of those political and economic policies, is only one part (or section) of a series of antiblack policies and arrangements, extending forward and backward. It is interesting that Kendrick claims in an interview that "when I say *Section.80*, I say everything from 1980–2012, everything between that, from start to finish."[93] On the one hand, Kendrick seems to be positing a definite beginning and end to the Reagan era. On the other hand, there is an acknowledgment that this era extends beyond discernible limits. The strategies and operations that make up the time of Reagan—war, antiblackness, cutting of government funds for the indigent, using racist and sexist images of black women to galvanize white support, unwillingness to respond to the emerging AIDS epidemic—cannot be framed within the president's two terms. Rather, the effects and consequences reverberate, haunt, and get attached to subsequent regimes, administrations, and periods of time. In addition, the time of Reagan is itself derivative of previous eras, antecedent iterations of sovereign time that actualized progress, growth, and the reclamation of whiteness at the expense of poor black people among other groups and subject positions.

It is important to consider the specific timing of Kendrick's album. *Section.80* was released in 2011, under the regime of hope, optimism, the first black president, and the post-racial. The Obama presidency was a moment when black artists and celebrities (including Kendrick) were regularly invited to the White House, when black people were warned that they have no more excuses, and when the first black president said that he embodies and corroborates the fact of racial progress and the concomitant perfectibility of American democracy and freedom (often in response to another incident of antiblack violence). Kendrick would seem to fall in line with the post-racial fantasy, as he begins the album with "Fuck Your Ethnicity," a track that boasts about not caring if you, the listener or fan, are "black, white, Asian, Hispanic." At the same time, on this opening track Kendrick underscores that "racism is still alive, yellow tape and colored lines," suggesting some kind of interplay between racialized lines of demarcation, crime, and the fear of contamination. In addition to dropping the album amid the Obama presidency, *Section.80* came out in a year when Gallup polls indicated that Americans were more inclined to regard Reagan as the greatest US president than any other.[94] In light of these realities, it is difficult not to think of Kendrick's debut album as an instance of what Benjamin refers to as the blasting of a time interval from the clutches of progress and sovereign conceptions of history. This blasting, for a moment, extricates the 1980s from ascendant narratives of freedom as well as grammars of recovery in a manner that both freezes and remobilizes this era. If progress is a conception of temporality, or a movement of time, that is not incompatible with yearnings for the past, a better time, an era marked by a lost plenitude that needs to be recovered, then this album performs a break into dreams of progress, recovery, and a previous plenitude. It also indicates how these dreams are predicated on disavowing the violence internal to the arrangements that the presidency is designed to defend and preserve. Consequently, I read *Section.80* as not only a form of counterremembrance regarding the epoch of Reagan; I read it as a refusal to elevate the figure of the president, the sovereign, and the highest office above the suffering and anguish, the wildness and disorder, that gets unduly indexed to blackness, black women, the impoverished, and so forth.

Consider the track "Ronald Reagan Era," in which Kendrick demonstrates his verbal dexterity while invoking a series of allusions, images, and sounds—police sirens, gang antagonisms, hunger, opioid consumption, the music of Big Daddy Kane, pornography actors, and "squad cars, neighborhood wars, and stolen Mazdas." One might listen to this song and hear a pathological account of Compton, the black ghetto, and working-class, urban black collectives and places. In other words, Kendrick is describing stigmatizing qualities and characteristics that appear to be inherent to and naturalized within these spaces. Yet there is a moment when Kendrick refers to himself and his generation (he was born in 1987) as the "children of Ronald Reagan." What does it mean to consider oneself the offspring and product of an instantiation of white male sovereignty? How does this reference reach back to the regime of slavery, in which the white master/settler could father and reproduce slave labor without taking responsibility, or only respond to this offspring as a fungible object, thing, and instrument? As a metaphor, the "children of Ronald Reagan" alludes to what gets produced and engendered by a succession of pernicious political-economic decisions, policies, and arrangements, factors that have a disproportionate, or exorbitant, impact on black subjects. Moreover, the line in question suggests that while the position of the impoverished black subject exists in opposition to the white patrimonial sovereign, that relationship entails a moment of what Christina Sharpe calls a monstrous intimacy,[95] a perverse kinship, or a deadly entanglement. At times, this wounded kinship engenders desires within blackened subjects to mimic and emulate the figure of the sovereign and acquire the power and territory that accompanies this status. Consequently, the pathology typically attached to Compton, and blackness more generally, is relocated. It becomes a mark and an effect of a violent (and disavowed) interaction between the proper, idealized human, the figure of the white sovereign, and the position of the black (who appears improper and unfit within this pathological matrix).[96]

But more is going on in songs like "Ronald Reagan Era." I take it that Kendrick is also showing us what it looks and sounds like to flow, move and be moved, maneuver words and metaphors, and take on the damages of the long Reagan era without being completely determined by that iteration of sovereign time. Or perhaps the damage, the fracture, is rearticulated through cadence, rhythm, vocal tone, rhyme scheme, and sonic imitation (of gunshots and police sirens, for instance). Think, for instance, of the moment when Kendrick raps, "I'm hungry, my body's antsy," in a manner that connects his passion as an emcee with memories of being without adequate sustenance. (There is also a subtle identification with the ant, the insect, etc.) In this utterance, we hear an unrest or agitation in his voice that cannot be easily contained or stabilized; he becomes the agitation that he describes regarding his body. Or think when he raps, "Peeling off like a Xanny," a simile that plays on the phonic resemblance of pill and peel. In this simile, we can appreciate Kendrick's poetical prowess and the sonic variations and slippages of black vernacular without being untouched by his concern about the overreliance on drugs to deal with pain, anxiety, and depression. Or perhaps the references in the song to Xanax and Vicodin ("take it in vain/vein") point to how the ordering of things generates disorder that certain kinds of subjects are forced to endure. This concern is amplified on the track "A.D.H.D," in which Kendrick addresses the excessive drug and alcohol consumption within his generation, an excess he ascribes to being crack(ed) babies and born in the 1980s. In opposition to the more aggressive and fierce flow on "Ronald Reagan Era," this song is slowed down, melancholic, and torpid. It carries a heavy emptiness. And yet the video shows Kendrick and his friends cruising, laughing, and joking in slow-motion shots and scenes, a pace that invites us to linger with the details and minutiae of movements, interactions, moods, and facial expressions. At one point, Kendrick and his friends are in an empty office, playing at simulating a work environment. The abandoned office points to an existential emptiness that Kendrick and his friends have inherited; and yet the moments of make-believe indicate the significance of invention and intimacy within and through the abyss.

Throughout *Section.80* one hears Kendrick identifying with and distancing himself from a "who gives a fuck" temperament that is unfairly blamed on black youth and contemporary hip hop. To some extent, this disposition prompts thoughts and reflections about black nihilism, care, and what makes life worthwhile (not unlike Biggie's *Ready to Die* album). If the specter of nihilism brings to mind Nietzsche's claim that "the highest values devaluate themselves,"[97] then it also recalls Cornel West's lament about the nihilistic tendencies that proliferate in black communities in a post–civil rights era. According to West, "This threat is not simply a matter of relative economic deprivation and political powerlessness. . . . It is primarily a question of speaking to the profound sense of psychological depression, personal worthlessness, and social despair so widespread in black America."[98] For West, nihilism is not so much the philosophical inability to find universal foundations for truth and moral claims; it has more to do with "a life of horrifying meaninglessness, hopelessness, and (most important) lovelessness."[99] On West's reading, this nihilistic menace, exemplified by the "I don't give a fuck" posture, has always been a part of black people's existential situation within a white supremacist world. And yet, for West, our black ancestors found ways to develop habits and practices of care, love, and community to protect themselves from the nihilistic threat. They created structures of meaning and value in response to social death, which have been severely jeopardized in a post–civil rights world.

While I take West's concerns seriously, I wonder if we might twist and twerk these worries about "meaninglessness, hopelessness, and lovelessness" that supposedly pervade black communities and rap music. According to Moya Bailey, who links the "I don't give a fuck" attitude to an ethics of care, it could be that Kendrick's generation has discovered that it is too painful to care.[100] It could be, as Bailey points out, that in a world that denies black men, especially, space to grieve and express hurt, a world that denigrates emotions and affects that are not productive and lucrative, a world that has decimated black peoples while relying on blackness for the renewal of life, expressing care and vulnerability is too hurtful, too risky. Or it could be that black care happens in undetected ways and spaces. Or that vulnerability and wounded exposure to others gets dissimulated by postures of coolness, indifference, or aggression.[101] To be sure, Kendrick's musical corpus, more often than not, reveals a willingness to sit with and express vulnerability, uncertainty, complicated love, self-care, mortality, depression, and so forth. In fact, in Kendrick's view, his music is a portrayal of blackness that "represents being happy, being sad, being angry, being mad, being depressed, being stressed [and so on]."[102] Consequently, there are moments when he identifies with the hopelessness that West understandably bemoans, an identification that is often split between the various perspectives and positions that Kendrick takes on—I, you, and s/he.[103]

My aim is not to defend or dismiss the "I don't five a fuck" posture toward the world, but to sit with and alongside it. While this stance replicates pernicious attitudes and dispositions, it also gives voice and witness to the violent conditions that systemically withhold care, attention, and concern from certain subjects, communities, and life-death worlds. Riffing on the work of Calvin Warren, we might ask: Why should black people invest energies and hopes in arrangements and institutions that are predicated on disavowed black death and suffering?[104] But as Warren points out, even if one abandons a circumscribed conception of hope and redemption (where hope is required to find its end in American democracy, humanism, the idea of progress), this does not mean that other ways of enacting hope and possibility are not available.[105] I take it that this possibility has something to do with making a cut into narratives and imaginaries that promise to make us whole and complete, at the expense of those bearing the burden of the void.

One of the ways that this cut, this intimacy through the wound, can happen is when a redemptive project falters. It can occur when one's attempt to integrate another into their story does not quite work, does not quite contribute to the production of sense and meaning. Here I am thinking about Kendrick's relationship to individual women, such as Tammy and Keisha, who are singled out in the opening skit, a fireside gathering led by a quasipreacher figure. On the song dedicated to Tammy (subtitled "Her Evils"), Kendrick suggests that lesbianism, or "turning dyke," is primarily a response to being "tired of these niggas."[106] In other words, erotic intimacy between women is an effect of a failed heteronormative framework and male infidelity, rather than its own set of self-generating relationships, desires, and practices. In addition, this song indicates that Tammy's evil consists of her sliding away from a heteronormative and monogamous relationship and imitating the infidelity of her partner. And yet something else can be heard. Each iteration of the hook consists of a repetition with a difference. Riffing on C-Murder and Snoop Dogg's classic track "Down for My Niggaz," we hear a voice that is almost choral. The first iteration is "Fuck them other niggas cuz I'm down for my nigga," which indicates a fidelity to the point of death (i.e., ride or die). The second iteration, "Fuck that other nigga, when she tired of her nigga," indicates a refusal to take on the burden of black feminine devotion and sacrifice at the expense of expressing anger and disappointment and pursuing sexual pleasure. And as described above, the third iteration, "Fuck with other bitches when they tired of these niggas," demonstrates that erotic and romantic intimacy cannot be fully contained within a heteronormative framework. Observe and hear how the reiterations of the hook move from the *I* to the less personal *she* and then to a more collective *they*. This movement between pronouns suggests that Kendrick and the listener might assume different subject positions and various ways of relating to black gender, sexuality, trust, power, and the interplay between anguish and intimacy. Finally, the sound of this track, the video game–type beat that accompanies the disjointed flow, unsettles the listening experience. This is supplemented by a video in which the images of the bodies are cut, fragmented, doubled, and recomposed. One's sense of coherence is undone. One's desire to locate, interpret, and even judge a unified subject named Tammy, and her evils, runs into a cutting that the listener/viewer cannot escape unscathed.

On "Keisha's Song (Her Pain)," Kendrick tells the story of a seventeen-year-old sex worker. Listening to this painful track, we find out that Keisha gives most of her money to her daddy/pimp; that she has been solicited by police officers who force her to exchange sex for remaining free or getting out of jail; and that she was molested and raped by her mother's boyfriend (which for Kendrick is the primary cause of her current predicament). At the end of the song, Keisha is raped, killed, and "left for dead" in the street. Her life ends due to a cycle of repetitive violence. And the listener encounters this terrifying sequence as Kendrick's voice and flow reaches an intensity that can only end in exhaustion, a fall. There is too much to think and feel about. And as I listen to this song and try to write, I am hesitating and fumbling. I think of the refrain, "Lord knows she's beautiful," and the proximity between Keisha's "sore body" and her anatomy as "God's temple." Is this a way for Kendrick to anticipate a transcendence of Keisha's wounds, or do the notions of the divine and the idea of the beautiful undergo a wounding, an aching? And then I reflect on the juxtaposition of Rosa Parks and Keisha performing sexual acts in the "back seat." Kendrick raps, "Rosa Parks never a factor when she [Keisha] making ends meet." On the one hand, Rosa Parks has been incorporated into a sanitized, respectable version of the civil rights movement that would seem to be of little relevance to Keisha's predicament. On the other hand, Parks was involved in grassroots efforts to investigate and redress patterns of sexual violence against black women, a site of struggle that has been diminished by these bowdlerized accounts of black liberation practices. I also think of Kendrick's reference to nuns, Catholic religion, and sinner's redemption, allusions in the third verse that suggest if only Keisha had been exposed to these possibilities, her life might have turned out differently. What kind of redemption is being imagined here? Is Kendrick rehearsing the proverbial virgin/prostitute binary while describing it as "foolish" at the same time? Is religion immune from routinized sexual abuse and violence? Does a kind of religious disciplining, and punishment, of (black) female sexuality point to another, less explicit form of containment and suppression? Shouldn't we be mindful of how Christianity has contributed to racial-religious mechanisms that have reviled black people because they don't perform gender and sexual desire properly?

At the end of "Keisha's Song," Kendrick informs the listener that he made his eleven-year-old sister listen to the track after its completion. There is a sense of urgency here as he looks into the face of his sister, knowing that she inhabits a world that is inimical to black women. Consequently, he seems to turn Keisha's song, life, and death into an instance of instruction and warning. Death might become useful, productive, and not be in vain. The track becomes an occasion to use Keisha's life and death to ensure that his sister does not repeat the cycle of abuse and exploitation. The apostrophe, the possessive has been taken up by Kendrick; her pain has become an opportunity to make life more livable and meaningful for him and his sister. But things are more complicated. He ends his verse with "The day that I wrote this song, sat her down and pressed play" before we hear the last iteration of the hook, "Fancy girls on Long Beach Boulevard." I consider this interval between play and repetition to be one that both recreates the conditions of Keisha's precarious situation and offers a space to imagine a different future, while allowing each listening experience to bring a new perspective on her life, sex work, and death. The language of "play," among other possibilities, brings to mind Jacques Derrida's turn to play as a kind of repetition and rhythm that conditions and undermines commitments to ideas and objects that would anticipate closure, the fulfillment of meaning, or the end of "signifying and substitutive references inscribed in a system of differences and the movement of a chain."[107] Play, for Derrida, resists the will to completion that tries to arrest it, allowing for a repetition that permits a kind of supplement, an addition and subtraction to a signifier, concept, or narrative.

This sense of the supplement can be heard in "Sing About Me, I'm Dying of Thirst," a song on Kendrick's 2012 *good kid, m.A.A.d city* album, when he assumes the voice and position of Keisha's sister, who expresses anger over Kendrick using Keisha's death for his advancement. She accuses Kendrick of judging Keisha and putting her on blast to propel his own story. In other words, he attempts to turn a death in vain into his own gain, a death that has no purpose and ultimate meaning into a story that will attach meaning and significance to it in a manner that primarily benefits the storyteller. She also reveals that her sister's past is her future, a reality that includes sex work, involves a sense of urgency, and brings exhaustion. The subject position and pronoun *I* here is split between Kendrick and Keisha's sister; the *you* that is being addressed is Kendrick, which connotes an additional sort of self-splitting. Keisha's sister is being subsumed into Kendrick's song and narrative even as s/he refuses the possibility of identification ("You can't fit the pumps I walk in"; "Just make sure I'm not in the song") and incorporation. Through a tortuous internal dialogue, a simultaneous endeavor to become Other and internalize a black feminine voice, this verse enacts and makes audible the failures and limits of endeavors to make and be made whole through narrative, meaning-making, and storying others. During the process, the listener is compelled to ponder the ethical implications of making another person's pain your own, a transference that elicits the dynamics of possession and dispossession. And as the sister's (i.e., Kendrick's) voice fades away at the conclusion of the verse, as s/he promises that she will never fade away, we can barely hear utterances like "Fuck your glory" and "Don't ignore me." The fade and gradual transition to silence punctuates the confidence in words being able to capture anguish, exhaustion, rage, or painful pleasure. It is the very breakdown of words that indicates the necessity and failure of language, even in its poetic variations, in the face of the heterogeneous.

To some extent, "Keisha's Song" exemplifies a pattern within hip hop, a succession of rap songs in which black men tell stories about a particular black woman or character who is a stand-in for a type of black female subject. Sometimes these stories involve comedy and romance; at other times they involve a story about trauma, moral vice, promiscuity, and so forth. Here I think of Tupac's "Brenda's Got a Baby," which, according to Kendrick, was Keisha's favorite song. I also think of tracks like Diamond D's "Sally Got a One Track Mind" or Brand Nubian's "Slow Down," in which the black female figures positioned in the narratives are ridiculed for being promiscuous, irresponsible, wayward, and exchanging sex for material objects. In these latter two songs, there is scant allusion to the structuring conditions that might lead to this behavior, no sense that sexuality can be a survival weapon and an instrument of pleasure in a world organized by patrimonial strictures, and no sense that black women have complicated relationships to these predicaments. While hip hop has been a space to articulate and work through the racial and gendered relations of power and subjugation that mark black masculinity (black men are not properly human and therefore not fully men[108]), it has also been a site where black male subjects work these tensions out on and through black women. To put it more precisely, hip hop has both permitted and prescribed certain kinds of black masculine (cishet, homolatent) expression that often rely on an antagonistic relationship to black women, even when there are displays of intimacy. As Imani Perry points out, "Masculinity in hip hop reflects the desire to assert black male subjectivity and it sometimes does so at the expense of black female subjectivity."[109] Kendrick participates in and agitates this legacy. His music also brings into relief the structural limits to narrative and meaning-making, to the ways the structural features of storying require exclusion, selectivity, undesired assimilation, and the conversion of another's anguish into something productive and sensible. This is one of the many lessons of Hartman's "Venus in Two Acts," especially when she questions whether one can "recuperate lives entangled with and impossible to differentiate from the terrible utterances [and conditions] that condemned them to death."[110] So, while a particular narrative will to coherence occasionally only permits women to enter Kendrick's acoustic story as problems to be fixed or unruly objects that need reform,[111] there are moments when a cut is inserted into this paradigm, which exposes and thwarts all too familiar desires to use another's anguish to fortify and protect the fantasy of becoming whole and undivided beings.

The image and sound of the cut segues into a conversation about spilling over and excess. In Lupe Fiasco's case, the exorbitance of violence that has been a precondition for the formation and development of US nation-state sovereignty overflows and dismantles any reliable contrast between the idea of America and terror. By retrieving images and memories of that violence, Lupe works against the ways US exceptionalism operates as a self-justifying paradigm. For Kendrick, the Reagan era, the time of the sovereign, cannot be contained in the 1980s, as the effects and consequences remain with Kendrick's generation. In addition, the violence that defines the relationship between the white sovereign and the (impoverished) black individual cannot be sutured alongside the rehabilitation of Reagan, the presidency, whiteness, and so forth. Finally, Kendrick's attempt to use and instrumentalize the unruly lives and deaths of black feminine subjects stumbles into an excess that cannot be incorporated into standard narratives and frameworks of meaning-making. (If hip hop can save lives, it can also bring into relief how the will to make, and be made, whole founders and breaks down.) In the next chapter, I address more explicitly a site of excess in hip hop that is expressed through performances of monstrosity. I explore monstrosity and the figure of the monster in hip hop in a manner that brings together, perhaps more fully than the first two chapters, the left-hand sacred, blackness, and black gender.

Monster/Monstrosity

The figure of the monster looms large in rap music and hip hop performance. One notices the presence of the monstrous in the names and alternate personas of artists like Rockness Monsta, Jean Grae (a play on the mutant character from the Marvel series *X-Men*), and Flatbush Zombies. In these cases, the naming prepares the listener for some identification with or mutation into that which is not quite human—an expectation of sounds, images, energies, and verbal skills that hang at the edges of the normal and proper. Consequently, one also hears the monstrous through various allusions and references within rap lyrics or through the modifications and amplifications of the voice and vocal tone.[1] Think, for instance, of Rakim's metaphorical utterance on "Microphone Fiend": "After twelve, I'm worse than a gremlin. Feed me hip hop and I start tremblin'. The thrill of suspense is intense, you're horrified. But this ain't the cinemas of *Tales from the Darkside*."[2] There is a lot going on in these lines. On the one hand, Rakim is alluding to the 1984 film *Gremlins*, in which a cute, harmless pet named Gizmo turns into a destructive and aggressive reptilian monster after certain rules are broken, such as feeding the fictional creature after midnight. The gremlin metaphor continues as Rakim mentions consuming or being fed hip hop, a process that causes him to tremble as he presumably begins to transform. Rakim's transformation on the mic, alongside the beat and production, leaves the listener suspended in a state of excitement and anticipation. These feelings, he instructs us, are mixed with a sense of the horrifying, but in a slightly different manner from a horror film or television series. In fact, Rakim warns us, and other emcees, that he is "worse" than the gremlin, more terrible and dangerous than the fictional monstrous figure. Consequently, if Rakim claims on another track that MC means "move the crowd,"[3] then he is indicating on "Microphone Fiend" that hip hop, when consumed, heard, or brought into contact with the emcee and the audience, creates a scene of reversible affectivity and unrest. Both the emcee and the second-person referent, the *you*, tremble, shake, and experience in different ways what Bataille might call an "inexorable movement."[4]

The figure of the monster continues to appear through more recent artists and compositions. Lil Wayne, for instance, asks his imaginary competitor, "Okay, you're a goon, but what's a goon to a goblin?"[5] This goblin figure is taken up by Tyler, the Creator in "Goblin," which connects the mischievous character to the activity of gobbling, eating, and consuming.[6] And 21 Savage confesses that "pain and hunger made a savage [and a superstar]" and that the "money and the fame make a monster."[7] What is interesting here is that the artist is not claiming that being/becoming a savage or a monster is intrinsic or congenital, as is the case in modern racist discourses. There is something about the conditions of pain and hunger that can create behaviors that appear to exist somewhere between and beside the human and the animal. Money and fame, according to 21 Savage, similarly can turn a rap artist into a creature that is not quite human, that exceeds the parameters of the proper human, or that indicates the monstrous traits that always accompany and haunt human subjectivity and desire. The link 21 Savage makes between money and fame and monstrosity bring to mind Karl Marx's description of the horrifying quality of capital. Marx writes, "Capital is dead labour, that, vampire-like, only lives by sucking living labour, and lives the more, the more it sucks."[8] We can be sure that capital, as a mechanism that lives off the life and blood of labor, produces subjects whose capacity to reproduce life depends on quenching the thirst for blood. And if there is a vampire-like dimension of capitalism's relationship to labor, we also know that the relentless pursuit of surplus value, land, and resources since the "rosy dawn of capital" has relied on the "conquest, enslavement, robbery, and murder" of non-European peoples.[9] This exorbitant violence has been facilitated by an imaginary that, among other things, equates blackness with the monstrous, positioning black people in the undefinable gap between the civilized human and the undomesticated animal. In other words, what Marx calls the primitive accumulation of capital is justified by relocating the monstrosity of racial capitalism and attaching it to black flesh.

In what follows, I contend that the figure of the monster within hip hop prompts us to bring together two trajectories of thought. On the one hand, the horrifying *and* alluring force of the monster exemplifies the left-hand, form-shattering sacred, articulated powerfully in the work of Georges Bataille, whose thought I work through in the first section. In addition, the performance of the monstrous within hip hop invites an engagement with authors within black studies, such as Frantz Fanon, Hortense Spillers, Christina Sharpe, and Zakiyyah Jackson, who interrogate and unravel the affiliation of blackness and black gender with monstrosity and the extrahuman. While thinking at the nexus of religious thought and black studies, I offer a reading of Kanye West's 2010 song and video "Monster." I contend that the artists on this track, such as Kanye, Jay-Z, and Nicki Minaj, identify with the monster in a manner that directs the viewer and listener to the exuberant and form-dissolving qualities of (black) life and death, while also becoming an occasion to reintroduce pernicious aspirations toward sovereignty. I end the chapter by moving to Minaj's video for "Anaconda," reading this instantiation and parody of hip hop's visual and erotic economy alongside Spillers's suggestion that the monstrosity that has been historically imposed on black women might be reclaimed and rewritten.[10]

Bataille and the Excessive Sacred

As discussed in the introduction, Georges Bataille takes and runs with Durkheim's understanding of the doubleness internal to the sacred, or that which is set apart and separated from the profane and everyday through taboos and prohibitions. To recapitulate, while sacredness refers to objects, spaces, and ideas that need to be protected from contaminating forces, it also refers to those latter forces that are cordoned off and managed so that they will not violate or sully precious and protected things. Among other implications, this means that religious experience necessitates reflection on the dynamics of separation, contact, the forbidden, and transgression; it also means that practices of the sacred involve some fraught interplay between the will to purity and exposure to the dirty and opaque, and between the attachment to form and susceptibility to form-dissolving excess. As Jeremy Biles points out in his provocative study of the French author, Bataille is "fascinated with the left-hand sacred . . .

not transcendent, pure, and beneficent but dangerous, filthy, and morbid."[11] As Biles describes further, the macabre quality of the sacred is embodied and revealed by the figure of the monster,[12] a figure that not only represents contradiction, horror, and anguish, but also the possibility of overcoming the limits of the profane self. In this section, I draw on Bataille's ideas to examine how this monstrous dimension of life, death, and desire is enacted, played with, and resignified in hip hop performance and visual culture. Furthermore, I am interested in how the figure of the monster can become an occasion to both reveal a horrifying and beautiful excess and a way to enact pernicious forms of sovereignty that are predicated on taming and domesticating that exuberance. Finally, I want to think through how Bataille's ideas about the sacred, intimacy, and the monstrous get modified when blackness and racialized gender slide into the foreground.

I begin with a brief analysis of Bataille's central ideas. Not unlike Walter Benjamin, Bataille is concerned about the ways modern life diminishes and forecloses certain kinds of intimate experiences. As Amy Hollywood has shown in her definitive text *Sensible Ecstasy*, Bataille turns to mysticism and other religious resources to think and feel beyond the restrictions of the social order.[13] This desire for a beyond, according to Hollywood, introduces a duplicity—a wish to be everything and a confrontation with human finitude and mortality.[14] Influenced by an array of diverse thinkers—from Teresa of Ávila to Karl Marx and Friedrich Nietzsche—Bataille is invested in the possibility of religious experience in a (Western/European) world in which god has been declared dead, a world also increasingly dominated by the logic of instrumental reason. For Bataille, this religious experience does not necessarily include some transcendent power that exists outside of time; rather, the quality of this experience involves the (im)possibility of recovering a lost connection with the immanent world. Or as he puts it, "Religion . . . is the search for lost intimacy."[15] In *Theory of Religion*, where Bataille lucidly develops these ideas, the French philosopher seems to make a rather stark distinction between the sacred and the profane realms. For Bataille, the profane realm is marked by what he calls discontinuity, instrumental reasoning, and the postponement of pleasure. Within this domain, human selves treat human and nonhuman beings as useful objects within future-oriented schemes and projects. In other words, I relate to and interact with others insofar as they support and buttress my sense of becoming a coherent self, enduring into an endless future. While this investment in a discrete and coherent self that treats the world in an instrumental manner is all too human and inescapable for Bataille, he contends that it prevents the kind of intimacy that humans long for. For Bataille, the sacred realm is associated with the possibility of intimate relationships with others, self-undermining encounters that are marked by excess, vulnerability, and anguish. While profane existence is constituted by production, accumulation, and self-preservation, sacred existence includes events, interactions, and practices that lead to the loss/expenditure of the coherent, discrete self and an opening to the painful contradictions that mark our lifeworlds. For Bataille, intimacy between self and Other is not devoid of pain and anguish; it is a "disheveled form of communication" that entails "despair, madness, love and even more: laughter, dizziness, vertigo, nausea, loss of self to the point of death."[16]

It is important to linger on this relationship between discontinuity, intimacy, and the loss of coherence, a relationship that anticipates the monstrous quality of the sacred. For Bataille, discontinuity, or a split in the immanent and intimate relationships within existence, is a result of the fact that humans possess consciousness, a quality that enables them to distinguish between subject and object, to imagine themselves as separate from other parts of the world, and consequently to treat beings as subordinate or transcendent things, instruments, and tools. According to Bataille, "Insofar as tools are developed with their end in view, consciousness posits them as objects, as interruptions in the indistinct continuity."[17] While consciousness and the making of distinctions enables meaning, which is something that humans cannot live without, meaning comes at a cost. Meaning-making for Bataille can only be reproduced by preserving the profane order of things, by placing objects, events, and relationships into future-oriented schemes and frameworks. For Bataille, "meaning [is] sought on the plane of utility, of the tool," a process that snatches objects out of the "undifferentiated continuity" or the immanent "flow of all that is."[18] The requirement of duration, without which there would be no meaning or the possibility of distinguishing objects, and the commitment to preservation foreclose certain kinds of experiences for the future-oriented subject, experiences that entail an undergoing of death, anguish, ecstasy, and the shattering of one's sense of being a discrete and coherent self. Bataille sums this up well in the following passage: "No thing in fact has a separate existence, has a meaning, unless a subsequent time is posited, in view of which it is constituted as an object. . . . Future time constitutes the real [profane] world to such a degree that death no longer has a place in it. But it is for this very reason that death means everything to it. The contradiction of the world of things is that it imparts an unreal character to death even though man's membership in the world is tied to the positing of the body as a thing insofar as it is mortal."[19] As I take it, human attachments to preservation and futurity, which are certainly necessary and valuable, rely on regular ways of avoiding and displacing death and self-loss. While death and life are clearly intertwined, death cannot have a real place, or death must be instrumentalized and made productive, as in the case of progress narratives discussed in the previous chapter. Conversely, this commitment to duration makes death and its intimations seem all the more daunting and filled with anguish. Thus Bataille claims, "The real/profane order does not so much reject the negation of life that is death as it rejects the affirmation of intimate life, whose measureless violence is a danger to the order of things, an affirmation that is fully realized only in death."[20] The sacred world for Bataille, in opposition to the world of things, duration, and accumulation, is defined and epitomized by a difficult intimacy with life's excessive features, an intimacy that can seem horrifying because of our attachments to preservation, self-coherence, and futurity.

Bataille is very much invested in identifying practices and activities that reconnect us to this sacred existence, that provide a sense of intimacy through loss, ecstasy, and anguish. While he infamously celebrates premodern rituals of sacrifice (an occasion where the sacrificing community identifies with the death/loss of the sacrificed body), he is aware that these practices are no longer legitimate in most contemporary communities and contexts. In fact, he claims in *Theory of Religion* that "the most solemn sacrifice may not be bloody."[21] For Bataille, sacrifice alludes to those experiences and events that disrupt our inclination to render the world intelligible, to place these episodes in some meaning-producing scheme or telos that would preserve form and order. As he puts it, "Sacrifice is the antithesis of production, which is accomplished with a view to the future; it is consumption [expenditure] that is concerned only with the moment."[22] Therefore, sacrifice is a kind of gift, offering, or relinquishment that undermines the logic of utility or exchange; it connotes an excess that escapes all too human tendencies to grasp, pin down, control, and render the world useful. The sacred order, in other words, takes the self outside itself, so to speak, into a tension-filled space of pleasure, pain, woundedness, and intimacy. As Bataille puts it, "Paradoxically intimacy is violence, and it is destruction, because it is not compatible with the positing of the separate individual."[23] Here the term *violence* signifies some disturbance or agitation to the general attachment to a separable self (or collective entity) untouched by the heterogeneous. Therefore, in lieu of actual sacrifices, Bataille directs our attention to self-undermining experiences and moments marked by excess, contradiction, and tension—such as laughter, tears, erotic life, friendship, and love. More generally, he also looks to art as a site where the self undergoes a puncturing and becomes more receptive to life's contradictions. His appreciation of art underscores how certain kinds of literature, paintings, films, and photographs take the reader/viewer outside their comfort zone, even if only for a moment. We might think of images or sounds of torment and suffering that disrupt familiar attempts to find some kind of redemptive narrative or reassuring meaning in suffering, representations that prompt us to sit with tensions, paradoxes, and horrors that permeate everyday life. As Jeremy Biles points out, the figure of the monster embodies for Bataille these horrifying qualities of the sacred, which appear horrifying in part because of our investment in "the integrality of the individual form."[24]

Bataille's understanding of religion and the sacred/profane is informed by an ontology of excess. In other words, Bataille locates an exuberance in the movements and circulations of energy that constitute planetary existence. He writes, "A movement is produced on the surface of the globe that results from the circulation of energy at this point of the universe. . . . The living organism, in a situation determined by the play of energy on the surface of the globe, ordinarily receives more energy than is necessary for maintaining life."[25] Consequently, the living organism can direct some of this energy toward discrete ends and goals. And while this channeled energy can lead to growth and expansion, the "excess [energy] cannot be absorbed in growth" and must be expended without a return or profit.[26] It must be wasted and rendered unproductive according to a framework defined by utility. Here Bataille is getting at an exuberant tumult that has its own patterns, interactions, and directions that cannot be contained by limited human goals. While the projection of goals and ends, and the concomitant formation of boundaries and limits, are necessary and significant, these processes tend to lead to the displacement of the ineluctable excess or to projects that harness that energy in catastrophic ways. Perhaps this is why Bataille gestures toward the possibility of cultivating projects that go against the logic of project and production, that counter the compulsion to accumulate and safeguard. What is crucial for my purpose is this interplay between excessive movement and a discrete end or form, one that can be redescribed as a polymorphous motion (what the emcee calls flowing or spitting) that inundates and disrupts the attachment to a singular form, or form as such. This "inexorable movement" is monstrous or multiformed, and it ruins a certain devotion to order, transparent borders, and so forth. And perhaps it prompts a rethinking of the relationship between form and the unformed, keeping in mind Eliade's claim that the monster, alongside water, darkness, and death, is that which "has not yet acquired a 'form.'"[27]

There are moments in Bataille's thought when his ideas arrive at an explicit allusion to and elaboration on the monster and the monstrous. In his essay "The Deviations of Nature," Bataille reminds the reader that the figure of the monster, always seen as a kind of deviation from normality, tends to generate fear and terror as well as fascination and curiosity.[28] The monster is a creature, being, persona that incites attraction and repulsion, not unlike Rudolf Otto's depiction of the holy. Alluding to this tension between repulsion and attraction, Bataille proclaims, "Mankind cannot remain indifferent to its monsters."[29] Consequently, Bataille suggests that the figure of the monster (he gives the examples of "freaks" at the carnival or eighteenth-century depictions of conjoined twins) allows us to represent, identify with, and also distance ourselves from contradiction and abnormality. He writes, "It is possible to state that [aggressive incongruity] manifests itself to a certain degree in the presence of any given human individual. But it is barely perceptible. That is why it is preferable to refer to monsters to determine it."[30] To put this differently, incongruity and deviation are a part of the movement of life that traverses and marks any individual. The lack of regular discernibility requires some object, a designated monster, to give form and shape to the incongruity internal to movement and becoming. But of course by making the monstrous quality determinate, a perceptible object, we can imagine ourselves as separate from it, we can locate the monster elsewhere, at a safe distance from our protected sense of self. But Bataille quickly reminds us that insofar as any individual form escapes any kind of common measure or aesthetic standard, it is somewhat monstrous, or a deviation from what is considered standard or normalizing.[31]

Elsewhere, Bataille describes that the human search for transcendence does not lead to God or to some ascendant notion of the human; rather, it leads to the tragicomic figure of the monster. As Bataille puts it, referring to a drawing of a headless body by André Masson, "Beyond what I am, I meet a being who makes me laugh because he is headless; this fills me with dread because he is made of innocence and crime. . . . He reunites in the same eruption Birth and Death. He is not a man. He is not a god either. He is not me but he is more than me: his stomach is the labyrinth in which he has lost himself, loses me with him, and which I discover myself as him, in other words as a monster."[32] As already described, Bataille is suggesting that transcending the limits of the human, the constraints of the self-contained individual, involves an opening to the monstrous qualities of existence (contradiction, abnormality, horror, fascination, dread and laughter, and loss of coherence). The reference to the stomach as a labyrinth indicates an entity that is noncoherent, an entangled network of relationships and desires without a clear end or direction. Similarly, this picture by Masson of a headless figure refuses to subordinate the interactions and desires between self and Other to the power of reason, the clutches of consciousness, the head of state, or the political body. Therefore, to identify with the monster, as Richard Kearney suggests, is to embrace those "border-line experiences of uncontainable excess, reminding the [self] that it is never wholly sovereign."[33] But of course this embrace is a difficult, maybe even impossible task, since the investment in preserving coherent identities and narratives tends to locate the monstrous elsewhere, at a distance from one's sense of possession and self-identity.

Before making a passage from Bataille, I note several caveats (or distinctions) in my use of the language of monster and monstrous. First, as suggested above, it is important to distinguish between the monstrous as a quality of human life, existence, and desire and the monster as a determinate position, object, or thing (even though the two are clearly related for Bataille and in hip hop music). The latter tendency is intertwined with a history of designating certain kinds of subjects and communities as excessive, violent, not so human, animal-like, and unnatural, designations that are employed to justify violence, subjugation, and erasure of these communities. Here we might think of how the vampire traditionally articulates and displaces fantasies, fears, and anxieties about eastern Europeans. We might remember how the trope of the monster was used in Nazi Germany to justify violence against Jews, Bolsheviks, and anarchists. And of course there is the King Kong character as a metaphor for black male aggression and sexuality, or the witch as a signifier for unruly and subversive women who practice religion in an errant manner.[34] Recently the grammar of monstrosity, or human-animals, has been mobilized to enact and justify a relentless siege on Gaza and the obliteration of Palestinians by the Israeli/US military machine. The monster is typically imagined and employed to make invidious and stark distinctions between self/Other, us/them, human/not so human, acceptable violence/terror.[35] (And these distinctions, as the above examples show, are mediated and informed by racial, gender, and sexual paradigms of power, regulation, and subjugation.) On the other hand, aesthetic allusions to the monstrous quality of existence, as I take it, use the figure of the monster to trouble and unravel these binaries, potentially rendering selves more open, receptive, and vulnerable to the contradictions, horrors, seductions, and coherence-undermining qualities of life, which we all participate in, contribute to, but often deny or locate elsewhere. The second related caveat has to do with the ambivalence involved when artists, like Kanye, assume the position of the monster. If the figure or persona of the monster is repulsive because of its excessive and deformed features, this figure can also be appealing insofar as it represents extrahuman qualities and powers. Consequently, identifying with the monster thwarts desires for an impermeable self, even as it also prompts further fantasies of triumph, sovereignty, and invincibility. It is this play, and tension, between a triumphant figure and a vulnerable, wounded subject that I intend to focus on in my discussion of hip hop, blackness, and monstrosity. In other words, I am interested in how the desire to transcend the profane, the limited and discontinuous subject, can lead to exaggerated expressions of self-deification, and how this desire can propel us toward a space of incoherence—what Nietzsche might call an undergoing, but without the longing to reach a summit.

Introducing this particular duplicity within the embrace of the monster—as a way of embodying and performing contradiction and noncoherence and as a way of gaining access to the fantasy of self-sufficient power and sovereignty—requires a rethinking of the very notion of sovereignty. For many people thinking about religion and politics, Carl Schmitt is a key author who defines sovereignty as the capacity to decide on the exception to the law; the sovereign is the one who can legally act outside the norm in the case of danger to a political body. This power to act in response to the exception is done for the sake of reestablishing order and preventing anarchy.[36] While Schmitt acknowledges an excess to the legal order, the sovereign is constituted at the moment of acting in the name of preservation and order. For Bataille, on the other hand, the sovereign names those practices, desires, and interactions that cannot be confined or enslaved by the logics of instrumentality. Consequently, Bataille describes sovereignty as an identification with a "general movement of exudation (of waste)" and positions sovereignty as a summit—but a summit that precedes a collapse and falling.[37] Following Bataille's understanding of sovereignty as an effect of movements that overflow discrete ends and limits, Biles describes Bataille's notion of sovereignty as a "relinquishment of power" and an "identification with the tortured other."[38] The monster is a strange kind of sovereign; we might say, juxtaposing Schmitt and Bataille and highlighting a crucial difference in their notions of sovereignty, that the figure (when performed, enacted, and identified with) can become an embodiment of self-aggrandizing forms of power and a moment when the kind of subject that undergirds fantasies of invincibility collapses and breaks down.

Alongside these connections between the monster and the sovereign, it is important to underscore how the relationship between the coherent, discontinuous self and the exuberant movement can become frozen and congealed. Certain kinds of subjects and beings have been systemically denigrated and pulverized under the heading of the monster, as the extra and not quite human, and as the excess to the ideal human that fascinates, arouses, and repels. More specifically, I want to examine the mechanisms and arrangements that have positioned black people as objects that give determinate shape to the monstrous (not unlike Calvin Warren's description of black subjects giving form to the terror of nothingness).[39] I wonder what happens when we shift our theoretical analysis from descriptions of the self-contained subject that is undermined by exuberant movements, to modes of black thought that, without refuting the general framework delineated by Bataille, articulate the predicament of being hailed as the monster or monstrous form that the will to coherence defines itself through and against. In the next section, I think alongside authors associated with black studies and black feminist thought to pursue these difficult lines of inquiry.[40]

Blackness, Monstrosity, and Erotic Fascination/Repulsion

Drawing on the pioneering work of Winthrop Jordan, who documents how early modern encounters between Europeans and Africans were mediated by a schema that associated Africans with fleshliness and carnal sin,[41] Zakiyyah Jackson contends that from the perspective of these Europeans, "Africa was seen as a land of new monsters."[42] Within a long-standing Christian imaginary, the African was a heathen, a figure that resisted the redemptive promise of Christianity. According to Kathryn Lum, among the many invidious qualities attached to heathens, they were described as participating in filthy and sordid acts (sexual, ritualistic, worship) that were not much different from those engaged in by animals.[43] Furthermore, from the perspective of Western enlightened reason, the African lacked the capacity of self-consciousness and autonomy, meaning that black people could not govern themselves properly and needed to be mastered and civilized from without, by the European agents of reason and law. Think, for instance, of Immanuel Kant's claim that "the Negroes of Africa have by nature no feeling that rises above the ridiculous. . . . So essential is the difference between these human kinds [whites and blacks] and it seems to be just as great with regard to the capacities of the mind as it is with respect to color."[44] Notice that for Kant the essential difference in color maps onto a difference in kind regarding reason and mental capacity. Also notice that Kant inserts an essential difference within the human such that the European and the Negro can both be included within the sphere of the human but represent essentially disparate kinds of human beings. It is almost as if black people are positioned at the lowest levels of the human in a manner that borders the animal and provides a bridge between human and animal. As Jackson puts it, "While also human, [black people] are nevertheless defined by their animality. Rather than being animal-like, [they] are animals occupying the human form."[45] Among other implications, this indicates that, under the political and epistemic dominion of Western imperial Man, blackness has been configured as some combination of animality and the human, a tertium quid, or a monstrous form.

Frantz Fanon in *Black Skin, White Masks* gives a devastating account of the experience of being hailed as a monstrous object, which is part of the process of a white subject's early formation. In a particular scene in the text, as a white child gesticulates to his mother, says, "Look, a Negro!" and subsequently fears that Fanon is going to eat him, Fanon reflects on the lived experience of being an object fixed and predetermined by the gaze of the white, European subject.[46] He articulates the anguish and absurdity (wishing that he could laugh himself to death) of being "woven out of a thousand details, anecdotes, and stories."[47] The child and his mother dramatize the imposition of a racial schema that defines the black as an ontological "impurity or a flaw."[48] In response, Fanon reveals, "My body was returned to me, spread-eagled, disjointed, redone, draped in mourning on this white winter's day. The Negro is an animal, the Negro is bad, the Negro is wicked, the Negro is ugly."[49] As the young boy and Fanon both tremble and shake, acknowledgment of a bidirectional affectivity, the boy runs to his mother for safety, to be protected from the black creature that the child fears is going to consume him. The child's coherence and safety, and the intimacy between mother and child, is constituted through a fear and fascination with black people, an ambivalent affective charge that accompanies a certain image of them as animalistic, wicked, deformed, and grotesque. Interestingly, a particular deforming is activated, according to Fanon, by the white gaze, by a colonial imaginary that seizes and extracts from his body, giving it back to him in a twisted, distorted form. Consequently, within a colonial matrix, the coherence of the European/white self is made possible through the phobogenic black object, through the ideal subject's anxious, trembling, and oppositional relationship to blackness. The child's subject formation involves an excess, a surplus of desire, fear, anxiety, and repulsion that finds its repository in the Negro. To be more precise, the child can only get on his way to subject formation by displacing a moment of reversible trembling, one that locates the horror, the source of frightened agitation, in the black object.[50]

This conception of black people giving form to a monstrous excess has implications for sexual and erotic fantasies. Because, as Fanon describes, black men are reduced to the biological, the body, and the penis, the repulsion initially experienced by the young child is, in other cases, intertwined with attraction and arousal. Fanon writes, for instance, "No longer do we see a black man; we see a penis. He is a penis. We can easily imagine what such descriptions can arouse in a young woman from Lyon. Horror? Desire? Not indifference, in any case."[51] The reduction of the black to the somatic, to the sexual organ, produces an affective predicament that is ambivalent (i.e., it includes desire and horror), but not a situation in which one is generally unmoved or unaffected. As mentioned in the introduction, Fanon discusses how white women sexually experiment with black men in order to "break with their being and to volatilize at a sexual level."[52] (Even when a sexual experience with a black man does not lead to the expected orgasmic ecstasy, Fanon claims that some white women still remain attached to the fantasy and speculation of black men's secretive sexual powers.)[53] The black male body, in this case, becomes an occasion for the white woman to lose herself and reach a state of frenzy. To reintroduce Bataille, we might say that the black (male) subject, determined by a reductive image of the black body as equivalent to sexuality, is, for the white women in Fanon's account, an opportunity for a sacred experience of self-dissolution. Based on Fanon's controversial account, it could be that the dynamics of the European (female) subject and her potential dissolution is dependent on a fixed conception of the black male as an available and convenient excess against which European/white subjectivity loses and refinds itself.[54]

Hortense Spillers also has something to say about the erotics of black flesh and the complexities of black gender, even as she takes the discussion in a slightly different direction from Fanon. In "Mama's Baby, Papa's Maybe," Spillers begins with a description of how black women are marked and framed by a particular American grammar. Not unlike Fanon's concern about the black person being predetermined by images and myths, Spillers writes, "Let's face it. I am a marked woman, but not everybody knows my name. 'Peaches' and 'Brown Sugar,' 'Sapphire' and 'Earth Mother,' 'Aunty,' 'Granny.' . . . I describe a locus of confounded identities, a meeting ground of investments and privations in the national treasury of rhetorical wealth. My country needs me, and if I were not here, I would have to be invented."[55] There is much to be unpacked in this opening passage. For one, there is something, some "it" that the author wants the reader to encounter and address, to look at and beneath. As a meeting ground of an abundance of names, images, and strategies, Spillers is identifying an interplay between lack and excess, privation and investment, that finds its playground in/on the figure of the black woman. By riffing on Sartre's powerful account of anti-Semitism,[56] Spillers claims that her country would need to invent her were she nonexistent. One wonders if Spillers is getting at how the outlines of a nation, the formation of a nation, requires some acknowledgment (and displacement) of an exorbitance that some group, being, or object is forced to take on and assume. The constitution of peoplehood and national space is tethered to a fundamental violence that, in the case of the United States, has been unfairly imposed on black women, who are expected to bear, embody, and facilitate its repetition. When Spillers uses terms like "overdetermined nominative properties," "signifying property *plus*," and "made an excess in time,"[57] she underscores how a certain grammar, a particular system of naming, framing, and predetermining the appearance of black women, identifies a surplus to that grammar while simultaneously trying to capture and confine that black feminine excess.

One way to think about this enduring dynamic is through Spillers's oft-cited distinction between flesh and body, which is "a central one between captive and liberated subject-positions."[58] And even as this distinction finds its initial context in transatlantic slavery, Spillers claims that "even though the captive flesh/body has been 'liberated,' the symbolic activity, the ruling episteme that releases the dynamics of naming and valuation, remains grounded in the originating metaphors of captivity and mutilation."[59] In other words, the aftermath of slavery is partly located, and hidden, in American grammars and ways of knowing. For Spillers, "Before the body, there is flesh, that zero degree of social conceptualization that does not escape concealment under the brush of discourse, or the reflexes of iconography. . . . If we think of the flesh as primary narrative, then we mean its seared, divided, ripped-apartness, riveted to the ship's hole, fallen, or escaped overboard."[60] As I take it, Spillers is claiming that prior to and alongside the coherent body is that basic level of existence, that fleshy, slippery stuff that the outline of the body is carved out of and defined against. The primary grammar of flesh allows her to draw attention to both the everyday cuts and dismemberments that slaves endured and a quality about black flesh that escapes the clutches of reason, discourse, and the hold of the ship (even if escape and liberation is achieved through death). Consequently, as Tiffany King points out, flesh is both a signifier that underscores how racial slavery created fungible, exchangeable black bodies and a concept that "connotes [blackened] flux, process, and potential" or "escape from the current entrapments of the human."[61] It will be important to keep in mind this duplicity internal to black flesh when we turn to artists like Nicki Minaj in the next section.

For Spillers, the flesh/body distinction, which should be seen as a cut within the black subject as much as a contrast between the captive and the liberated position, accompanies the legacy of New World slavery, a brutal system that produced a predicament of ungendering. Here Spillers offers a series of examples—from African men and women being mutilated and tortured with a similar degree of brutality to Africans being classified and stored on the ship based on space occupied rather than gender distinctions—to show how "in the historic line of dominance, the respective subject positions of 'male' and 'female' adhere to no symbolic integrity."[62] Here we must be careful. I do not take Spillers to be arguing that gendering or gender distinctions do not exist within blackness, black people, et cetera. I do take her to be making a claim about how blackness, as it has been positioned and subordinated within the coloniality/slavery matrix, interrupts conventional sex/gender systems, especially those that derive from white domesticity. Drawing on the work of Spillers, Jackson reminds us that "the masculine-feminine dichotomy is racialized . . . [and] that anti-blackness constitutes and disrupts sex/gender constructs."[63] Sex/gender constructs are informed by what is considered to be properly human; gender and sexual difference within the properly human have been shaped by antiblackness, by legacies that associate blackness with the improper or not quite human, with those who do not practice family, kinship, gender norms, or sexuality appropriately. This notion of ungendering/regendering has tremendous implications for hip hop's gender and sexual politics.[64] If blackness inserts a sort of cut into sex-gender systems, then hip hop (primarily associated with black male and female artists) is a space where these systems are reinscribed and intensified, but also where they break down. To put it differently, if blackness and black thought show conventional sex/gender binaries to be based on an "order with its human sequence written in blood," where this order is based on systemic "mutilation and dismemberment,"[65] sexual violence and torture, could it be that hip hop artists have been given the burden to embody and perform these disavowed antagonisms and incoherencies? Could it be that artists who assume the figure of the monster compel us to confront the horrifying quotidian, or the horrifying quality of the order of things written in blood?

What is crucial for Spillers is that black flesh messes with and confounds what Gayle Rubin calls the sex/gender system and its binary strategies and logics.[66] For Spillers, black men and women, within a ruling episteme haunted by racial slavery, have been positioned (perhaps with differences in degree rather than kind) as both things/objects and as the "sources of irresistible, destructive sensuality."[67] Here Spillers notes a contradiction. Black flesh is subordinated as an instrument to further white supremacist projects; at the same time, the black subject is imagined as having uncontainable sexual powers that are dangerous and destructive. Recall that Bataille associates the profane with instrumentality and treating the world as a tool for various future-oriented endeavors. The sacred names those experiences (erotic, religious, aesthetic) where one encounters the heterogeneous, or self-shattering otherness. By bringing together objectification and an excessive "otherness," Spillers approaches and deviates from Bataille. While she acknowledges some interchange between objectification and violent intimacy, she also suggests that the grammar of "destructive sensuality" or dangerous "otherness" is itself a tool, a way to codify, contain, and displace an exorbitance that is the result of what Sharpe would call monstrous intimacies (between the master, mistress, and slave for instance). Black flesh becomes the locus and gathering site of a sea of violence that propels and sustains racial capitalism. Perhaps this is one way to understand what Spillers calls the pornotroping, a term that brings together obscene sexual activity (*porneia*) and metaphor, figure, and turning (*tropos*). It could be that the pornotroping of black flesh, a mechanism that extends from the plantation to the strip club and the music video, is a way of configuring, ordering, and turning/twisting black sexuality toward certain ends, projects, and schemes. And while Spillers associates the pornotropic with powerlessness, one wonders if black subjects within this visual framework might find ways to turn this powerlessness into (while not quite agency) laughter, parody, satire, moments of anguish-filled pleasure, and revelations of absurdity.[68] It could be that certain ways of appearing, sounding, and performing within pornotropic visual regimes might implicate and cut against the fantasies and complacencies of the viewer and the prevailing gaze.

To bring Bataille into conversation with black (feminist) thought creates a field of friction that prepares us for a foray into the performance of the monstrous within hip hop by artists like Kanye West and Nicki Minaj. Bataille provides a grammar of the sacred and profane that accentuates the human's double character—one foot in the realm of tools, utility, and preservation of self, and the other foot in form-undermining experiences of the ecstatic. The sacred appears monstrous, to some extent, because of the human attachment to form and coherence in the face of exuberant energies, movements, and interactions. In Bataille's writings, there is a fascination with blackness and the opaque. (Intimacy brings about a beclouded consciousness; in the final scene of his novella *Story of the Eye*, the characters, after a series of brutal sexual pursuits, escape punishment in a boat staffed by Africans.[69]) One gets a sense that Bataille's discontinuous self is coterminous with the European subject while blackness is a vestibule for religious experience and the unraveling of the transparent *I*. Authors such as Fanon, Jackson, and Spillers underscore a racial/colonial/capitalist legacy of designating black people as animal-like, not quite human, and monstrous. Black people, within the matrix of racial capitalism and antiblack racism, have been positioned as the monstrous excess that the idealized human needs to contain, locate, and displace. As Sharpe describes, there is a history of "attempts to make manifest, measurable, and readable an essential black inferiority and black monstrosity, not the monstrosity of slavery [and its aftermaths] . . . and not the violence of the law and the gaze."[70] The violent intimacies and rituals that convert the African into enslavable flesh become the burden and inheritance of blackened peoples.

In what follows, I show how hip hop artists assume the role of the monster to elicit, dramatize, and parody this racial/sexualized conflation of blackness and monstrosity. In a track like Kanye West's "Monster," which features Rick Ross, Jay-Z, and Nicki Minaj, the figure of the monster certainly becomes an opportunity to enact self-aggrandizing power (which parodies and refracts white sovereign subjectivity). At the same time, the performance of monstrosity on this track, especially Minaj's contribution, draws the viewer into contradictions, tensions, wounds, and streams of anguish and pleasure that cut against the pursuit of coherence and self-possession. Part of my argument will involve examining how the viewer becomes implicated in the music video's scenes of horror, laughter, and absurdity. After examining the final, and best, verse by Nicki Minaj, I then turn to her 2014 track "Anaconda." Reading the song and video alongside Spillers's suggestion that the black female subject might rewrite the monstrosity imposed on her by white supremacist imaginaries, I highlight moments in the song and video where prevailing racial, gendered, and sexual fantasies and expectations get cut, parodied, and laughed at as the viewer must confront Minaj's haunting proclivity to look back.[71]

I, Monster

Kanye West's fifth studio album is aptly described by the eponymous title—it is beautiful, dark, and twisted. Among other things, it gives the listener a sense of an exaggerated drama of the baroque mixed with a tinge of the darkness associated with the gothic. The album is replete with tensions, paradoxes, and fractures. Consequently, the listener cannot easily disentangle the brilliance (production, beats, sophisticated sonic sequences, the rhyme patterns delivered by him and his peers) from the misogyny and narcissism displayed throughout. While Kanye, in the tradition of the boasting, self-aggrandizing emcee, admits to tripping off his phallic power as the proverbial "clock is ticking," he also hints at the possibility of letting go of power in the process of undergoing a "beautiful death."[72] On the track "Gorgeous," Kanye boasts about being a pimp on Mount Olympus, which underscores masculine power, possession, height, and stature. On a later song, "Runaway," he calls himself an asshole (void, filth) whom you/we should do our best to escape from. And while he is in front of all the lights, some of which are fleeting and momentary, this immersion in the light includes cop lights, or the scrutiny of the police and the surveillance of the state. It is almost as if being a star, with all the connotations of belated light and darkness, cannot prevent a black male subject from being, to some degree, "an abomination." As I write this section, I think broadly about what Julius Bailey calls "the multiple representations of [Kanye's] public self, his perceived image, and his self-selected branding."[73] More specifically, as I write about Kanye, I am beleaguered by the series of antiblack and anti-Semitic utterances, claims, and modes of reasoning he has expressed in interviews. Kanye is spiraling within and before public scrutiny and condemnation, not to mention broken contracts with major corporations and bastions of capital. (Moreover, indications of mental unwellness and bipolarity remind me of the pleasures and enjoyments that we derive from those who explicitly visualize the excesses and reason and self-possession.[74]) Even as my analysis is not *about* Kanye (he is only one moment in the track and video I examine), it is important to position myself in some place between and alongside the alternatives of apology and cancellation. I don't justify or mollify the hurtful claims that he has been making for years. At the same time, I also don't want to circumvent a moment to think about the continuities between the old and new Kanye, the Kanye that has been touted as a musical genius and the artist who is enamored with fascism. Furthermore, Kanye's public personas and exclamations are painfully instructive and emblematic. They invite us to explore the gap between the monster as an aesthetic figure embodying racial, gendered, and sexual anxieties, and the monster as a tool to express and chase fantasies of power and control, traditionally reserved for white propertied men or those resembling Western imperial Man. The distinction is precarious, no doubt. In fact, the latter possibility and trajectory might be an enduring enticement within the general performance of, and conversion into, the monstrous within hip hop.

Before turning to "Monster," it is important to linger on the language of fantasy, to reflect on the song and album as fantasy, and to situate hip hop and rap within a framework of fantasy. While hip hop is frequently conflated with autobiography, experiential reality, and keeping it real, there has always been an emphasis on imagination, hyperbole, metaphor, and constructing and becoming different personas. Regarding the last tendency, think, for instance, of Missy Elliott and Da Brat dressed as superheroes flying through space in the 1997 "Sock It to Me" video. Or consider how RZA from Wu-Tang Clan created the character of Bobby Digital, a darker and more unruly version of his former persona. Along these lines, Imani Perry contends that "rap music . . . combines poetry, prose, song, music, and theater. It may come in the form of narrative, autobiography, science fiction, or debate."[75] Rap is just as much about theater and spectacle as it is about telling stories as they actually occurred. It has always included inflated self-depictions and outrageous, self-aggrandizing descriptions in the spirit of verbal competition, battle, and rivalry. This is why Robin D. G. Kelley, in his early engagement with the genre of gangsta rap, reminds the reader that rap lyrics should not always or only be taken literally. Rather, rap lyrics involve play, signifying, and the turning of words against their ordinary meaning, qualities that are exemplified in rhyme schemes where the mic becomes a weapon that figuratively murders or maims imaginary competitors.[76] While authors like Perry and Kelley refuse the tendency to reduce hip hop and rap to a direct expression of reality, they also initiate further thinking about the general relationship between fantasy, imagination, and reality. Instead of viewing reality and fantasy as oppositions, I maintain that the two are always imbricated. Our relationship to the empirical world is mediated and constituted by the imagination, by what we crave and fear, our imaginary identifications with fictional characters and scenarios (cinema, television, music) and the crafted representations of actual people and events, and the pursuit of speculative objects and ideals we are told will bring satisfaction. Inversely, when we actively fantasize about an alternative world, or create an alternate reality, this does not simply involve an escape from reality. More precisely, it entails a reconfiguration or reassemblage of ideas, desires, interactions, and scenarios that compose everyday experiences and practices. Artistic fantasies are produced within the order of things, even as they point to, and are animated by, a surplus to this order. One might even say that artistic fantasy is a framework and a form of experience that prompts unrecognized desires, anxieties, and attachments to be articulated and visualized, even if only momentarily.

In "Monster," this fantasy-reality conjunction is made audible as the track and video draw from genres that involve vampires, zombies, torture, and so forth. Alluding to popular televisual works like *The Walking Dead* and *Saw*, the artists on this track reenact, play with, and implicate the viewer in racial and sexualized frameworks of meaning and desire that have associated blackness with monstrosity. As a viewer and listener, I attempt to confront the inseparability between the horrifying and the fascinating within this iteration of black performance, staying attuned to what gets overshadowed by the spectacular quality of the monstrous and inversely what aspects of hip hop and the broader world get amplified by the monstrous, those anguish-filled aspects that are generally treated casually. The song and video begins with Bon Iver's Justin Vernon singing in a haunting tone about shooting the lights out and preparing the listener/viewer to enter a dark space, a twisted fantasy. Vernon also asks, "Are you willing to sacrifice your life?" Recall that for Bataille sacrifice (or a particular sort of sacrifice) is the "antithesis of production," as it counters the demand to interact and behave with an eye toward future accumulation. At the same time, this song is very much a product within a market-driven circulation of commodities, consumer desires, and expectations of profit. Furthermore, there is a spectacular quality to the song, and as Guy Debord describes it, the spectacle is "both the outcome and goal of the dominant mode of production."[77] While Debord associates the spectacle with a commodified world that permits the separation of the image from the real while making the image a kind of stand-in for reality (or that which mediates a social world marked by alienation), one wonders if the monstrous can be a way of showing us that, in Moten's language, commodified objects cry, scream, and laugh.[78]

While this possibility is most audible in Minaj's verse and segment, there are other moments in "Monster" when racial/gendered/sexual tensions and wounds are articulated, dramatized, and even inverted. In fact, the various performances insert a cut or gash into the unified spectacle in a manner that requires the viewer to confront their complicities and fraught enjoyments and revulsions during the visual and aural experience. After the Justin Vernon introduction, we hear Rick Ross's voice appear with self-deprecating descriptions—"No-good bloodsucker, fat motherfucker." Here Ross's allusion to fatness brings to mind Deshaun Harrison's claim that in a world where antiblackness and antifatness comingle, "to be Ugly is to be a Monster . . . to be Undesirable is to be the Beast."[79] As Ross makes an allusion to "run[ing] through my jungles," such that the forced rhyme pattern draws and heightens a connection between movement and identification with animality, the use of the possessive pronoun indicates ownership and reinforces his self-described status as the "boss." In the video, Ross is sitting in a regal chair while smoking a proverbial, phallic cigar, and he is surrounded by three half-naked women hanging/dangling from the ceiling with chains around their necks. The viewer can only see the legs of one of the victims, which heightens the sense of fragmented or a fractured viewing experience and relationship to the twisting, contorted body. The lifeless woman in the middle of the frame appears white/whitened by the light, while the other two figures are shadowed, opaque, and blackened in a way that frustrates racialization. It is not clear how we are supposed to read, describe, and be affected by this scene. For one, Ross's monstrosity is exemplified by the juxtaposition with these women hanging from the ceiling.

His self-deprecating lyrics contrast with a posture of coolness and indifference to the comatose women that surround him. This harrowing scene contains an irony, since the images of the hanging women resemble and invoke the ritual of lynching, that sexually violent liturgy that was often justified as punishment for black men's "predatory" desire for white women. As David Marriott describes, the lynching of black men brought together "the horror of black men's [mutilated and castrated] bodies" with "the pleasure of the mob," within a public spectacle reproduced through the photograph and postcard.[80] Consequently, one might read this opening scene in "Monster" as a twisted reenactment that brings together the fantasies and fears about black men that coalesced during the lynching ceremony. At the same time, women (blackened, whitened, ambiguous) become the substitutes for the punished black male body, the figure who was the primary target of this form of extrajudicial violence after the US Civil War.[81]

Kanye's subsequent verse intensifies the horrifying qualities that Rick Ross's persona briefly takes on. At first, Kanye's half-naked body appears with his back against a gate, through which the arms of zombie- and vampire-like characters are trying to grab and confine him. It is almost as if he is both enjoying and trying to escape from these creatures that exist at the edge of life and death, or whose continued life depends on taking, consuming, and sucking the life and flesh out of others. There is even an instant when his facial expression brings together anguish and ecstasy. Immediately after this scene, Kanye is in bed with two women who resemble mannequins; they appear as stiff, lifeless bodies that Kanye treats like puppets, nonchalantly manipulating their arms and bodies. (Later on in the track, Kanye will recite the hook while holding a woman's decapitated head, an object that we notice gradually as the camera moves from Kanye's cool pose to the head in his hands.) There is also a moment during Kanye's verse when he is juxtaposed with an image of zombies who are positioned outside, on the opposite side of a glass door. At one point, he seems to be gesticulating toward the zombie-like creatures, as if they are a crowd that requires control and manipulation. At another point, Kanye is trying to keep the door shut, to prevent an exterior expression of the monstrous from entering his domain. Consequently, while Kanye embraces the monster in a manner that permits him to casually treat women as manipulable puppets, props, and divisible objects, he also must hold at bay the invasion of a multitude of creatures that vividly blur the line between life and death. There is a zombie-populated outside or a wild, unruly outdoors that Kanye needs to subdue and prevent from undermining his posture of self-possession.[82] Kanye tells us on the hook, "Profit, profit, I got it," which underscores the activity of turning surplus value into a possession. Thus Kanye's performance of the monster looks more like a desire for sovereign control or the yearning for a constrained space that permits him to live out and reenact fantasies of the sovereign subject, whose indifferent and casual relationship to violence and mutilation bears resemblance to a certain description of the monster. Perhaps this is inverting and refracting the indifference to, and reproduction of, the paradigms of violence that have conditioned and beleaguered black masculinity.

The figure of the monster also facilitates exaggeration and hyperbole regarding Kanye's lyrical prowess, greatness, and sexual capacity. He begins his verse by both boasting and asking, "The best living or dead hands down, huh?" This of course has become a familiar trope, as contemporary artists make implicit allusions to figures like Biggie and Tupac, deceased rappers who remain objects of veneration, comparison, and competition. Throughout the verse, Kanye attempts to convince the listener that he is "more than" or greater than his competitors or, more precisely, that his presence and aura evinces a superior surplus. He claims, that he is about to "take it to another level," that "ain't nobody cold as this," that "my eyes more red than the devil is." The latter comparison exemplifies Ebony Utley's point about a pattern within hip hop of rappers identifying, conversing, and competing with Lucifer or the devil.[83] (Here we can think of the late DMX's internal conversation with "Damien" or Lil Nas X entering and queering the underworld by seducing and giving the devil a lap dance in the video for "Montero.") Toward the end of the verse, Kanye continues the "living or dead" motif introduced earlier, as his sexual power and vitality relies on the figurative death of the female Other, or the killing of a part that stands in for the whole. After claiming that nobody can "top" him, he raps, "So mommy [mummy] best advice is to get on top of this. Have you ever had sex with a pharaoh? I put the pussy in a sarcophagus." In addition to the wordplay between mommy and mummy, Kanye extends and suspends the second syllable of *pharaoh* to make the listener linger with the hyperbolic comparison. Here Kanye likens himself to a supreme ruler while associating the heterosexual act with putting to death, crushing, beating, smashing, et cetera. The assertion of sexualized sovereignty, whose affiliation with mummification would indicate a will to immortality even through death, involves figurative death to the female/ mommy's body part, which acts as a synecdoche while highlighting divisibility and fragmentation of (black) female flesh. At the same time, Kanye's continued boasting ("bruising her esophagus" in the allusion to oral sex) plays on and into Fanon's account of how black men are conflated with the penis; this also places women as embodiments of a cavity, a passage, or an available opening.

One could respond to Kanye's verse with a reminder that rap music is playful, ludic, and not meant to be taken too seriously. The identification with the monster is part of this play and masquerade. Furthermore, rap music is meant to be enjoyed on many levels besides lyrical content—poetics, rhythm, creativity, style, wittiness, vocal accent, and the ability to put words and syllables together in unfamiliar ways. While Adam Bradley draws attention to these facets of rap and rhyme, he also admits that there is a perennial problem that hip hop fans and critics face—being put in a position "of defending the indefensible, of making the case to excuse the coarse language and misogynistic messages behind some of rap's best-known lyrics."[84] For Bradley, "there is no defense for the sexism, homophobia, and violence found in certain rap lyrics . . . or the broader culture that sanctions such beliefs."[85] While I agree with Bradley's argument about the indefensibility of these recurring themes, and his implicit claim that rap is an arena where the broader world's sanctioned beliefs are dramatized and contested, it is important to acknowledge the moments of pleasure and enjoyment that derive from, and not despite, the discursive violence and sexism. To put it differently, one cannot easily disentangle the enjoyments and satisfactions within hip hop's sonic and visual culture from the violent imageries and displays. Something remains exciting about the fantasies of invincibility, of taking on the persona of the indomitable and punitive ruler, sovereign, or rap god and separating oneself from the all too often feminine object, instrument, and symbol of male power. Listeners and spectators identify with, get drawn into and repelled by, narratives and depictions that are animated by (imaginary and actual) black violence, death, and anguish and the compensatory responses to these predicaments of black vulnerability, precarity, and existential abjection. The hook on "So Appalled" sums up this predicament: "This shit is ridiculous." The very conjunction of the appalling and the ridiculous reminds us that laughter, or the laughable, is not always separable from the horrifying, the anguish-filled, and the violently absurd. It is appalling and ridiculous that the contours of freedom and power are so often imagined within, and confined to, the rubrics and grammars of Western imperial Man ("Donald Trump, taking money from y'all;" "We above the law") by the very subjects and subject positions that this figure has decimated. When we place Kanye's enduring anxiety about being positioned as a "new slave"[86] and having his ideas dictated by the masses next to moments of identifying with and yearning for a form of freedom that is configured according to the imperial machinations of Western Man, we might begin to understand his recent white supremacist sympathies and collaborations. We may also begin to understand the slippery relationship between fantasy and reality, or how fantasy structures actual desires and attachments.[87]

But more must be said in light of Kanye's predilection for Nazis, his claim that slavery was a choice, or his argument that the cause of George Floyd's death was a drug overdose rather than state murder. As Monica Miller has described, Kanye's corpus, especially his electropunk-inspired 2013 album *Yeezus*, tends to oscillate between the position of god and the position of the slave.[88] On *Yeezus*, the track "I Am a God" precedes the song "New Slaves," in which Kanye makes allusions to slavery continuing in a different form through racialized capital and the profitability of prisons. In the former song, Kanye boasts, "I am a god . . . even though I'm a man of god." Here Kanye combines an instance of self-deification with a Christian-inspired acknowledgment of a higher power that demands submission. But as Miller points out, we should think beyond the framework of a particular tradition and interrogate how the term *god* functions and reverberates more generally. As she puts it, "[Kanye] knows that god is an idea that easily translates something of power, authority, and omniscience."[89] Consequently to be a "man of god" is to be a man possessed by god, but also a man who claims the power associated with god, the divine sovereign. As Kanye's music brings together god and the slave, with different permutations and lines of flight, it could be that one of the more enticing trajectories is to aspire to the vertical power and brutalizing freedom of the divine and human sovereign at the expense of those (including Kanye) who have been burdened to take on the qualities, signifiers, and legacies of the black slave. It could be that this aspiration, even for wealthy black subjects, will always run up against the dominion of racial capital, a limit that for Kanye appears as a lack of autonomy and the threat of new slavery, a structural stumbling block that Kanye resolves in an all too familiar manner by blaming a Jewish conspiracy. Here my aim is not to single out Kanye or to argue for some necessary, causal relationship between his artistry and his political speech acts. I am trying to identify a set of tensions and conundrums internal to this interplay among monstrosity, sovereignty, and the position of the slave. Alongside other factors, this has something to do with hip hop, and blackness, being positioned to take on the antagonisms and rifts of a social world that disavows the fascist and imperial underpinnings of Western Man and liberal notions of freedom. It has something to do with blackness, and black masculinity, being a well-established object of violence, enjoyment, fascination, thrill, and repulsion *and* the horizon of power and freedom that entices and grips subjects in myriad ways being strongly determined by Western imperial sovereignty. One might think of Kanye as a caricature that can never really approximate those who defend their fantasies with bombs and tanks. At the same time, Kanye's monstrous expressions, which have been informed by a fascination with, and subordination to, the figure of the divine/human/white sovereign and anxiety about not being able to escape the slot of the slave (and over the predicament of one's *choices* being structurally constrained), are more emblematic than his extreme and shocking public statements might suggest.

Jay-Z's verse, and identification with the monstrous, moves in a slightly different direction from Kanye, even as he cannot escape the tensions and conflicted aspirations that his former partner renders audible. In fact, Jay-Z has for a long time referred to himself as J-Hova, the rap god, and has boasted about "owning his masters,"[90] which is a double entendre that corresponds to musical copyrights and the assumption that access to capital can reverse the master/slave relationship. In his segment on "Monster," Jay-Z verbalizes an interplay between life and death, but in a manner that sounds more vulnerable and hesitant than Kanye's. After introducing a litany of proverbial monsters (from King Kong to Godzilla to Sasquatch), a list that elicits the legacy of associating black men with monstrous characteristics, Jay-Z's verse becomes a tense back and forth between triumph and vulnerability, cruel indifference and exposure to the outside. For instance, while he raps about killing blocks and murdering avenues (both a figurative and literal allusion, considering his drug-dealing past), he also admits, "I still hear fiends scream in my dreams." In other words, there are moments when he is unhinged and haunted by sonic reminders of the carnage he has experienced, seen, and participated in. He is unsettled by the cry of the Other, the fiend that is frequently linked to the zombie, the other that is trapped inside Jay Z's narrative and memories. Throughout his verse, we find out that while others have tried to take or suck the life out of him, he has also played the role of the zombie, the reanimated, the socially dead that lives off the flesh of others positioned at the lowest frequencies of life, to survive within a social order, a world, that relies on exploitation and instrumental logics. Consequently, the monster persona, while being a site of cruelty and destruction, also enables Jay-Z to remember and register anguish and suffering, to express a moment of painful intimacy with those he exploited in the past. In addition, while the Brooklyn artist suggests that he has "ice-cold veins" that bloodsuckers, adversaries, and former allies cannot draw from, he also admits that his weakness, or Achilles' heel, is love. His monstrous performance, which includes the posture of being above and indifferent to his detractors, is therefore an attempt to shore up and fortify a cohesive form of self in response to fragility, betrayal, and painful memories. This dovetails with his confession in "Song Cry" that the song, especially the feminine-sounding wail (or the modified vocal sample of Bobby Glenn), serves as a substitute for his tears, in a manner that personifies the track and permits a distance between the emcee/I and the objectified cry or the tears that drip from the eye.[91]

According to Justin Adams Burton, Nicki Minaj's concluding performance of the monster departs from the "stock characters" that Kanye and Jay-Z take on.[92] As Burton puts it, "In a song about monsters, Minaj proves the most monstrous of them all, cowing the beat and chasing off both the hook and her fellow rappers."[93] While Minaj boasts in a typical manner about being "hotter than a Middle Eastern climate" or "pockets eatin' cheesecake," she does so in a way that the surplus associated with boasting is matched by a verbal flow and intensity that the beat cannot quite catch up to. As Burton describes, "when her voice hits the track, she destabilizes everything further," which touches or pricks the listener/spectator.[94] A significant part of this instability has to do with Minaj's externalization of a division, a split subjectivity, as she takes on the roles of two of her alter egos, Roman Zolanski (gay, male, aggressive, twin sister, androgynous) and Harajuku Barbie (femme, submissive, doll-like). At the beginning of her verse, RZ—dressed in black leather and tights, bearing fangs and a whip—is tormenting HB, who is confined to a chair with her head hooded to present and stress a scene of torture. After RZ takes off the covering, which is accompanied by the camera shifting to the captured HB, we hear a drastic change in Minaj's voice, from an aggressive and ferocious sounding tone and flow to one that sounds innocent, sweet, and naive.[95] Throughout the back and forth transitioning between these two personas, an oscillation that is both fluid and unsettling, RZ taunts, torments, silences, seduces, and offers a lap dance to their pink-haired counterpart. It is almost as if the splitting, and the self-objectification, visualizes and externalizes some kind of internal dissonance, a multiplicity, that involves tormenting, being tormented, and a wounded intimacy across different subject positions. Something here cannot be contained within a unified form.

There are a variety of ways to situate and interpret this final verse and scene, in which Minaj performs this tortured interaction between two personas. Following the work of Savannah Shange, we can frame the oscillation between RZ and HB as an example of Minaj's "strategic queerness."[96] According to Shange, Minaj deploys race, queer sexuality, and femme gender performance through a variety of different personae, but in a manner that "appears to perform 'straight' or 'queer' but upon closer examination, refuses both."[97] For Shange, Minaj refuses "the laws of [sexual] normativity" and the demand to be legible within "any parochial rendition of black sexuality."[98] This helps explain why over her career, Minaj has flirted with and suggested a predilection for women without identifying as a lesbian.[99] The strategic queerness motif also allows Shange to draw attention to those moments in songs and concert performances when Minaj refers to herself as possessing a penis, wearing the phallic object, pissing on her opponent, et cetera.[100] Within the specific frame of her part in "Monster," this strategy allows Minaj to transition from RZ to HB, in a way that maintains a sense of twoness, movement, and transness. Another way to assess Minaj's performance on the track is through Uri McMillan's idea of the avatar. Alongside the conception of the avatar as the Hindu deity that comes down to earth and the image of a virtual, computer-generated persona, McMillan thinks of the avatar as a way to describe black women performers who use self-objectification as a strategy of agency.[101] This self-objectification ironically opens a space for subjectivity largely through "highlighting (and stretching) the subordinate roles available to black women."[102] Situating Minaj's enactment of the monster within a line of black feminist art, McMillan writes, "Her multiplicity of selves, rather than simply self-fragmentation, elucidates how objecthood is harnessed for self-actualizing effect, producing a fecund-expansion of roles, especially those available to women in this fantastic fantasy."[103] For McMillan, Minaj's enactment of the monstrous, which involves an expression of the multiple, demonstrates how black women have found ways to "create meanings from within problematic representational structures,"[104] such as the pornotropic as described by Spillers. In other words, instead of only thinking of Minaj's self-objectification as evidence of constraint and confinement, McMillan contends that Minaj's spectacular display of fabricated characters "propels us toward planets, and personas, yet undiscovered."[105]

Combining the insights of Shange and McMillan, Minaj's scream at the end of her verse and the visualization of a split that is also a multiplication and an excess, serves as a strategy that works both within and against racial/gender/sexualized frameworks that constrain black women and femmes for the sake of the world's coherence and legibility. What we need to linger with here is the strange agency that transpires in the moment of self-objectification, for instance, when HB is tormented, tortured, and silenced by her other within the scene, RZ. How does this succession of images, where violence is mixed with pleasure and seduction, replicate and amplify ingrained tendencies within hip hop's visual economy of female objectification and exploitation? To put it differently, how does the tortured interaction between RZ and HB demonstrate both an internalization and externalization of the whip—that is, the forms of subordination that (black) women endure and resist in a world where antiblackness is gendered even as blackness presents a problem for conventional gender paradigms and binaries?[106] What should one make of HB's response to those who call Minaj "fake," a fabrication that Minaj embraces and embellishes in an arena that touts authenticity and keeping it real?[107] As we reflect on these questions, it is imperative to think about how the monstrous, the doubling, and the excess point beyond the artist and performer, implicating the viewer in what Hartman calls the "terrible spectacle."[108] As Minaj becomes the object of torment and the tormentor, she takes on a burden to both distance herself from the mutilated women that appear throughout the video and to identify with the manipulable objects and props of masculinized power and control. This double burden draws attention to and prompts reflection on the ways that consumers and spectators derive pleasure and enjoyment from depictions of black violence, (black) gendered anguish, and the quotidian sexualization of blackness within the regime of capital, which converts a surplus associated with blackness into surplus value and profitability.[109] The excess that the black (feminine) monster takes on and embodies might direct attention to and disconcert the mundane and quotidian, bringing into relief the ways we become inured to the pleasure that is derived from seeing blackness, black women, and women more generally, placed as objects of subordination and sexual consumption. Therefore, Minaj's verse and contribution to "Monster" begins to expose and interrupt what Sharpe refers to as the violence of the gaze, a violence that black women have disproportionately suffered. Pursuing this volatile trajectory, I contend in the closing section that the video for "Anaconda" further messes with and disturbs, while replicating, a visual and libidinal economy that functions to render black women, and men, legible through imprisoning constructs of gender and sexuality.

Exorbitance Beside the Excess: "Anaconda," Black (Female) Flesh, and the Severing Phallus

In this concluding section, I read Nicki Minaj's 2014 video "Anaconda" *alongside* Spillers's hope that black women might "claim the monstrosity . . . which her culture imposes in blindness."[110] We need to proceed with caution and care here. I am not claiming that this controversial video (accused of being vile by critics like television personality Al Roker and banned in some countries) necessarily exemplifies Spillers's appeal at the end of "Mama's Baby, Papa's Maybe." In fact, Spillers concludes the essay on a subjunctive note, with the verb "might," such that the reader is left with a sense of possibility, open-endedness, and uncertainty regarding what this reclamation would look like. I also recognize that one could very well read "Anaconda" as a quintessential example of what Spillers calls the pornotropic or the conflation of the black (female) with destructive sensuality, an Otherness that "slides into a more general power-lessness, resonating through various centers of human and social meaning."[111] This resonance through various centers of meaning, pleasure, and entertain-ment is even more significant in an era where images can be circulated, modi-fied, and appropriated with an unprecedented speed and frequency.[112] (At this writing, "Anaconda" has over 1.1 billion views on YouTube.) More generally, I acknowledge that mobile images of this kind that focus on and turn black women's bodies and body parts into objects of consumption and enjoyment have become so mundane, excessively repetitive, and no less painful. I acknowl-edge that hip hop's visual rituals reenact legacies that include the slave ship, the plantation, systems of sexual coercion and terror, the forced "freak show" exhibition of Sarah Baartman, and a general confinement, narrowing, and punishment of black (female) sexuality. Consequently, my aim here is not to make any confident claims about black female agency or to impose on Minaj the burden of being representative of black women or a harbinger of libera-tion and empowerment. My task is humbler and more hesitant. I am simply after an excess alongside the spectacular performance in "Anaconda," beside and below what Aria Halliday names as "viral mimetic violence."[113] This excess, which involves Minaj, her coperformers, and the spectator, does not escape the quotidian violence of objectification, the gaze, the search engine, virtual extraction, and self-satisfying fantasies about blackness and black women. But perhaps by teasing out aspects of the video that halt the mimetic onslaught, that cut against prevailing economies of racial and sexualized desire and affect, a different relationship and exposure to the divisibility of black flesh might be available.

There are many aspects that stand out in Nicki Minaj's "Anaconda"—the sampling of, and response to, Sir Mix-A-Lot's 1992 hit "Baby Got Back"; the dif-ferent scenes and wardrobes that Minaj and her coperformers take on through-out the video; the forest- or junglelike hut that also serves as a gym and a kitchen throughout the sequences; Minaj's identification with and separation from the background dancers; her verses, which, among other pleasures, em-phasize the length of her former partner's anaconda-like package; the succes-sion of sarcastic, silly facial expressions and the instances of self-deprecating humor ("I'm on some dumb shit");[114] the exaggerated bodily movements and gyrations, occasionally in slow motion; the lap dance that Minaj offers Cana-dian rapper Drake, the only male in the video, before walking away and leav-ing him unsatisfied; the way the video makes comparisons and substitutions between food/fruit and bodily parts and their secretions; the way the song changes from an accelerated to a slower tempo, a shift that is noticeable in

MONSTER/MONSTROSITY   137

the transition from the hook to the verses; the all-white background in the scenes where she and her coperformers are dancing in cut-off shorts, which reminds the viewer of old-school videos like J. J. Fad's 1988 "Supersonic" as well as the atmosphere of whiteness that cannot be fully escaped; and finally, the continuity between human and animal, as demonstrated by conflation of the anaconda with the black male phallus and the instances when Minaj is crawling, moving on all fours, and so forth. While there is too much to delve into here, my interest in the possibility of rewriting the monstrous draws attention to three facets of the song and video: the call-and-response relationship between "Anaconda" and "Baby Got Back"; the anaconda motif as an occasion to both uphold and sever phallic power and signification; and the persistence of Minaj's look, the looking back, or the return of the gaze.[115]

Throughout Minaj's track, we hear the refrains "My anaconda don't want none" and "Look at her butt" intercut into the song, lines that are sampled from Sir Mix-A-Lot's *Billboard* hit. The beginning of his video shows two white women looking at and speaking in a disgusted manner about a black woman's buttocks. The look, the gaze, is directed at the rear body part; for these white women, its bigness and roundness is immediately associated with rap and prostitution. Moreover, black femininity is, under this white female gaze, labeled as gross and "just *so* black."[116] And yet the video shows that the grossness and disgust is what prevents them from looking away and spurs a fascination with the part, the object, the backside that "baby *got*" but that has been temporarily taken or grasped by the look. This slippage between disgust and fascination, which is in line with Bataille's description of the monstrous, is also similar to Julia Kristeva's understanding of the abject, which "beseeches, worries, and fascinates desire . . . [and acts as] a vortex of summons and repulsion."[117] One might initially think that Sir Mix-A-Lot's verses represent an attempt to revalorize thickness and roundness, qualities that, as he boasts, make him "act like an animal." Throughout the video there are actual black women dancing and enjoying themselves; at the same time, there are butt props scattered throughout that the artist and dancers stand on, forcing the viewer to sit with the function of a prop, an instrument, and an exploitable support. Yet things get complicated as it becomes clear that, like the white women, Sir Mix-A-Lot cannot escape conflating black women with the backside, fetishizing the black woman's part. Similarly, in the moment of referring to what his anaconda does and does not want, the artist both substitutes an animal for the penis and gives the penis its own power and autonomy. It is also significant that throughout the song, Sir Mix-A-Lot makes an essentialized distinction between the idealized black woman's body as round and juicy and the body of the white model, displayed on the cover of *Cosmopolitan* or *Playboy* magazine, as either too thin or fabricated. Of course, as described above, Minaj upends this kind of contrast between the natural and the synthetic (i.e., the doll). And for Sir Mix-A-Lot, this contrast between full flesh and fabricated bodies is his attempt to invert the aesthetic hierarchy between black and white women.

In the call and response between Minaj and Sir Mix-A-Lot, Minaj replicates, signifies on, and reworks sounds, images, and themes from her predecessor's track. Part of this reworking involves the cutting and chopping of the sample such that the phrase "Look at her butt," for instance, undergoes what sounds like a stuttering and even a hesitation alongside a repetition and overflowing. If Sir Mix-A-Lot focuses on what pleases him, what he likes about big butts, then Minaj reveals what she enjoys about her previous "boy toy named Troy" and her former intimate partner Michael, whom she describes as "bigger than a tower, a "real country nigga," and a rifle that she can play with. Throughout the video, the viewer is presented with a series of phallic images, including the slithering snake in the opening scene that slowly approaches Minaj and the four other women (who are positioned in a stationary manner in front of hut, with their bodies arranged as if they were both blocking and enticing the viewer's desire to enter, to come inside). To some extent, this initial scene, in which the camera pans and closes in on the women such that they are situated within their forestlike environment, makes an allusion to the biblical Book of Genesis and the Garden of Eden. The snake and the absence of men in this opening segment brings to mind the ways Eve, women, and feminine desire have been unduly impugned for and associated with fleshly temptation, transgression, the forbidden, and the fall/descent from a former plenitude. As the snake, or the mobile phallus, moves toward the women, the movement of the snake also sets into motion the verbal flows and choreographies that compose the song and video. The phallic imagery is also reproduced with the bananas that circulate on a spinning turntable, a repeated trope that can be interpreted as the circulation, rotation, and repetition of masculine power within hip hop and the broader androcentric world. And yet the rotation can always be taken as a spiraling and a potential undoing of this mechanism of power and control, a spiraling that involves the groove and fissure of the record. This undoing anticipates a scene toward the end of the video when Minaj chops up and throws away a banana while wearing an exotic maid's outfit. If, as Shange points out, Nicki has been willing to take on and wear the phallic object, in this instance, she expresses a desire to destroy it. And yet the poaching of "My anaconda don't want none" from Sir Mix-A-Lot, especially the possessive adjective *my*, indicates that the destruction accompanies a moment of possession. In both cases, the phallic object is treated as detachable (especially from male), divisible, and susceptible to a severing, not unlike Spillers' notion of blackened flesh.

These sequences in "Anaconda" demand further elaboration on the relationship between the phallic, the fetish, and black flesh. This is difficult and overwhelming territory to enter, but Minaj's music and performances take us there. According to Freud, there is an intimate relationship between the penis and the fetish, or an object that stands out as a source of power, attraction, and fixation. For Freud, "the fetish is a substitution for the penis . . . [and more specifically] a substitute for the woman's/mother's penis that the little boy once believed in and does not want to give up."[118] Here Freud is building on his description of the oedipal economy of desire and subject formation, a description that privileges the male child's fear of castration, which is occasioned by seeing and experiencing his sister's lack of a penis as well as the possibility of being punished by the parent for touching himself.[119] What is crucial here is that the possession of the penis represents both access to fullness and coherence as well as a defense against castration (i.e., the threat of becoming those qualities of lack and incompleteness assigned to the sister). And yet the fetish for Freud is also a way to hold onto and "not give up" a belief in the woman's penis, the mother's access to fullness and plenitude, especially since there was a moment when the child was inseparable from the mother. The fetish is therefore a substitute and a protective mechanism. The fetish, and the relationship to the fetish, internalizes the fantasy of being indivisible while retaining "the horror of castration."[120] For Lacan, who famously moves away from Freud's biologism and toward semiotics and the system of signs, the phallus is not an organ as much as a signifier. The phallus, according to him, is "the signifier destined to designate meaning effects as a whole."[121] The phallus is a master signifier that anchors and structures meaning, while the organ that takes on this function can become a "fetish" that stands in the place of a fundamental lack, a sort of castration that happens as the subject enters language, the gaps between signs, and the alienating relationship between subject and Other.[122] And while Lacan anchors sexual difference in the contrast between the male having the phallus and the female being the phallus (or the sign, reflection, and instrument of male power), then perhaps Minaj's response to "Baby Got Back" shows some fluidity between these positions.[123] While there is much more to say about the heteronormative foundations of psychoanalytic thought, I am interested here in how the phallic object as fetish, especially for Freud, both indicates and protects against the subject's exposure to castration, the void, the wound, the maternal, et cetera.

Things get even more complicated when blackness and black gender enter the picture. Here we should think of the racial, colonial, and religious origins of the very term *fetish*. As authors like William Pietz and J. Lorand Matory have argued, the concept derives from the truculent encounters and hierarchical relationships that have developed between Europe and Africa over the last five hundred years, beginning with Portugal and West Africa in the fifteenth century.[124] Within the colonial matrix, the term was used to describe uncivilized and unrational religious beliefs and practices, exemplified by Africans depicted as worshipping particular objects, without the capacity of transcending these objects to attain the universal beyond the material.[125] Along these lines, for an author like Hegel, fetish worship indicated the African incapacity for self-consciousness, the inability to rise above the subjection to and immersion within the object.[126] Authors such as Marx and Freud famously draw on this Christian European discourse about the African fetish to make sense of the mystery of the commodity and anxieties about the threat of castration, respectively. And yet, in a strange twist, we might see Minaj's "Anaconda" as a response to how blackness, black gender, and black people's body parts have been subject to a form of fetishization, one that brings together erotic desire, fascination, and repulsion, as well as the extraction and accumulation of surplus value. The ritual of lynching, as discussed above, involved a perverse fascination with, and fear of, black male genitalia, exemplified in those moments when the penis was excised as part of the spectacle of violence and torture. In these terrifying liturgies, castration was not a symbolic condition of entering what Lacan calls the Symbolic, but an actual process that operated to fortify whiteness and solidify white subject formation. The black penis, as a symbol of dangerous vitality, had to be removed in this liturgy of punishment and death. It is almost as if Freud's notion of the fetish, which incorporates a stubborn belief in indivisibility *and* the "horror of castration," is projected onto the black body in a manner that allays a tension within the white subject. In Minaj's track, there is a haunting reliance on tropes that reduce black men to the imagined size and enormity of their genitalia, with the rifle metaphor bringing to mind the link between sex, sexuality, and death. In addition, her terse reference to Troy's "shootouts with the law," which might get lost in a song with an up-tempo, pop-like rhythm, relies on the ways black men are disproportionately punished under the law, an antagonistic relationship that regularly becomes the occasion for entertainment and thrill. As Wilderson might put it, the subject that is figuratively castrated as part of the entrance into civil society can still define itself against those who "magnetize bullets."[127]

While Minaj's "Anaconda" works within and disturbs prevailing econo-mies of desire and pleasure through possessing and cutting the phallic ob-ject, she also performs an interruption by the way she looks back throughout the video. Alongside the various forms of exorbitance, the viewer cannot avoid the multiple ways that Minaj stares and peers at the camera. As Imani Perry argues, many of the women who appear in rap videos are positioned within the visual field in a manner that "allows the viewer to have a voyeuristic relation-ship to them."[128] This trite pattern has been especially noticeable when women performers "avert their eyes" or "look at the camera, eyes fixed in a seductive invitation, mouth slightly open."[129] Among other things, Perry worries that this positioning leaves little to no room for "thought, humor, irony, anger."[130] While Minaj mimics and exaggerates these tendencies and qualities, there are moments when something like a cut happens in the gap between voyeur and performer, subject and object, fantasy and flesh. Think, for instance, of the early part of the video, right before the first verse, when there is a shot of Minaj looking seductively at the camera, on all fours, while her backside is shaking in slow motion. More precisely, the shaking motion gets split (accelerates and de-celerates) alongside the looping of Sir Mix-A-Lot's voice. The look, the staring eyes, do not move; they remain fastened on the camera, such that the contrast between movement of the body and persistence and severity of the look po-tentially frustrates the viewing experience. As I watch, I am being watched; the usual dynamics of circulation and consumption, of image availability and the ac-tivity of watching, is traversed by a cut, a stare that prompts a rethinking of the casual ways that viewers are trained to look, absorb, and derive pleasure. These possibilities invite a reconsideration of the banana-cutting sequence. After Minaj sprays whipped cream on herself and acts as if she is going to consume the banana, or simulate the act of oral sex, she cuts the fruit and then looks at the camera with disgust, rolling her eyes and sucking her teeth. There is a different sort of eye contact that throws something off, that blocks the circuit of desire. For a moment, pornotropic expectations and desires are thwarted and returned, or rerouted, to the viewer. How am I, as viewer, implicated in the kinds of networks of pleasure, desire, and spectatorship that rely on, pilfer from, and freeze-frame black women and black feminine sexuality? Even as an author such as bell hooks might describe this video as an example of "eating the Other," in which "all the nasty unconscious fantasies and longings about contact with the [exoticized] Other"[131] percolate to the surface, there is also a way to think about this track alongside hooks's notion of the oppositional gaze. While not a blueprint for liberation, there are instances when Minaj's ways of looking back and making a different kind of eye contact "resist the imposition of dominant ways of knowing and looking."[132]

And yet hooks's concerns remain salient as we think about Minaj's "Anaconda" alongside Spillers and the possibility of black women reclaiming and rewriting the monstrous, especially within the realm of hip hop. I think, for instance, about hooks's description of how "getting a bit of the Other [and] engaging in sexual encounters with non-white females [those seen as more primitive, closer to animal life]" has been a rite of passage and a ritual of transcendence for white hetero-male subjects.[133] This interplay across race, gender, sexuality, and the desire to lose and rediscover oneself in the Other reveals a set of connections and tensions between the volatile sacred and blackness. While the left-hand sacred entails experiences and encounters that expose selves to the monstrous, to a flow and movement that shatters form and coherence, this excess, a quality that escapes the human-animal binary, has a history of being unduly attached to blackness in a way that consolidates the prevailing configuration of the human. Consequently, while Bataille makes a distinction between intimacy and utility, we know that antiblackness and the desires and anxieties attached to blackness demonstrate how a particular paradigm of monstrous intimacy has been an enduring project of accumulation and violence. This means that when the monstrous gets performed and dramatized by black artists, one has to be attentive to the slippage between the monstrous and the monster, the monster and the sovereign, and self-satisfying consumption and interruption (of the self, viewer, fantasy, the will to coherence). While there is no way to handle or contain the slippage, my guess is that hip hop's sonic and visual terrains will continue to be a disturbing presence, an unsettling inhabitation, a horrendous and beautiful flow, that frustrates the relentless demand for coherence and integrity and exposes us to the irresolvable contradictions, wounds, and cuts that compose our world. Hip hop, situated at the intersection of blackness and the contaminating sacred, is a sonic witness to the monstrosity that is our earthly existence.

Conclusion

On Blackness, Religion, and Hip Hop's Kinetic Anguish: An Un/freestyle

When I tell people that I teach and write about hip hop and religion, I'm often met with a mixture of surprise, confusion, and curiosity. The extreme version of the response is something like "I had no idea those two went together," betraying some assumption about the separation between the two, the holy and the profane. I usually respond by giving examples of rappers whose projects are deeply influenced by religious traditions—such as Poor Righteous Teachers (Nation of Gods and Earths) or Jeru the Damaja (whose musical content combines Taoism and Rastafarianism). Or I cite artists, videos, and album covers that draw on religious imagery (e.g., Nas's *Street's Disciple* album cover, which resembles Leonardo da Vinci's *The Last Supper*), motifs, or names (e.g., the rapper Psalm One). This can lead to a discussion about blasphemy and the prohibition on representing certain figures or scenes, an anxiety that is heightened when black people are placed in the place of the iconic.[1] While I very much enjoy and learn from these kinds of conversations, in the back of mind I am always wondering, inspired by Monica Miller's work, about the unquestioned assumptions attached to everyday invocations and usages of the term *religion*. What are the different ways that *religion* signifies, circulates, and condenses meaning, and what work does its discursive use accomplish? What is the difference between religion and the religious, or the religious and the spiritual? How does one talk about religiosity without necessarily centering recognizable traditions, institutions, and formations? Where does one find religion, and what are the connections and differences between religious practice and the production of religious meaning and sense?[2] What is the place of the sacred within the religious (and the secular), and how does any appeal to sacrality, even a blackened and volatile sacred, generate suspicions in certain circles, especially in the academy? How does one situate themselves in a tradition of what Julia Kristeva calls the two-sided sacred, with its capacity to name protection and defense as well as transgression, rupture, and contamination,[3] while simultaneously maintaining a faith in blackness and black people? Is it possible to embrace the profanation that is internal to the (left-hand) sacred?

These questions lead to a discussion about black religion, black religious thought, and the tendency to leave religion unthought within black studies. Much of black religious thought is contained within the fields of theology, history, and social science, which have produced brilliant work on an array of subjects: from the identification of God with the poor, oppressed, and enslaved, to the queer and ungendering qualities of Afro-Atlantic gods and orishas, to the forged affinities between African-derived religions and those rituals and practices scattered throughout the diaspora, to the long-established presence of Islam in the Americas. Building from authors like Anthony Pinn and Charles Long, my contribution and intervention into black religious thought begins with a general conception of the religious—as orientation, disposition, attunement, exposure, and contemplation of my place in the ordering of the world.[4] But almost immediately, this awareness involves a disorientation as one comes to realize that this ordering relies on systems of signification and meaning-making that designate opaque peoples as signifiers of disorder, negation, and excess, a process that has been the source and justification of unremitting devastation (in the name of protecting the order of things). For Long, black people have responded in a multitude of ways to the arbitrariness and terror of the signifier, a response that includes religious and spiritual practice, the creation and resignification of symbols, different invocations of Africa as place and signifier, and a persistent remembrance of the disturbing presence of black people within the Americas and the very idea of America. Following James Baldwin, this disturbance has something to do with a history that includes "a past of rope, fire, torture, castration, infanticide, rape, death, and humiliation."[5] An opaque piety does not reduce blackness to this history. Yet it refuses a general will to transparency that would resolve or explain away this discordance, the contaminating and form-shattering experiences and encounters that for Long constitute the "contact zone" of the Americas.[6]

For Long, black religiosity inundates and flows under and around the proverbial boundary between the secular and the religious. In fact, Long maintains that creative and critical power has been found in black folklore, music, styles of life, and literature.[7] Referring to these elements as the "extra-church," where

church does not just refer to Christianity but to formal, institutionalized re-
positories of piety, Long broadens our understanding of religion to include the
indeterminate experiences and expressions within blackness that cannot be
reduced to or contained by the more recognizable rituals and arrangements
that signify the religious. As mentioned in the introduction, this prompts an
inquiry into the sparks and embers of sacrality within black literature, music,
and aesthetics. Similarly, this more fugitive conception of the religious allows
us to interrogate how black studies has always been invested in resignifying,
deconstructing, and reconfiguring prevailing, world-ordering conceptions
of religion, piety, spirit, and the sacred, even if it hasn't always been explicit.
Think, for instance, of Du Bois's description of whiteness as a new religion that
revolves around the dictum "ownership of the earth forever and ever, Amen."[8]
For Du Bois, whiteness is not reducible to pigmentation, but names an array of
beliefs and drives structured by the fantasy of planetary and temporal ownership and control. Similar to Durkheim, Du Bois describes religion as the "life
of the nation," or what ties and binds life together, a binding that is predicated
on terror, death, and murder. We also know that Du Bois gestures toward a
different conception of *religare*, a different understanding of blackened piety),
one that is tied to the cry that precedes the thought, the frenzy, black gatherings and wanderings at the edges of the Master's gaze and patrol, identification
with lynched, dismembered flesh, and stubborn memories of death and disappointment in the face of ascendant nation-building projects and narratives.

Similarly, consider an author like Hortense Spillers (who wrote a dissertation on the rhetorical strategies of black sermons). According to her, the
formation of racial hierarchies in early modernity, or the interplay between
European transcendence and African degradation, is a "symptom of the sacred."[9] The sacred here is a synonym for the ahistorical, the reified, or an imaginary that is based on racial antagonism and mutual exclusion. Sylvia Wynter
is another author within black studies who understands how a particular configuration of the sacred has propelled and funded racial hierarchies and antiblack racism. For Wynter, Western imperial Man, celebrated as the pinnacle
and highest representation of humanity, is inaugurated through a series of
planetary divisions and demarcations that have theological roots—redeemed
and unredeemed, spirit and flesh, Christian and pagan, and symbolic life and
symbolic death.[10] Even as her narrative of transition between different iterations of Man can sound like secularization, there is also a sense that the theological, the symptom of the sacred, remains with ever new ways of carving up
the globe and affixing death to the black, the indigenous, the poor, the global
South, et cetera. For Wynter, what remains is a logic of nonhomogeneity,

which for Eliade is precisely the essence of religiosity. And yet Wynter's work also gestures toward an alternative sacred, a demonic sacred, where the term *demonic* alludes to the unrepresentable, the uncertain, and the indeterminate.[11] At the threshold of the order of things, Wynter thinks about the potential of a new poetics, strategies for creating and reconfiguring thoughts, concepts, and modes of affect, feeling, and knowing. She invites us to move toward an opaque sacred within and alongside imperial paradigms that can never completely contain the excess that these paradigms help to produce and bring into being.

For an author like Fred Moten, this other way of inhabiting the sacred entails a belief in blackness.[12] This belief is synonymous with what Moten calls an "ode to impurity" that brings together celebration, diffusion, and a "rich, rigorous, powerful, and utterly necessary analytic of anti-blackness that enables that devotional practice."[13] For Moten, this devotion is directed toward blackness as a disruptive movement, a "deformational force" that catalyzes strategies of containment; he is after a tumultuous motion that black people have been called to give form to and embody.[14] This necessarily raises questions about the interaction between form and the unformed, norm and rupture, and structure and improvisation. It also raises questions about the relationship between devotion and witnessing the terrible weight and perdurance of antiblack violence that has something to do with black people giving shape to movements, and modes of stillness, that appear impure and defiling to the law, the sovereign, and a will to purification. There is a resemblance here between Moten's understanding of blackness as disruptive tumult and Bataille's understanding, discussed in chapter 3, of a perpetual movement of energy that exceeds the logic of utility, that cannot be subordinated to human limits (without terrible violence). And yet part of Bataille's tragic vision is that we cannot escape form, norm, and the will to preservation as much as we cannot evade exuberance, the unproductive, and interactions that dissolve attachments to form, structure, accumulation, and progressive growth. This intersection between Moten and Bataille propels us to think, paradoxically, about forms, genres, and strategies that cut against the general attachment to form. They also suggest that a commitment to the left-hand aspects of religion, those that involve the dissolution of form and coherence, will never be completely separate from religious operations that function to defend, protect, ground, and establish control (like the religion of whiteness or the schemes of Western imperial Man). Perhaps what is necessary is a radical rethinking and reworking of the interactions between form and the unformed, or form and that which thwarts the drive toward containment.

What I am getting at is a conception of black religion, a religion of black-ness, a way of being bound or called by blackness, that stays with the wound, the antagonism, the cut that is sustained by this interplay between preservation and exuberance, form and dissolution, structure and flow. While this is an in-terplay that can take many shapes, under the paradigm of racial capital and Western imperialism it has reached catastrophic proportions—for the sake of the maintenance of dis/order. I am after something like what Alexis Gumbs, in her fascinating ode to Spillers and black women writers more generally, calls "a space, which is a temporary space . . . a sacred dedicated space . . . libation for the named and nameless . . . the black women who made and broke narra-tive . . . the quiet, the quarreling, the queer."[15] What would it mean to develop spaces and practices, those that we know are fleeting and susceptible to un-timely destruction, dedicated to the unfit, the unnamed; those who have been excised because they cut against and got cut from narrative; those whose desires and movements strained against the normal and normalizing; those whose very appearance in certain places indicated a quarrel or a problem for propriety; and those whose passions and thoughts never found a home in the clutches of dis-course? What kind of piety would this look like and what kind of evanescent form could it take, if any at all? How does one cultivate rituals for the dead and dying, the life lived within social death? Where can we create rendezvous that spill over, that honor and bear the trace of the dead that haunt life, espe-cially black deaths that are never safe from being reaccumulated by progress, redemption narratives, the regime of happiness, or even academic study?

Through writing this book, I have arrived here, wherever that place is. I have attempted to interpret, listen to, and experience hip hop as an instantia-tion of blackness meeting the volatile sacred, a meeting that involves experi-mentation with words, flows, sounds, and images that disturb and cut against a collective will to coherence. Similar to Fumi Okiji's reading of jazz, I read hip hop as a musical genre that continues to "call the integrity of the world into question."[16] It remains a site and sound of contradiction, friction, and ambiva-lence. Hip hop, among other things, reexpresses the (antiblack) violence that structures the world and in the process makes available the possibility of being exposed and attuned to that violence differently. It is an expression of a con-stitutive wound, a kinetic anguish that black people have been positioned and designated to bear in specific and overwhelming ways. To read rap music and hip hop in this direction is not to deny the pleasures, enjoyments, and forms of relaxation that often come with listening to hip hop. It is not to diminish the playfulness, hyperbole, erotics, and self-deprecating humor, or the signifi-cance of style, ingenuity, fantasy, and competition. In fact, this study draws attention to the presence of these qualities and attributes as they appear along-side and intertwined with the persistence of death and violence, conditions that rap artists relate to as targets, agents, participants, griots, critics, and witnesses. Consequently, the *re* in reexpression acknowledges an iterative process, a repetition that, in addition to call and response and signifying, includes a rearticulation of the violence that shapes and structures our world, a redirection and deflection that often targets women, the queer, the adversary, et cetera. (And yet this repetition also reveals that hip hop is a space where gender and sexual binaries and formations are thrown into disarray.) More generally, hip hop occasions a kind of devotional practice that stages and breaks down the striving for wholeness and solidity. It prompts attunement to the wound (or re-wound, as Moten puts it) as a general condition; it is an exposure to cuts and breaks, opacity, and disturbing movements that can get (us) carried away. This devotional practice, which includes motion and stillness, affective flights and contemplation, is no less anguish-filled because it is enjoyable.

To think about and reimagine hip hop and rap music as occasions to contemplate and linger with the wound, this study gathered pertinent themes and expressions within hip hop, in conversation with black studies, religious thought, and critical theory. Sorrow brings together anguish and pleasure, pain and subversive joy, death and life or the death within life, in accordance with the right to opacity. In the process, this affect, mood, and existential disposition enables artists and listeners to question and interrogate god's absence and silence even, or especially, in the midst of prayer. Along this line, redemption is not always a recovery of the whole or a will to fulfillment; it can also sound like a striving after the ruin, the rupture, the hole in the face of relentless endeavors to rehabilitate progress, US exceptionalism, sovereignty, a time of white plenitude, or a futurity based on the recovery of an idealized (and antiblack) past. And the monstrous within hip hop is both horrifying and beautiful. The enactment of the monster can be a vehicle to aspire to and parody the figure of the sovereign, and it can be an opportunity to dramatize and expose racial/gendered/sexual contradictions, wounds, and (twisted) fantasies that accompany the legacy of depicting blackness as monstrous, not quite human, and closest to the animal. Within the monstrous, which is immediately associated with the hypervisible and the ostentatious, there is room for layers, surface-level depth, concealment, and that which cannot be readily disclosed. This study does not pretend to be exhaustive. It barely scratches the surface. But it hopes to encourage and propel studies that wrestle with the uncanny religiosity within hip hop as that which cuts, stirs strangely, and exposes us to the monstrosity and uncoherence that is our world. This uncanny religiosity enacts and makes available a kind of left-hand sacrality (through sound, image, silence, rupture) that exposes the underside, and calls into question, the sanctity of life (apart from death), wholeness, form, and coherence. This might be a fleeting and impossible grammar and practice of the sacred in light of the deeply ingrained assumptions that freedom and liberation, especially for black people, will be synonymous with fulfillment and wholeness.

This was a difficult book to write. I wanted to complete it in 2020, but COVID-19 happened . . . and continues to take lives. Over the past decade, this project has been interrupted by the regular deaths and murders of rappers: MF Doom, DMX, Nipsey Hussle, Prodigy, Ecstasy, Young Dolph, Hurricane G, Coolio, PnB Rock, Takeoff, Chynna Rogers, Gangsta Boo, Kangol Kid . . . the list goes on. (And during that time, the artists and figures examined in this book have taken on different personas, lives, and reputations within the order of things.) I cannot pretend that the series of deaths are reducible to one condition or predicament. And yet the undisclosed health conditions that are taking rap artists before they reach the age of fifty-five and the gun violence that takes younger rappers when they are entering the field of success/progress/escape has something to do with the asymmetrical distribution of death that blackness and black people have been positioned to take on and endure. One ritual that my friends and I have created in response to the untimely deaths of these artists involves texting each other lines, bars, or verses from deceased rappers. Sometimes the lines are silly and ridiculous; sometimes they speak to a particular situation or event; sometimes they become an occasion to appreciate, remember, and lament. In general, this practice of exchanging lines becomes a way for us to communicate through multiple absences and the recurring wound. It might not be a way to communicate with the dead, but a means of communing with the death within life and that which lives on or remains through sound, silence, citation, and mourning. By sending a line from Prodigy through a text ("There's a war going on outside; no man is safe from. Lord forgive me, I don't know how to act, I'm fallin' and I can't turn back"),[17] we can reminisce, smile, tear up, and remember friends of ours who enjoyed these lyrics with us but are no longer here . . . in the flesh, at least. The war outside, the war that gets pushed outside, the war that no one is safe from, even if some are protected from the immediate effects of the violence that shapes and organizes social life. And then there is Prodigy's allusion to a fall that is permanent, that there is no coming back from, as one attempts to survive in a Darwinian world ruled by what Wynter names as the figure of biocentric Man. And perhaps this fall, this collapse, is the condition for a new modality of being with, of contact, of *getting down* together. As much as hip hop strives to fit, to appear as the fittest, it is a reminder of the persistence of the unfit, of those who don't quite belong within the domain of coherent and livable human subjects.

Along this line, I think about that moment in July 2020 when Megan Thee Stallion was shot in the foot (since then, Tory Lanez has been convicted of the assault). The general discourse, and the commentary within hip hop, has been both hurtful and all too familiar—the jokes and dismissals, the misgendering, the trans- and queerphobic vitriol, the death threats hurled at Megan, and the refusal to believe or trust her grief, her tears.[18] It would be too easy to say that the shooting, the unabashed misogynoir, and the accompanying discourse on social media are not representative of all of hip hop. The more difficult endeavor is to contemplate how the everyday (celebrity worship, profitability, the silencing that accompanies celebration, unequal distributions of grievability and believability) is the site of repeated cruelty and aggression; this is a repetition that blurs the line between words and action, fantasy and actual life, the entertaining and the terrifying. This scenario in which Megan Thee Stallion becomes the object of physical and discursive animosity is also a reminder that, as Spillers tells us, blackness and black culture constitute a wound, a rupturing. (Intramural, or intracommunal, forms of life and relationality are also made possible by creating targets of hostility, rallying points of sociality against those who fail to conform to normalizing ideas of blackness, sexuality, and gender expression.) This wound is where hip hop lives; this is where blackness meets the volatile sacred. Hip hop is a disturbing sonic presence that demands a confrontation with the disavowal of the black gendered anguish that is inseparable from the culture industry's vending of entertainment and pleasure within the general drive toward accumulation and surplus value. Hip hop has become a crucial part of this accumulative drive, while being a testament to that which falls by the wayside and cannot be fully assimilated. Or at least this is my blackened and torn faith—a faith in blackness that is never far from the abyss.

Notes

INTRODUCTION

1　OutKast, "SpottieOttieDopaliscious," on *Aquemini*. For a brilliant study of OutKast, see Bradley, *Chronicling "Stankonia."*

2　Baldwin, *Fire Next Time*, 33.

3　Baldwin, *Fire Next Time*, 39.

4　Crawley, *Blackpentecostal Breath*.

5　Jon Michael Spencer anticipates my argument when he suggests (following Albert Murray) that the early juke/blues joints were sacred spaces, liturgical practices that prompted black bodies to confront musically the harsh realities of their existence. See Spencer, *Protest and Praise*, 113.

6　Quashie, *Sovereignty of Quiet*, 6.

7　2Pac, "Trapped," on *2Pacalypse Now*.

8　On Tupac as martyr and saint, see Dyson, *Holler If You Hear Me*, 247–68. On Tupac as a kind of prophet, see Hodge, *Soul of Hip Hop*, 141–56.

9　For an insightful essay on the virtual and spiritual afterlife of Tupac, see Peterson, "PARTICULAR PAC."

10　On how Tupac can be perceived as saint who watches over and protects his constituency from death (placing him within traditions like Santería and Palo Monte), see Ralph et al., "Saint Tupac."

11　Dyson, *Holler If You Hear Me*, 13.

12　Benjamin, "Critique of Violence," 239.

13　MC Breed and 2Pac, "Gotta Get Mine," on *The New Breed*.

14　James Perkinson makes this argument to show the limitations of Western notions of the divine that often imagine good and evil as strongly opposed to each other. See Perkinson, "Tupac Shakur as Ogou Achade."

15　In contrast to "Dear Mama," listen for instance to "Wonda Why They Call U Bitch," on *All Eyez on Me*. For some commentators, the more "positive" depictions of women in Tupac's music can be just as confining as songs that allude to women in a derogatory manner. In fact, the more positive depictions often limit black women's roles and responsibilities to being maternal reproducers of the black community. On these concerns, see Lubiano, "Black Nationalism and Black Common Sense."

16 Dyson, *Holler If You Hear Me*, 177.

17 According to Luce Irigaray, this is because women have historically provided a container for male desire without having a place of their own. As container, female desire is contained and regulated. See Irigaray, *Ethics of Sexual Difference*.

18 Dyson, *Holler If You Hear Me*, 21–45.

19 Georges Bataille uses the language of heterogeneity to describe this position of being set apart from the ordinary. See, for instance, Bataille, "The Psychological Structure of Fascism," in *Visions of Excess*. I discuss Bataille's work in detail later.

20 Spillers, "Mama's Baby, Papa's Maybe," 80.

21 On a powerful articulation of the relationship between religion, race, and modern spatial imaginaries, see Jennings, "Building Landscapes."

22 For a description of the notion of black gender, see Douglass, "Black Feminist Theory for the Dead and Dying," 106–11.

23 To some extent, I am picking up on P. Khalil Saucier and Tryon Woods's concerns that hip hop studies has increasingly been disconnected from its roots in black studies and struggles against antiblackness. See Saucier and Woods, "Hip Hop Studies in Black." While this is a provocative article, my sense is that the authors downplay scholarship that already makes explicit links between hip hop and radical black traditions. For a response to Saucier and Woods that echoes this sentiment, see Forster, "What Is This Thing Called Hip Hop Studies?"

24 Throughout this book, I use hip hop and rap interchangeably because much of my focus is on rap music. Yet I recognize that rap is only one part of a hip hop culture that includes DJing, dance, graffiti, literature, sartorial styles, and other practices.

25 Here I am thinking of critics like C. Delores Tucker, Bob Dole, William Bennett, and the Reverend Calvin Butts. For an engagement with early concerns about the obscenities of gangsta rap, see Dyson, *Between God and Gangsta Rap*, 176–86.

26 Dyson, *Between God and Gangsta Rap*, 184–85.

27 Lomax, *Jezebel Unhinged*, 10.

28 Smooth featuring 2Pac, "P.Y.T. (Playa Young Thugs)."

29 For a reading of the image of Jesus in rap music and culture, see Utley, *Rap and Religion*, 49–68.

30 For insightful scholarship on the Five-Percenter influence on hip hop, see McKnight, *Five Percenters*; and Miyakawa, *Five Percenter Rap*.

31 Utley, *Rap and Religion*, 7.

32 Utley, *Rap and Religion*, 7.

33 I engage Utley's particular concern about how hip hop reproduces Christianity's patriarchal sensibilities in chapter 1.

34 Pinn, "'Handlin' My Business,'" 86.

35 Pinn, "'Handlin' My Business,'" 86.

36 On the connections between hip hop and its musical precursors, see Pinn, "Introduction."

37 Talal Asad's famous critique of Clifford Geertz's description of religion, a description that supposedly reduces religion to the establishment of meaning and order, is fitting here. See Asad, *Genealogies of Religion*, 27–54.

38 Pinn has shifted his understanding of religion in his recent work. Instead of thinking of religion as a search for complex subjectivity, he describes religion as a technology for understanding the porous nature of the human and its interaction with other things. See, for instance, Pinn, *Interplay of Things*.

39 Miller, *Religion and Hip Hop*, 12.

40 Miller offers insightful readings of how religion operates in these texts in chapter 2 of her book. See Miller, *Religion and Hip Hop*.

41 Miller, *Religion and Hip Hop*, 70. Here and throughout the text, one notices the heavy influence of Russell McCutcheon, particularly his *Manufacturing Religion*. For McCutcheon, scholars of religion that emphasize its universal quality or its autonomy with respect to other domains conceal their own political interests and investments.

42 On this distinction between religious meaning and religious doing, see Jones, "What the Doing Does."

43 Perry, *Prophets of the Hood*, 6.

44 On this separation of religion and erotic desire, see Bataille, *Tears of Eros*. For how this plays out in the black church, see Douglas, *Sexuality and the Black Church*.

45 I have shown and taught the video for "Shesus Khryst" in my hip hop and religion class. At times, the response is fascinating—people are visibly repelled and shocked by the image of Remy Ma on the cross.

46 Part of the problem is that secularism is not necessarily antireligious, but names a particular way of managing and regulating religion. On this, see Lloyd, "Introduction."

47 One author who has thought about this dissonance between the stabilizing and disruptive aspects of religion is Tyler Roberts. Borrowing from the work of J. Z. Smith, Roberts highlights a distinction in the former's work between the locative and utopian, where the locative registers the order-preserving function of religion while the utopian gestures toward excess and incongruity. Roberts wants to maintain the both/and of the locative and the excessive. See Roberts, *Encountering Religion*, 23–47. See also Hollywood, *Acute Melancholia*, 9–10.

48 Eliade, *Sacred and the Profane*, 20.

49 Eliade, *Sacred and the Profane*, 20.

50 For a discussion of these passages between the two domains, see Eliade, *Sacred and the Profane*, 25.

51 Eliade, *Sacred and the Profane*, 24.

52 Jeremy Biles shows how Eliade's understanding of sacred value is more complicated than his detractors assume. See Biles, "Sacrifice of Domestication."

53 Here I am alluding to Otto's famous notion of the God as *mysterium tremendum*. See Otto, *Idea of the Holy*. Eliade pays tribute to Otto in the introduction of *The Sacred and the Profane*.

54 Eliade, *Sacred and the Profane*, 31.

55 Eliade, *Sacred and the Profane*, 49.

56 Eliade, *Sacred and the Profane*, 65. This becomes complicated in light of the fact that creation and destruction (bringing form to chaos or eliminating the chaotic) are intertwined in Eliade's reading of myths and creation stories. In other words, the original moment of creation entails a violence that undermines any notion of sacred purity.

57 Durkheim, *Elementary Forms of Religious Life*, 21–44.

58 Durkheim, *Elementary Forms*, 44.

59 Durkheim, *Elementary Forms*, 44.

60 Durkheim, *Elementary Forms*, 227.

61 Durkheim, *Elementary Forms*, 216–21.

62 Durkheim, *Elementary Forms*, 232.

63 For a reading of the athletic protests that includes a Durkheimian interpretation of the flag's sacredness, see Zeller, "Why Kaepernick's Refusal to Stand." For my response, a reading of these matters that underscores more than Zeller's the connections between religion and race, see Winters, "How Protesting Black Bodies Are Imagined as a Threat to National Pride."

64 Durkheim, *Elementary Forms*, 412–13.

65 Douglas, *Purity and Danger*, 196–220.

66 See, for instance, Goodie Mob, "Dirty South," on *Soul Food*; and Snootie Wild, "Made Me," on *Go Mode*.

67 Chandler, *X*, 16–30.

68 Here I am indebted to Jeremy Biles's reading and description of Bataille's work. See Biles, *Ecce Monstrum*, 3.

69 Bataille, *Theory of Religion*, 57.

70 Bataille, *Theory of Religion*, 45.

71 Bataille, *Accursed Share*, 21.

72 Bataille, *Inner Experience*, 22.

73 Bataille, *Inner Experience*, 5.

74 For an insightful essay on the connections between Bataille's understanding of the sacred and black poetics, see Carter, "Black Malpractice."

75 For an interesting use of Long's ideas to examine the particular genre of Christian rap, see Baker-Fletcher, "African-American Christian Rap."

76 Long, *Significations*, 209.

77 For a protracted account of how this theological imaginary serves as a precursor to modern colonial regimes and world ordering frameworks, see Wynter, "Unsettling the Coloniality of Being/Power/Truth/Freedom."

78 Long, *Significations*, 211.

79 Long, *Significations*, 7. See also Long, *Ellipsis*, 14.

80 Long, *Significations*, 7.

81 Long, *Significations*, 7. For a critical reading of this notion of extra-church that highlights the vagueness of the concept and the way Long locates the authenticity of black religion in what is outside the church, see Sorett, *Black Is a Church*, 9–10.

82 Glissant, *Poetics of Relation*, 189.

83 Hartman, *Scenes of Subjection*, 36. Here Hartman is indebted to Glissant's reflections on opacity in *Poetics of Relation*.

84 Hartman, *Scenes of Subjection*, 36.

85 Rose, *Black Noise*, 39.

86 Stoever, *Sonic Color Line*, 1–28.

87 Love, "Good Kids, Mad Cities."

88 Damage, "Infrasonic Sound."

89 Marriott, *Of Effacement*, 9–19.

90 Some have suggested that hip hop introduces a new racial politics, particularly between black and white populations in the United States. See, for instance, Kitwana, *Why White Kids Love Hip Hop.*

91 Moten and Harney, *Undercommons*, 47.

92 Moten and Harney, *Undercommons*, 47.

93 Wynter, "Unsettling the Coloniality of Being /Power/Truth/Freedom."

94 Park, *Race and Culture*, 280.

95 Fanon, *Black Skin, White Masks*, 118.

96 Cohen, *Boundaries of Blackness*, 13–16.

97 Here I am indebted to the arguments made by Calvin Warren in his provocative text *Ontological Terror.*

98 Tate, *Flyboy 2*, 246.

99 For concerns about this last use of hip hop, see Saucier and Woods, "Hip Hop Studies in Black."

100 I think here of the "black Trump" refrain from artists like Raekwon The Chef, Cocoa Brovaz, and Yung Joc.

101 Spence, *Knocking the Hustle.*

102 Kanye West featuring Jay-Z, "Diamonds from Sierra Leone (Remix)," on *Late Registration.*

103 Spence, *Staring in the Darkness*, 27.

104 Spence, *Staring in the Darkness*, 28.

105 Here I am thinking of how Jacques Lacan associates the real with trauma, the unassimilable, and missed encounters. See Lacan, *Four Fundamental Concepts of Psychoanalysis*, 51–55.

106 Quinn, *Nuthin' but a "G" Thang*, 11.

107 Quinn, *Nuthin' but a "G" Thang* 11.

108 Quinn, *Nuthin' but a "G" Thang*, 15.

109 Adorno and Horkheimer, *Dialectic of Enlightenment*, 94.

110 Adorno and Horkheimer, *Dialectic of Enlightenment*, 115–16.

111 Adorno, *Aesthetic Theory*, 6.

112 Adorno, *Aesthetic Theory*, 135.

113 Adorno, *Aesthetic Theory*, 237.

114 Adorno, *Aesthetic Theory*, 245, 331.

115 Adorno, *Prisms*, 257.

116 Moten, *In the Break*, 1.

117 Moten, *In the Break*, 6.

118 Moten, *In the Break*, 10.

119 Bailey, "Homolatent Masculinity and Hip Hop Culture," 190.

120 Wilderson, *Red, White, and Black*, 82.

121 See, for instance, Sharpe, "Black Studies," 60.

122 Reiland Rabaka's work traces the traditions and legacies that hip hop participates in, carries on, and excludes. See, for instance, Rabaka, *Hip Hop's Inheritance*, 1–47.

CHAPTER 1. SORROW/DEATH

Material in this chapter first appeared in "Contemporary Sorrow Songs: Traces of Mourning, Lament, and Vulnerability in Hip Hop," *African-American Review* 46, no. 1 (Spring 2013): 9–20.

1 Ghostface Killah featuring Raekwon, "Motherless Child," on *Ironman*.

2 Baldwin, *Price of the Ticket*, 65.

3 Rose, *Black Noise*, 25.

4 Rose, *Black Noise*, 25.

5 Other authors have noticed this link between Du Bois and hip hop. See, for instance, Rabaka, *Hip Hop's Inheritance*, ix–xiv. See also McCarthy, *Who Will Pay Reparations on My Soul?*, 109–32. In addition, see Bradley and Vaught, "Of the Wings of Traplanta."

6 I have previously written on the work of sorrow in Du Bois's *Souls of Black Folk* as an affective strategy that resists the complacencies and comforts of progress narratives. In this section, I provide a remix of sorts and cling more to the idea of sorrow than melancholy or melancholia. See Winters, *Hope Draped in Black*, 31–84.

7 Perry, *Prophets of the Hood*, 19.

8 Du Bois, *Souls of Black Folk*, 9.

9 Here I am thinking of Adolph Reed's concern that contemporary black intellectuals have taken Du Bois's concept of double-consciousness out of its historical context and inflated its importance. See Reed, *W. E. B. Du Bois and American Political Thought*, 93–125. For Reed, the increasing interest in this concept of twoness within African American studies and the decreasing interest in his political disagreements with Booker T. Washington betrays the conservative bent of contemporary black intellectuals. Although I take Reed's critique seriously, I think he too easily separates Du Bois's notion of twoness from the latter's political commitments.

10 Du Bois, *Souls of Black Folk*, 8.

11 On this relationship between the self and non-Other, an encounter that vexes Hegel's logic of recognition, see Gordon, *Existentia Africana*, 85.

12 Fanon, *Black Skin, White Masks*, 89–95.

13 Chandler, *X*, 11–67.

14 Cheng, *Melancholy of Race*, 3–7.

15 Cheng, *Melancholy of Race*, 20.

16 For I. August Durham, there is a black aesthetic and literary tradition that links melancholy and genius, even as the expression of genius (usually tied to masculinist notions of autocreation) is connected to the maternal. See Durham, *Stay Black and Die*.

17 Sharpe, *In the Wake*, 19–20.

18 Du Bois, *Souls of Black Folk*, 167.

19 Eric B. and Rakim, "Eric B. Is President," on *Paid in Full*.

20 Du Bois, *Souls of Black Folk*, 129.

21 Ferreira da Silva, *Toward a Global Idea of Race*, 117.

22 Du Bois, *Souls of Black Folk*, 169.

23 Du Bois, *Souls of Black Folk*, 169.

24 Ahmed, *Promise of Happiness*, 12–20.

25 Ahmed, *Promise of Happiness*, 13.

26 Ahmed, *Promise of Happiness*, 195.

27 Cervenak, *Wandering*, 23.

28 Du Bois, *Souls of Black Folk*, 175.

29 Bataille, *Inner Experience*, 11.

30 Here I am indebted to Crawley's play on the term *aspire* in *Blackpentecostal Breath*.

31 Du Bois, *Souls of Black Folk*, 175.

32 Glaude, *Exodus!*

33 This is a major argument in Sylvester Johnson's book *African American Religions, 1500–2000*.

34 Jones, *Is God a White Racist?*

35 Hartman, *Scenes of Subjection*, 49–78.

36 Pinn, "Introduction," 3.

37 Glissant, *Poetics of Relation*, 6.

38 Pinn, "Introduction," 3.

39 Du Bois, *Souls of Black Folk*, 167.

40 Hurston, "Art and Such," 24.

41 Stewart, *Politics of Black Joy*, 3.

42 *Narrative of the Life of Frederick Douglass*, 11.

43 Douglass, *My Bondage and My Freedom*, 99–100.

44 Du Bois, *Souls of Black Folk*, 171, 169.

45 As Eric Lott has pointed out, blackface minstrelsy is a complicated cultural development that denotes both white culture's ridicule of and fascination with black culture. It is a form of appropriation and appreciation. See Lott, *Love and Theft*. For a different take, see Jones, *Captive Stage*.

46 Perry, *Prophets of the Hood*, 34.

47 Rose, *Black Noise*, 21.

48 Rose, *Black Noise*, 36.

49 Grandmaster Flash and the Furious Five, "The Message," on *The Message*.

50 Benjamin, *Origin of German Tragic Drama*, 176–77.

51 Bruce, *How to Go Mad Without Losing Your Mind: Madness and Black Radical Creativity*, 4.

52 I am thankful for previous discussions with Tehama Lopez on this point.

53 In this verse, there is a reference to prison taking away one's manhood. Melle Mel recites, "Got sent up for a eight-year bid. Now your manhood is took and you're a Maytag, Spend the next two years as a undercover fag." A Maytag is slang for a male in prison who becomes the sexual slave of another male. The term refers to the reality of rape and sexual violence in prison. At the same time, these lines also express anxieties about performing manhood properly and "authentically," concerns that are pervasive in hip hop culture.

54 Scarface, "I Never Seen a Man Cry," on *The Diary*.

55 Morrison, *Jazz*, 113.

56 A Tribe Called Quest, "Steve Biko," on *Midnight Marauders*.

57 For a reading of this line that situates "The Message" within the framework of theodicy, black suffering, and divine power, see Nelson, "'God's Smiling on You and He's Frowning Too,'" 135.

58 Gilmore, *Golden Gulag*, 25–29.

59 Cairns, "1982."

60 Smalls, *Hip Hop Heresies*, 24.

61 On how funk works on the sensorium, or the multisensory, see Stallings, *Funk the Erotic*.

62 Arrested Development, "Tennessee," on *3 Years, 5 Months and 2 Days in the Life of . . .*

63 Griffin, *"Who Set You Flowin'?,"* 179.

64 Holloway, *Passed On*, 29.

65 For a reading of how the group generally tries to implement an integrative and unifying approach to blackness, see Taylor, "Bringing Noise, Conjuring Spirit," 124. For Taylor, this integrative quality to spirituality is always in tension with liminality and division.

66 Ghostface Killah featuring Ox, "The Prayer," *Big Doe Rehab*.

67 50 Cent, "Many Men," on *Get Rich or Die Tryin'*.

68 Freud, *Civilization and Its Discontents*, 66.

69 See, for instance, Brown, "Sacrificial Citizenship."

70 See, for instance, Miller's section on 50 Cent and Robert Greene in *Religion and Hip Hop*, 47–56.

71 Utley, *Rap and Religion*, 46.

72 Utley, *Rap and Religion*, 47.

73 While Utley does not really explore it, we should remember that the relationship between submission, liberation, and agency is complicated. See, for instance, Griffith, *God's Daughters*.

74 Utley, *Rap and Religion*, 42.

75 Lauryn Hill featuring Mary J. Blige, "I Used to Love Him," on *The Miseducation of Lauryn Hill*.

76 The album name is of course an allusion to Carter G. Woodson's *The Mis-Education of the Negro*. For a recent account of the radical quality of Woodson's understanding of education, see Givens, *Fugitive Pedagogy*.

77 Refugee Camp All-Stars featuring Lauryn Hill, "The Sweetest Thing," on *Love Jones: The Music* (soundtrack).

78 Lauryn Hill, "When It Hurts So Bad," on *The Miseducation of Lauryn Hill*.

79 Lauryn Hill featuring D'Angelo, "Nothing Even Matters," on *The Miseducation of Lauryn Hill*.

80 Queen Latifah, "U.N.I.T.Y.," on *Black Reign*.

81 Spillers, "Mama's Baby, Papa's Maybe," 68.

82 Morgan, *When Chickenheads Come Home*, 48.

83 Ellis, *If We Must Die*, 5.

84 This tendency was also contested and criticized, most famously, by Fugees on their 1996 album *The Score*.
85 Mary J. Blige featuring Notorious B.I.G., "Real Love (Remix)," on *What's the 411? Remix*.
86 See, for instance, Banks, "Hip Hop's Long and Complicated."
87 Edelman, *No Future*, 3.
88 Edelman, *No Future*, 24.
89 Muñoz, *Cruising Utopia*, 91–96. This of course has changed in Edelman's recent work, where he engages various strands of black thought, such as Afropessimism and black nihilism. See Edelman, *Bad Education*, 1–44.
90 On how Biggie is part of a tradition of writers, thinkers, and artists who have thought about the perpetual threat of death, see JanMohamed, *Death-Bound Subject*, 3.
91 Morgan, *When Chickenheads Come Home*, 48.
92 Notorious B.I.G., "Intro," on *Ready to Die*.
93 Turner, *Ritual Process*, 95.
94 Notorious B.I.G., "Sky's the Limit," on *Life After Death*.
95 Here I am especially indebted to Butler's arguments in *The Psychic Life of Power*, 1–30.
96 Spillers, "Mama's Baby, Papa's Maybe," 80.
97 Sullivan, "Fat Mutha," 209.
98 Cooper, "Fallen."
99 Camus, *Myth of Sisyphus*, 4.
100 For a powerful reading of this song, see Pinn, *Deathlife*, 12–14.
101 Notorious B.I.G., "Suicidal Thoughts," on *Ready to Die*.
102 Miller, *Religion and Hip Hop*, 46.
103 Nas, "Hip Hop Is Dead," on *Hip Hop Is Dead*.
104 Adorno and Horkheimer, *Dialectic of Enlightenment*, 94–136.
105 Miller, *Religion and Hip Hop*, 46.
106 Eliade, *Myth and Reality*, 1 20.
107 Eliade, *Myth and Reality*, 112.
108 Common Sense, "I Used to Love H.E.R.," on *Resurrection*.
109 Morgan, *When Chickenheads Come Home*, 44–47.
110 Morgan, *When Chickenheads Come Home*, 40.
111 Wikipedia, "Hip Hop Is Dead," last modified August 29, 2024, 18:46 (UTC), http://en.wikipedia.org/wiki/Hip_Hop_Is_Dead.
112 Nietzsche, *Untimely Meditations*, 72.
113 Nietzsche, *Untimely Meditations*, 75.
114 Benjamin, "On the Concept of History."
115 Nietzsche's *Gay Science*, which includes the "god is dead" motif and allegory, is a sort of call for cultural renewal and overcoming of decadence.
116 See, for instance, Peterson, *Hip Hop Underground*, 36–37.
117 Here I am riffing on the language used by Gilles Deleuze and Félix Guatarri. See Deleuze and Guatarri, *Thousand Plateaus*, 285.
118 Smalls, *Hip Hop Heresies*, 13.

CHAPTER 2. REDEMPTION/RUPTURE

This chapter includes a fragment from "Constructing Constellations: Frankfurt School, Lupe Fiasco, and the Promise of Weak Redemption," in *Religion in Hip Hop: Mapping the New Terrain in the US*, edited by Monica R. Miller, Anthony B. Pinn, and Bernard "Bun B" Freeman (New York: Bloomsbury Academic, 2015).

1 Gilroy, *Darker than Blue*, 4–54. For a critical response to Gilroy's critical assessment of hip hop, see Brown, "Drive Slow."

2 See Robinson, *This Ain't Chicago*, for a discussion of how region plays a part in racial identity and how black southerners often see the Midwest as a site of inauthentic blackness.

3 Harris, "Porch-Sitting as a Creative Southern Tradition," 447.

4 Here I am thinking with Karen Bray's text *Grave Attending*.

5 Miller, *Religion and Hip Hop*, 46.

6 Drake, "Started from the Bottom," on *Nothing Was the Same*.

7 I develop these reflections keeping in mind Evylynn Hammonds's concept of black (w)holes in her discussion of black female sexuality and the politics of silencing and invisibilizing black women. In this formulation, the homophonic relationship between "whole" and "hole" registers a moment of contact between opposing concepts: completion and a kind of void or puncturing that refuses the will to completion. See Hammonds, "Black (W)holes," 126–45.

8 Schmitt, *Political Theology*, 36.

9 Bray, *Grave Attending*, 4.

10 Shulman, *American Prophecy*, 10.

11 Shulman, *American Prophecy*, 248–49.

12 Shulman, *American Prophecy*, 249.

13 Shulman, *American Prophecy*, 252.

14 On the primacy of redemption in Benjamin's thought, see Wolin, *Walter Benjamin*. According to Wolin, "The question of redemption was to [Benjamin] a foremost concern in his understanding of the past" (xlvii).

15 Joya, "Vision of Hell," 24. The relationship between Christian eschatology (in an author like Augustine of Hippo, for instance) and human progress is complicated. Something surely changes when human beings, rather than the Christian deity, become primarily responsible for overcoming human problems and making human life better, happier, and more peaceful. On how the imago of progress is related to Christian notions of time and the unfolding of history, see Adorno, "Progress."

16 Wynter, "Unsettling the Coloniality of Being /Power/Truth/Freedom," 262.

17 There are ways to make distinctions between progress as a critical principle and an idea to achieve, and progress as something that has already happened. See, for instance, Allen, *End of Progress*. Benjamin makes a similar distinction in the following passage: "The concept of history has run counter to the critical theory of history the moment it ceased to be applied as a criterion to specific historical developments and instead was required to measure the span between a legendary inception and a legendary end of history. In other words, as soon as it becomes the signature of his-

torical process as a whole, the concept of progress bespeaks an uncritical hypostatization rather than a critical interrogation." Benjamin, "N," 478.

18 Benjamin, "On the Concept of History," 392.

19 Benjamin, "On the Concept of History," 392.

20 Benjamin, "On the Concept of History," 392.

21 Benjamin, "Paralipomena to 'On the Concept of History,'" 402.

22 Benjamin, "On the Concept of History," 391.

23 Benjamin, "On the Concept of History," 392.

24 See especially the opening pages of *Dialectic of Enlightenment*.

25 Felman, *Juridical Unconscious*, 33. Survival is itself a complicated concept that has been very much shaped by Western Christian discourses and practices. See, for instance, Stern, *Survival*.

26 Felman, *Juridical Unconscious*, 33.

27 On the double silence of history, see Joya, "Vision of Hell," 44.

28 A full elaboration of these modes of composition is beyond the scope of this chapter. On the constellation, Benjamin introduces this idea in his early work *The Origin of German Tragic Drama*, 34. He claims that "ideas are to objects as constellations are to stars."

29 I have focused a lot on the catastrophic in Benjamin's late essay. But redemption for Benjamin also has something to do with involuntary and unconscious memories of tastes, smells, images from an individual's past, childhood, et cetera. He is very much indebted to the writings of Marcel Proust on involuntary memory. On these themes, see Masuzawa, "Tracing the Figure of Redemption."

30 Adorno, *Negative Dialectics*, 166.

31 Adorno, *Minima Moralia*, 151.

32 Adorno, *Negative Dialectics*, 203.

33 Hartman and Wilderson, "Position of the Unthought," 184–85.

34 Hartman, *Scenes of Subjection*, 7.

35 Hartman and Wilderson, "Position of the Unthought," 185.

36 Hartman and Wilderson, "Position of the Unthought," 183.

37 Hartman and Wilderson, "Position of the Unthought," 185.

38 Armstrong, "Losing Salvation," 325.

39 Hartman, *Lose Your Mother*, 6. See also Sharpe's engagement with Hartman in *In the Wake*, 1–22.

40 Hartman, *Scenes of Subjection*, 6.

41 KRS-One, "Sound of da Police," on *Return of the Boom Bap*.

42 Hartman, "Venus in Two Acts."

43 Hartman, "Venus in Two Acts," 2.

44 Hartman, "Venus in Two Acts," 11.

45 Wilderson, *Afropessimism*, 16.

46 Wilderson, *Afropessimism*, 16.

47 Wilderson, *Afropessimism*, 174.

48 Wilderson and Howard, "Frank B. Wilderson."

49 For a brilliant analysis of how redemption operates in black religion more generally (especially through the tradition of Ethiopianism), see Nicholas Andersen's dissertation "'Ethiopia Shall Soon Stretch Out Her Hands unto God.'"

50 Think, for instance, of X Clan's track "Fire and Earth," on *Xodus (The New Testament)* versus KRS-One's "Heal Yourself," part of the Human Education Against Lies project.

51 Pinn, "'Handlin' My Business.'"

52 Rabin, "Lupe Fiasco."

53 While the album cover seems to depict a random array of things, Lupe has said that these objects (Koran, notepad, toys, etc.) are things that he carries with him daily. See Endelman, "Few of Lupe Fiasco's Favorite Things."

54 Lupe Fiasco, "Intro," on *Food and Liquor.*

55 See, for instance, Said, "Orientalism Reconsidered," 12; and Asad, *On Suicide Bombing.*

56 See, for instance, Gomez, *Black Crescent*, prologue.

57 Floyd-Thomas, "Jihad of Words," 51.

58 For a fascinating article on the dimensions of the Five-Percenters that resonate with, but also contest, Western esotericism, see Gray, "Traumatic Mysticism of Othered Others."

59 Floyd-Thomas, "Jihad of Words," 50. Here Floyd-Thomas is drawing from the work of Richard Brent Turner. See Turner, *Islam in the African-American Experience*, 174–238. Also check out Alim, *Roc the Mic Right*, 20–50.

60 Khabeer, *Muslim Cool*, 7, 8.

61 Khabeer, *Muslim Cool*, 5.

62 Khabeer, *Muslim Cool*, 6.

63 Sorett, "'Believe Me,'" 14.

64 Main Source featuring Nas, "Live at the Barbeque," on *Breaking Atoms.*

65 Here one might think of connections between Kate Bowler's genealogy of the American prosperity gospel, in which the commitment to victory is paramount, as on DJ Khaled's "All I Do Is Win," on *Victory*. See Bowler, *Blessed*, 178–225.

66 Sorett, "'Believe Me,'" 19.

67 Sorett, "'Believe Me,'" 14.

68 See for instance, Levinas, *Totality and Infinity*, 38.

69 For response to this incident, see Volf, "Wheaton Professor's Suspension."

70 Lupe Fiasco, "Muhammad Walks," on *Muhammad Walks.*

71 On the limits of grievability in a post-9/11 America and during the early stages of the war on terror, where biopolitical distinctions between who can be mourned and who cannot are produced by obituaries, media, and everyday political discourse, see Butler, *Precarious Life*, 34–38.

72 Edwards, *Other Side of Terror*, 3.

73 I am intentionally eliding the difference between terror and terrorism, especially definitions of terrorism that exclusively focus on nonstate actors that use violence or coercion to achieve certain political ends. We must keep in mind that terrorism has had different meanings and uses in various contexts; it has been deployed routinely to make distinctions (between acceptable and unacceptable violence,

for instance) that protect nation-state sovereignty. See, for instance, Erlenbusch-Anderson, *Genealogies of Terrorism*.

74 Puar, *Terrorist Assemblages*, 3.

75 See note 29 of this chapter.

76 Wilderson, *Red, White, and Black*, 1–32.

77 For Wilderson, there is an important distinction between a conflict and an antagonism. A conflict involves some group or subject position being alienated from and by the social order. This conflict can be resolved by extending the sphere of recognition. An antagonism cannot be reconciled in this manner. An antagonism (between the black and the human, for instance) marks a form of violence that needs to stay in place so that various conflicts can be resolved. In other words, an antagonism is an irreconcilable conflict that prevents black people's suffering from being analogous to other people's suffering (i.e., those that can find a grammar of redress within the sphere of the human). For Wilderson, Native peoples have one foot in the antagonistic relationship and one foot in the conflictual one (insofar as they can claim a past sovereignty or a sovereignty that has been lost but could be regained). See, for instance, Wilderson, *Red, White, and Black*, 35–38, 149–51.

78 King, *Black Shoals*, 20.

79 Hartman, *Scenes of Subjection*, 4.

80 Pinn, *Terror and Triumph*, 49.

81 Du Bois, *Souls of Black Folk*, 111.

82 This is a term I take from the work of Mark Rifkin. See Rifkin, *Beyond Settler Time*.

83 For a powerful essay that shows the links and divergences between Lupe and Kendrick, see Gill, "From 'Blackness' to Afrofuture to 'Impasse.'" For Gill, Kendrick slides into an essentialized conception of blackness while Lupe (like Jimi Hendrix and Richie Havens) points to a set of possibilities beyond limited, narrow conceptions of black being and identity.

84 See, for instance, Bristout, "Kendrick Lamar's *Section.80*."

85 Floyd-Thomas, "Good, the m.A.A.d, and the Holy," 69.

86 Pinn and Driscoll, "Introduction," 4.

87 Miller, "Can Dead Homies Speak?"

88 Love, "Good Kids, Mad Cities," 3.

89 Guillory, "Can I Be Both?," 28.

90 Guillory, "Can I Be Both?," 26.

91 2Pac, "Words of Wisdom," on *2Pacalypse Now*. For a powerful account of the effects of militarized policing on the lyrical content of LA hip hop and gangsta rap in the 1980s and 1990s, see Kelley, *Race Rebels*, 183–227.

92 Here I am thinking with the work of Fred Moten and Édouard Glissant.

93 Guillory, "Can I Be Both?," 26.

94 See, for instance, Newport, "Americans Say Reagan."

95 Sharpe, *Monstrous Intimacies*. I will have more to say about this text in the next chapter.

96 For an interesting discussion of black pathology, see Sexton, "Social Life of Social Death." Here Sexton is responding to Fred Moten's concerns that Frantz Fanon's

work stumbles into a conventional understanding of blackness as pathology. See Moten, "Case of Blackness."

97 Nietzsche, *Will to Power*, 9.

98 West, *Race Matters*, 19–20. On how Kendrick's broader musical corpus responds to this threat of black nihilism, see Hills, "Loving You Is Complicated."

99 West, *Race Matters*, 23.

100 Bailey, "Homolatent Masculinity and Hip Hop Culture," 196.

101 Bailey, "Homolatent Masculinity," 196.

102 Etminan, "Kendrick Lamar Interview." For Kedrick blackness is not a simple essentialism but includes a multiplicity of colors and shades.

103 On this technique in Kendrick's music, see Thomas, "Singing Experience in *Section.80*," 61.

104 Warren, "Black Nihilism and the Politics of Hope."

105 Warren, "Black Nihilism and the Politics of Hope," 219.

106 Kendrick Lamar, "Tammy's Song (Her Evils)," on *Section.80*.

107 Derrida, "Structure, Sign, and Play," 292.

108 This has been addressed most recently by Tommy Curry in *The Man-Not: Race, Class, Genre, and the Dilemmas of Black Manhood*.

109 Perry, *Prophets of the Hood*, 118.

110 Hartman, "Venus in Two Acts," 3.

111 Here I am thinking with Hartman's concerns and reflections regarding a collective will to reform and rehabilitate black women (in early twentieth-century urban centers) who deviated from standard gender and sexual norms and expectations. Instead of seeing these women, who often enter the archive as problems, criminals, and deviants, as wounded and ruined, she reinterprets them as experimenting in forms of everyday anarchy. See Hartman, *Wayward Lives, Beautiful Experiments*.

CHAPTER 3. MONSTER/MONSTROSITY

Part of this chapter appeared in "The Horrifying Sacred: Hip Hop, Blackness, and the Figure of the Monster," *Journal of Africana Religions* 5, no. 2 (2017): 291–99.

1 Burton, *Posthuman Rap*. I will discuss this book in more detail below.

2 Eric B. and Rakim, "Microphone Fiend," on *Follow the Leader*.

3 Eric B. and Rakim, "Eric B. Is President," on *Paid in Full*.

4 Bataille, "The Practice of Joy Before Death," in *Visions of Excess*, 235.

5 Lil Wayne featuring Gucci Mane, "Steady Mobbin'," on *We Are Young Money*.

6 Tyler, the Creator, "Goblin," on *Goblin*.

7 21 Savage, "Monster," on *I Am > I Was*.

8 Marx, *Capital*, 163.

9 Marx, *Capital*, 507.

10 Spillers, "Mama's Baby, Papa's Maybe," 80. Burton makes a similar claim in the first chapter of *Posthuman Rap*.

11 Biles, *Ecce Monstrum*, 3.

12 Biles, *Ecce Monstrum*, 3.

13 Hollywood, *Sensible Ecstasy*, 25–110.

14 Hollywood, *Sensible Ecstasy*, 14–15.

15 Bataille, *Theory of Religion*, 57.

16 Bataille, *Inner Experience*, 37.

17 Bataille, *Theory of Religion*, 27.

18 Bataille, *Theory of Religion*, 29.

19 Bataille, *Theory of Religion*, 46.

20 Bataille, *Theory of Religion*, 46–47.

21 Bataille, *Theory of Religion*, 48.

22 Bataille, *Theory of Religion*, 49.

23 Bataille, *Theory of Religion*, 51.

24 Biles, *Ecce Monstrum*, 4.

25 Bataille, *Accursed Share*, 20–21.

26 Bataille, *Accursed Share*, 21.

27 Eliade, *Sacred and the Profane*, 48.

28 Bataille, "The Deviations of Nature," in *Visions of Excess*, 53.

29 Bataille, "The Deviations of Nature," in *Visions of Excess*, 55.

30 Bataille, "The Deviations of Nature," in *Visions of Excess*, 55.

31 Bataille, "The Deviations of Nature," in *Visions of Excess*, 55.

32 Bataille, "The Sacred Conspiracy," in *Visions of Excess*, 181. For a powerful reading of Bataille's interpretation of this drawing, one that underscores an aporia in his thought regarding the potential of the human embracing its animality, see Agamben, *The Open*, 5–8.

33 Kearney, *Strangers, Gods, and Monsters*, 3.

34 See, for instance, Federici, *Caliban and the Witch*.

35 See, for instance, Puar and Rai, "Monster, Terror, Fag."

36 Schmitt, *Political Theology*, 5.

37 Bataille, *Accursed Share*, 23.

38 Biles, *Ecce Monstrum*, 5.

39 Warren, *Ontological Terror*, 1–25.

40 For a brilliant piece that thinks more about the possibilities of Bataille's notion of the sacred (even with the Eurocentric limits within the tradition of thought that his writing derives from) alongside black poetics, see Carter, "Black Malpractice."

41 Jordan, *White over Black*, 17–20.

42 Jackson, *Becoming Human*, 6.

43 Lum, *Heathen*, 98–100.

44 Kant, *Observations on the Feeling of the Beautiful and Sublime and Other Writings*, 58–59. For a great reading of this passage and Kant's understanding of race more broadly, see Eze, "Color of Reason."

45 Jackson, *Becoming Human*, 22.

46 Interestingly enough, the term *monster* has an etymology that includes "sign" and "warning." On this, see Gordon and Gordon, *Of Divine Warning*.

47 Fanon, *Black Skin, White Masks*, 79.

48 Fanon, *Black Skin, White Masks*, 78. See also Marriott, *Whither Fanon?*, foreword.

49 Fanon, *Black Skin, White Masks*, 81.

50 For a brilliant reading of this scene that stresses the mobility of fear and the stickiness of affect, see Ahmed, "Affective Economies," 126–28.

51 Fanon, *Black Skin, White Masks*, 117.

52 Fanon, *Black Skin, White Masks*, 118.

53 Fanon, *Black Skin, White Masks*, 118.

54 I do not have the space to delve into the energetic discussions and debates regarding Fanon's understanding of gender, sexuality, women's liberation, and so forth. There have been strong critiques of Fanon's writings on black and white women, including charges of essentialism, double standards, and limited roles for Algerian women in the anticolonial struggle against France. According to Rey Chow, for instance, Fanon locks women of color into a position where their love for white men can only be a traitorous desire to be valued, recognized, and folded into the orbit of whiteness. Whereas Fanon shows more patience and sympathy for black men and their desires for recognition via white women, he shows no such generosity toward Mayotte Capécia, who is a kind of stand-in for the black woman's yearning for whiteness. On Chow's reading, Fanon allows black men to pursue sexual encounters with those outside the black community without being labeled disloyal or unfaithful to black people. This is not the case for black women, who are considered traitors when they transgress the taboo against miscegenation. There is something about the sexual desires of women of color that Fanon needs to police and constrain for the sake of community. See Chow, "Politics of Admittance." For a very different reading of Fanon's gender politics, see Douglass, "At the Intersections of Assemblages." According to Douglass, Chow misses the fact that Fanon's reading of Capécia's writings focus on her disdain for blackness and especially black femininity. For a text that deals generally with Fanon's relationship to feminism, see Sharpley-Whiting, *Frantz Fanon*.

55 Spillers, "Mama's Baby, Papa's Maybe," 64.

56 Sartre, *Anti-Semite and Jew*, 8.

57 Spillers, "Mama's Baby, Papa's Maybe," 64.

58 Spillers, "Mama's Baby, Papa's Maybe," 67.

59 Spillers, "Mama's Baby, Papa's Maybe," 68.

60 Spillers, "Mama's Baby, Papa's Maybe," 67.

61 King, "Labor of (Re)reading Plantation Landscapes," 1024.

62 Spillers, "Mama's Baby, Papa's Maybe," 66.

63 Jackson, *Becoming Human*, 9.

64 This language of regendering is indebted to the work of Haylee Harrell. She offers a brilliant interpretation of Spillers in her presentation "A Black Feminist Genealogy of the Monstrous Mulatta," Duke University, Durham, NC, January 25, 2022.

65 Spillers, "Mama's Baby, Papa's Maybe," 67.

66 Rubin, "Traffic of Women."

67 Spillers, "Mama's Baby, Papa's Maybe," 67.

68 For a reading of Spillers that exhibits a concern about reducing the representation of black women to trauma, pain, and exploitation, see Nash, *Black Body in Ecstasy*, 1–26.

69 See, for instance, Dean, "Black Bataille."

70 Sharpe, *Monstrous Intimacies*, 11.

71 Here my reading is indebted to Nash's interpretation of Renee Cox's self-portrait *Hot-En-Tot*, which reenacts the nineteenth-century public exhibition of Saartjie Baartman. Nash underscores how Cox attempts to reclaim the power of looking back. See Nash, *Black Body in Ecstasy*, 27–30.

72 Kanye West, "Power," on *My Beautiful Dark Twisted Fantasy*.

73 Bailey, "Preface," xviii.

74 See, for instance, Beshara, *Psychoanalytic Biography of Ye*.

75 Perry, *Prophets of the Hood*, 38.

76 Kelley, *Race Rebels*, 189–90.

77 Debord, *Society of the Spectacle*, 5.

78 Moten, *In the Break*, 1–24.

79 Harrison, *Belly of the Beast*, 16.

80 Marriott, *On Black Men*, 4.

81 See also Wood, *Lynching and Spectacle*.

82 Keetley, "Zombie Republic."

83 Utley, *Rap and Religion*, 69–92.

84 Bradley, *Book of Rhymes*, 86.

85 Bradley, *Book of Rhymes*, 89.

86 For a different and provocative reading of Kanye's allusion to modern-day slavery, see Curry, "'You Can't Stand the Nigger I See!'"

87 Lacan, *Four Fundamental Concepts*, 60.

88 Miller, "God of the New Slaves?"

89 Miller, "God of the New Slaves?," 173.

90 Jay-Z featuring Jay Electronica, "We Made It (Remix)." YouTube, March 23, 2024, https://www.youtube.com/watch?v=iaLIzQJLBzo.

91 Jay-Z, "Song Cry," on *The Blueprint*.

92 Burton, *Posthuman Rap*, 7.

93 Burton, *Posthuman Rap*, 6.

94 Burton, *Posthuman Rap*, 6.

95 Wiki Nicki: Nicki Minaj Fandom, "The Harajuku Barbie," last modified September 10, 2024, 15:11 (UTC), https://nickiminaj.fandom.com/wiki/The_Harajuku _Barbie; see also "Roman Zolanski: Roman v Ms.Kim," accessed December 20, 2024, https://nickiminaj.fandom.com/wiki/Roman_Zolanski:_Roman_v_Ms.Kim.

96 See Shange, "King Named Nicki"; and Ganz, "Curious Case of Nicki Minaj."

97 Shange, "King Named Nicki," 30.

98 Shange, "King Named Nicki," 30.

99 For a different reading of Minaj's queer identifications, one that focuses on how Minaj has rejected the position of the black cisfemme, see Tinsley, *Ezili's Mirrors*, 29–30.

100 Here I am thinking especially of "Did It On'em," on *Pink Friday*. Also check out "Stupid Hoe," on *Pink Friday: Roman Reloaded*.

101 McMillan, *Embodied Avatars*, 11–13.

102 McMillan, *Embodied Avatars*, 12.

103 McMillan, *Embodied Avatars*, 214.

104 McMillan, *Embodied Avatars*, 214.

105 McMillan, *Embodied Avatars*, 214.

106 See, for instance, Marquis Bey's sustained response to Nahum Chandler in *The Problem of the Negro as a Problem for Gender*.

107 See, for instance, McMillan, "Nicki-Aesthetics," 85.

108 Hartman, *Scenes of Subjection*, 3.

109 In other words, the idea and image of black feminine excess has always been subject to white supremacist containment, exploitation, and profitability. This is especially complicated within the realm of popular culture, where black artists and performers mobilize, take advantage of, and contest this all too familiar association of black women with a kind of surplus sexuality. See, for instance, Fleetwood, *Troubling Vision*, 105–45.

110 Spillers, "Mama's Baby, Papa's Maybe," 80.

111 Spillers, "Mama's Baby, Papa's Maybe," 67. Spillers has actually been critical of rap music and hip hop scholarship, especially when it treats hip hop as the measure and essence of black culture. See Leonard, "First Questions."

112 See, for instance, Halliday, "Miley, What's Good?"

113 Halliday, "Miley, What's Good?"

114 Nicki Minaj, "Anaconda," on *The Pinkprint*.

115 This is not quite bell hooks's notion of the oppositional gaze but, as I describe below, might be read alongside it. See hooks, "The Oppositional Gaze: Black Female Spectators," in *Black Looks*.

116 Sir Mix-A-Lot, "Baby Got Back," on *Mack Daddy*.

117 Kristeva, *Powers of Horror*, 1.

118 Freud, "Fetishism," 153.

119 Freud, "Dissolution of the Oedipus Complex."

120 Freud, "Fetishism," 154.

121 Lacan, "Signification of the Phallus," 579.

122 Lacan, "Signification of the Phallus," 583.

123 On this fluidity more generally, see Rae, "Questioning the Phallus." For a helpful reading of Lacan's distinction between being and having the phallus, see Butler, *Gender Trouble*, 56–60.

124 See, for instance, Pietz, "Problem of the Fetish"; and Matory, *Fetish Revisited*.

125 Pietz, "Problem of the Fetish," 7.

126 Hegel, *Lectures on the Philosophy of Religion*, 234–35.

127 Wilderson, *Red, White, and Black*, 82.

128 Perry, *Prophets of the Hood*, 176.

129 Perry, *Prophets of the Hood*, 175–76.

130 Perry, *Prophets of the Hood*, 176.

131 hooks, "Eating the Other: Desire and Resistance," in *Black Looks*, 21.

132 hooks, "Oppositional Gaze," in *Black Looks*, 128.

133 hooks, "Eating the Other," in *Black Looks*, 23.

CONCLUSION

1 Fleetwood, *On Racial Icons*.
2 See, for instance, Bender, "Practicing Religions."
3 Kristeva, *Powers of Horror*, 56–58.
4 Long, *Significations*, 7.
5 Baldwin, *Fire Next Time*, 98.
6 Long, *Ellipsis*, 15–16.
7 Long, *Significations*, 7.
8 Du Bois, *Darkwater*, 18.
9 Spillers, "Mama's Baby, Papa's Maybe," 71.
10 See, for instance, Wynter, "1492."
11 Wynter, "Afterword," 356. See also McKittrick, *Demonic Grounds*, xxiv.
12 Moten, "Black Op," 1745.
13 Moten, *Black and Blur*, 1, 2.
14 Moten, "Case of Blackness," 180.
15 Gumbs, *Spill*, xii.
16 Okiji, *Jazz as Critique*, 10.
17 Mobb Deep, "Survival of the Fittest," on *The Infamous*.
18 On this pattern of refusal to grieve Megan Thee Stallion as an object of brutality (because she embodies qualities and traits such as loudness and excessiveness that render her disposable, even as a celebrity), see Lane, "Ratchet Lives Matter." I am thankful to conversations with Rukimani PV on these matters.

Sources

DISCOGRAPHY

Arrested Development. *3 Years, 5 Months and 2 Days in the Life of . . .* Chrysalis, 1992.

A Tribe Called Quest. *Midnight Marauders.* Jive, 1993.

Banks, Azealia. *1991.* Interscope, 2012.

Blige, Mary J. *What's the 411? Remix.* Uptown, 1993.

Brand Nubian. *One for All.* Elektra, 1990.

Common Sense. *Resurrection.* Relativity, 1994.

Diamond D and the Psychotic Neurotics. *Stunts, Blunts, and Hip Hop.* Chemistry/ Mercury, 1992.

DJ Khaled. *Victory.* We the Best/EI, 2010.

Drake. *Nothing Was the Same.* Cash Money/Republic, 2013.

Eric B. and Rakim. *Paid in Full.* 4th and Broadway, 1986.

Eric B. and Rakim. *Follow the Leader.* MCA, 1988.

Fiasco, Lupe. *Lupe Fiasco's Food and Liquor.* Atlantic, 2006.

Fiasco, Lupe. *Muhammad Walks.* Chi Town Getting Down, 2006.

Fiasco, Lupe. *Lupe Fiasco's The Cool.* Atlantic, 2007.

50 Cent. *Get Rich or Die Tryin'.* Interscope, 2003.

Fugees. *The Score.* Columbia, 1996.

Ghostface Killah. *Ironman.* Epic Street/Razor Sharp, 1996.

Ghostface Killah. *Big Doe Rehab.* Def Jam, 2007.

Goodie Mob. *Soul Food.* LaFace, 1995.

Grandmaster Flash and the Furious Five. *The Message.* Sugar Hill, 1982.

Hill, Lauryn. *The Miseducation of Lauryn Hill.* Ruffhouse, 1998.

Jay-Z. *The Blueprint.* Def Jam, 2001.

KRS-One. *Return of the Boom Bap.* Jive, 1993.

Lamar, Kendrick. *Section.80.* Top Dawg Entertainment, 2011.

Lamar, Kendrick. *good kid, m.A.A.d city.* Top Dawg Entertainment, 2012.

Love Jones: The Music (soundtrack). Sony, 1997.

Main Source. *Breaking Atoms*. Wild Pitch, 1991.

Mill, Meek, featuring Rick Ross. "Tupac Back." Maybach Music Group, 2011.

Minaj, Nicki. *Pink Friday*. Young Money, 2010.

Minaj, Nicki. *Pink Friday: Roman Reloaded*. Young Money, 2012.

Minaj, Nicki. The *Pinkprint*. Young Money, 2014.

Mobb Deep. *The Infamous*. Loud/RCA, 1995.

Nas. *Hip Hop Is Dead*. Def Jam, 2006.

Notorious B.I.G. *Ready to Die*. Bad Boy, 1994.

Notorious B.I.G. *Life After Death*. Bad Boy, 1997.

OutKast. *Aquemini*. LaFace Records, 1998.

OutKast. *Speakerboxxx/The Love Below*. Arista, 2003.

Raekwon. *Only Built 4 Cuban Linx . . .* Loud/RCA, 1995.

Scarface. *The Diary*. Rap-A-Lot/Noo Trybe, 1994.

Sir Mix-A-Lot. *Mack Daddy*. American, 1992.

Smooth. *Smooth*. TNT/Jive, 1995.

2Pac. *2Pacalypse Now*. Jive/Interscope, 1991.

2Pac. *Me Against the World*. Out Da Gutta, 1995.

2Pac. *All Eyes on Me*. Death Row, 1996.

21 Savage. *I Am > I Was*. Epic, 2018.

Tyler, the Creator. *Goblin*. XL, 2011.

We Are Young Money. Cash Money/Universal Motown, 2009.

West, Kanye. *Late Registration*. Def Jam, 2005.

West, Kanye. *My Beautiful Dark Twisted Fantasy*. Roc-A-Fella, 2010.

West, Kanye. *Yeezus*. Def Jam, 2013.

Wild, Snootie. *Go Mode*. Epic, 2014.

Wu-Tang Clan. *Enter the Wu-Tang (36 Chambers)*. Loud, 1993.

X Clan. *Xodus (The New Testament)*. Polydor, 1992.

BIBLIOGRAPHY

Adorno, Theodor. *Aesthetic Theory*. Translated by Robert Hullot-Kentor. Minneapolis: University of Minnesota Press, 1998.

Adorno, Theodor. *Minima Moralia: Reflections on a Damaged Life*. Translated by E. F. N. Jephcott. New York: Verso, 2005.

Adorno, Theodor. *Negative Dialectics*. Translated by E. B. Ashton. New York: Continuum, 1973.

Adorno, Theodor. *Prisms*. Translated by Samuel Weber and Shierry Weber Nicholsen. Cambridge, MA: MIT Press, 1983.

Adorno, Theodor. "Progress." In *Critical Models: Interventions and Catchwords*, translated by Henry Pickford, 143–60. New York: Columbia University Press, 2005.

Adorno, Theodor, and Max Horkheimer. *Dialectic of Enlightenment*. Translated by Edmund Jephcott. Stanford, CA: Stanford University Press, 2002.

Agamben, Giorgio. *The Open: Man and Animal*. Translated by Kevin Attell. Stanford, CA: Stanford University Press, 2004.

Ahmed, Sara. "Affective Economies." *Social Text* 22, no. 2 (Summer 2004): 126–28.

Ahmed, Sara. *The Promise of Happiness*. Durham, NC: Duke University Press, 2010.

Alexander, M. Jacqui. *Pedagogies of Crossing: Meditations on Feminism, Sexual Politics, Memory, and the Sacred*. Durham, NC: Duke University Press, 2006.

Allen, Amy. *The End of Progress: Decolonizing the Normative Foundations of Critical Theory*. New York: Columbia University Press, 2017.

Alim, H. Samy. *Roc the Mic Right: The Language of Hip Hop Culture*. New York: Routledge, 2006.

An, Yountae. *The Decolonial Abyss: Mysticism and Cosmopolitics from the Ruins*. New York: Fordham University Press, 2016.

Andersen, Nicholas. "'Ethiopia Shall Soon Stretch Out Her Hands unto God': Ethiopianism, Conjure, and Repatriation in Black Religious Thought." PhD diss., Brown University, 2022.

Armstrong, Amaryah. "Losing Salvation: Notes Toward a Wayward Theology." *Critical Times* 6, no. 2 (2023): 324–44.

Asad, Talal. *Genealogies of Religion: Discipline and Reasons of Power in Christianity and Islam*. Baltimore: Johns Hopkins University Press, 1993.

Asad, Talal. *On Suicide Bombing*. New York: Columbia University Press, 2007.

Bailey, Julius, ed. *The Cultural Impact of Kanye West*. New York: Palgrave, 2014.

Bailey, Julius, "Preface." In Bailey, *Cultural Impact of Kanye West*, xvii–xxvii.

Bailey, Moya. "Homolatent Masculinity and Hip Hop Culture." *Palimpsest* 2, no. 2 (2013): 187–99.

Baker-Fletcher, Garth Kasimu. "African-American Christian Rap: Facing Truth and Resisting It." In Pinn, *Noise and Spirit*, 29–48.

Baldwin, James. *The Fire Next Time*. 1963. Reprint, New York: Vintage Books, 1993.

Baldwin, James. *The Price of the Ticket: Collected Nonfiction, 1948–1985*. New York: St. Martin's, 1985.

Banks, Alec. "Hip Hop's Long and Complicated Fascination with the Mafia." *Rock the Bells*, January 6, 2021. https://rockthebells.com/articles/john-gotti-hip-hop.

Bataille, Georges. *The Accursed Share: An Essay on General Economy*. Translated by Robert Hurley. New York: Zone Books, 1988.

Bataille, Georges. *Inner Experience*. Translated by Leslie Anne Boldt. Albany: SUNY Press, 1988.

Bataille, Georges. *Story of the Eye*. Translated by Dovid Bergelson. San Francisco: City Lights Publishing, 1987.

Bataille, Georges. *The Tears of Eros*. Translated by Peter Connor. San Francisco: City Lights Books, 1989.

Bataille, Georges. *Theory of Religion*. Translated by Robert Hurley. New York: Zone Books, 1989.

Bataille, Georges. *Visions of Excess: Selected Writings, 1927–1939*. Edited by Allan Stoekl. Minneapolis: University of Minnesota Press, 1985.

Bender, Courtney. "Practicing Religions." In *The Cambridge Companion to Religious Studies*, edited by Robert Orsi, 273–95. Cambridge: Cambridge University Press, 2012.

Benjamin, Walter. "N [On the Theory of Knowledge, Theory of Progress]." In *The Arcades Project*, edited by Rolf Tiedemann, translated by Howard Eiland and Kevin McLaughlin, 456–88. Cambridge, MA: Belknap Press of Harvard University, 1999.

Benjamin, Walter. "On the Concept of History." In *Selected Writings, 4*, 389–400.

Benjamin, Walter. *The Origin of German Tragic Drama*. Translated by John Osborne. New York: Verso, 1985.

Benjamin, Walter. "Paralipomena to 'On the Concept of History.'" in *Selected Writings, 4*, 401–11.

Benjamin, Walter. *Selected Writings, 4: 1938–1940*. Edited by Howard Eiland and Michael Jennings. Cambridge, MA: Harvard University Press, 2006.

Beshara, Robert K. *A Psychoanalytic Biography of Ye: The Legacy of Unconditional Love*. Cambridge: Cambridge University Press, 2023.

Bey, Marquis. *The Problem of the Negro as a Problem for Gender*. Minneapolis: University of Minnesota Press, 2020.

Biles, Jeremy. *Ecce Monstrum: Georges Bataille and the Sacrifice of Form*. New York: Fordham University Press, 2007.

Biles, Jeremy. "The Sacrifice of Domestication: Theorizing Religion." In *From Influence and Confluence to Difference and Indifference: Studies on History of Religions*, edited by Mihaela Gligor, 14–75. Cluj-Napoca, Romania: Presa Universitara Clujeana, 2015.

Bowler, Kate. *Blessed: A History of the American Prosperity Gospel*. New York: Oxford University Press, 2013.

Bradley, Adam. *Book of Rhymes: The Poetics of Hip Hop*. New York: Basic Books, 2009.

Bradley, Regina. *Chronicling "Stankonia": The Rise of the Hip-Hop South*. Chapel Hill: UNC Press, 2021.

Bradley, Regina, and Seneca Vaught. "Of the Wings of Traplanta: (Re)Historicizing W. E. B. Du Bois' Atlanta in the Hip Hop South." *Phylon* 54, no. 2 (Winter 2017): 11–27.

Bray, Karen. *Grave Attending: A Political Theology for the Unredeemed*. New York: Fordham University Press, 2020.

Brintnall, Kent. *Ecce Homo: The Male Body in Pain as Redemptive Figure*. Chicago: University of Chicago Press, 2011.

Bristout, Ralph. "Kendrick Lamar's *Section.80*: Reagan-Era Blues." In Driscoll, Pinn, and Miller, *Kendrick Lamar and the Making of Black Meaning*, 19–24.

Brown, Adrienne. "Drive Slow: Rehearing Hip Hop Automotivity." *Journal of Popular Music Studies* 24, no. 3 (2012): 265–75.

Brown, Wendy. "Sacrificial Citizenship: Neoliberalism, Human Capital, and Austerity Politics." *Constellations* 23, no. 1 (2016): 3–14.

Bruce, La Marr. *How to Go Mad Without Losing Your Mind: Madness and Black Radical Creativity*. Durham, NC: Duke University Press, 2021.

Burton, Justin Adams. *Posthuman Rap*. New York: Oxford University Press, 2017.

Butler, Judith. *Gender Trouble: Feminism and the Subversion of Identity*. New York: Routledge, 1999.

Butler, Judith. *Precarious Life: The Powers of Mourning and Violence*. New York: Verso, 2004.

Butler, Judith. *The Psychic Life of Power: Theories of Subjection*. Stanford, CA: Stanford University Press, 1997.

Caillois, Roger. *Man and the Sacred*. Translated by Meyer Barash. Champaign: University of Illinois Press, 2001.

Cairns, Dan. "1982: Grandmaster Flash: The Message." *Sunday Times*, September 28, 2008.

Camus, Albert. *The Myth of Sisyphus*. Translated by Justin O'Brien. New York: Vintage Books, 1991.

Carter, J. Kameron. *The Anarchy of Black Religion*. Durham, NC: Duke University Press, 2023.

Carter, J. Kameron. "Black Malpractice (a Poetics of the Sacred)." *Social Text* 37, no. 2 (June 2019): 67–107.

Cervenak, Sarah. *Wandering: Philosophical Performances of Racial and Sexual Freedom*. Durham, NC: Duke University Press, 2014.

Chandler, Nahum. *X: The Problem of the Negro as a Problem for Thought*. New York: Fordham Press, 2013.

Cheng, Anne. *The Melancholy of Race: Psychoanalysis, Assimilation, and Hidden Grief*. New York: Oxford University Press, 2001.

Chow, Rey. "The Politics of Admittance: Female Sexual Agency, Miscegenation, and the Formation of Community in Frantz Fanon." In *The Rey Chow Reader*, edited by Paul Bowman, 56–74. New York: Columbia University Press, 2010.

Cohen, Cathy. *The Boundaries of Blackness: AIDS and the Breakdown of Black Politics*. Chicago: University of Chicago Press, 1999.

Cone, James. "The Blues: A Secular Spiritual." *Black Sacred Music* 6, no. 1 (1992): 68–97.

Cooper, Cecilio. "Fallen: Generation, Postlapsarian Verticality, and the Black Chthonic." *Rhizomes* 38 (2022): 1–33.

Crawley, Ashon T. *Blackpentecostal Breath: The Aesthetics of Possibility*. New York: Fordham University Press, 2016.

Cruz, Jon. *Culture on the Margins: The Black Spiritual and the Rise of American Cultural Interpretation*. Princeton, NJ: Princeton University Press, 1999.

Curry, Tommy. *The Man-Not: Race, Class, Genre, and the Dilemmas of Black Manhood*. Philadelphia: Temple University Press, 2017.

Curry, Tommy. "'You Can't Stand the Nigger I See!': Kanye West's Analysis of Anti-Black Death." In Bailey, *Cultural Impact of Kanye West*, 127–49.

Damage, DB. "Infrasonic Sound: The Black Noise Kinship of David Bowie and William S. Burroughs." *Sound of Life*, February 1, 2023. https://www.soundoflife.com/blogs/experiences/black-noise-bomb-music.

Dean, Aria. "Black Bataille." *November* magazine 2 (2020). https://www.novembermag.com/content/black-bataille.

Debord, Guy. *Society of the Spectacle*. Translated by Donald Nicholson-Smith. New York: Zone Books, 1994.

Deleuze, Gilles, and Félix Guatarri. *A Thousand Plateaus: Capitalism and Schizophrenia*. Translated by Brian Massumi. Minneapolis: University of Minnesota Press, 1987.

Derrida, Jacques. *The Gift of Death*. Chicago: University of Chicago Press, 1995.

Derrida, Jacques. "Structure, Sign, and Play in the Discourse of the Human Sciences." In *Writing and Difference*, translated by Alan Bass, 278–93. Chicago: University of Chicago Press, 1978.

Douglas, Kelly Brown. *Sexuality and the Black Church: A Womanist Perspective*. Maryknoll, NY: Orbis Book, 1999.

Douglas, Mary. *Purity and Danger: An Analysis of Concepts of Pollution and Taboo*. New York: Routledge, 2002.

Douglass, Frederick. *My Bondage and My Freedom*. New York: Dover, 1969.

Douglass, Frederick. *Narrative of the Life of Frederick Douglass, an American Slave*. 1845. Reprint, New York: Barnes and Noble Classics, 2003.

Douglass, Patrice. "At the Intersections of Assemblages: Fanon, Capécia, and the Unmaking of the Genre Subject." In *Conceptual Aphasia in Black: Displacing Racial Formation*, edited by P. Khalil Saucier and Tryon Woods, 103–26. New York: Lexington Books, 2016.

Douglass, Patrice. "Black Feminist Thought for the Dead and Dying." *Theory and Event* 21, no. 1 (2018): 106–23.

Driscoll, Christopher, Monica Miller, and Anthony Pinn, eds. *Kendrick Lamar and the Making of Black Meaning*. New York: Routledge, 2020.

Du Bois, W. E. B. *Darkwater: Voices from Behind the Veil*. 1920. Reprint, Mineola, NY: Dover, 1999.

Du Bois, W. E. B. *The Souls of Black Folk*. 1903. Reprint, New York: Oxford University Press, 2007.

Durham, I August. *Stay Black and Die: On Melancholy and Genius*. Durham, NC: Duke University Press, 2023.

Durkheim, Émile. *The Elementary Forms of Religious Life*. Translated by Karen Fields. New York: Free Press, 1995.

Dyson, Michael Eric. *Between God and Gangsta Rap: Bearing Witness to Black Culture*. New York: Oxford University Press, 1996.

Dyson, Michael Eric. *Holler If You Hear Me: Searching for Tupac Shakur*. New York: Basic Books, 2006.

Edelman, Lee. *Bad Education: Why Queer Theory Teaches Us Nothing*. Durham, NC: Duke University Press, 2022.

Edelman, Lee. *No Future: Queer Theory and the Death Drive*. Durham, NC: Duke University Press, 2004.

Edwards, Erica. *The Other Side of Terror: Black Women and the Culture of US Empire*. New York: NYU Press, 2021.

Eliade, Mircea. *Myth and Reality*. Translated by Willard Trask. New York: Harper and Row, 1975.

Eliade, Mircea. *The Sacred and the Profane: The Nature of Religion*. Translated by Willard Trask. New York: Harcourt Brace, 1987.

Ellis, Aimé. *If We Must Die: From Bigger Thomas to Biggie Smalls*. Detroit: Wayne State Press, 2011.

Endelman, Michael. "A Few of Lupe Fiasco's Favorite Things." *Entertainment Weekly*, October 20, 2006. https://ew.com/article/2006/10/20/few-lupe-fiascos-favorite-things.

Erlenbusch-Anderson, Verena. *Genealogies of Terrorism: Revolution, State Violence, Empire*. New York: Columbia University Press, 2018.

Etminan, Nima. "Kendrick Lamar Interview." *DubCNN*, April 2012. https://www.dubcnn.com/interviews/kendricklamar2012.

Eze, Emmanuel. "The Color of Reason: The Idea of Race in Kant's Anthropology." *Bucknell Review* 38, no. 2 (January 1995): 200–241.

Fanon, Frantz. *Black Skin, White Masks*. Translated by Richard Philcox. New York: Grove Press, 2008.

Federici, Silvia. *Caliban and the Witch: Women, the Body, and Primitive Accumulation*. New York: Autonomedia, 2004.

Felman, Shoshana. *The Juridical Unconscious: Trials and Traumas in the Twentieth Century*. Cambridge, MA: Harvard University Press, 2002.

Ferreira da Silva, Denise. *Toward a Global Idea of Race*. Minneapolis: University of Minnesota Press, 2007.

Fleetwood, Nicole. *On Racial Icons: Blackness and the Public Imagination*. New Brunswick, NJ: Rutgers University Press, 2015.

Fleetwood, Nicole. *Troubling Vision: Performance, Visuality, and Blackness*. Chicago: University of Chicago Press, 2011.

Floyd-Thomas, Juan. "The Good, the m.A.A.d, and the Holy: Kendrick Lamar's Meditations on Sin and Moral Agency in the Post-Gangsta Era." In Driscoll, Pinn, and Miller, *Kendrick Lamar and the Making of Black Meaning*, 63–98.

Floyd-Thomas, Juan. "A Jihad of Words: The Evolution of African American Islam and Contemporary Hip-Hop." In Pinn, *Noise and Spirit*, 49–70.

Foreman, Murray, and Mark Anthony Neal, eds. *That's the Joint: The Hip Hop Studies Reader*. New York: Routledge, 2004.

Forster, Nicolas. "What Is This Thing Called Hip Hop Studies? A Response to Saucier and Woods." *Journal of Popular Music Studies* 27, no. 3 (September 2015): 343–52.

Freud, Sigmund. *Civilization and Its Discontents*. Translated by James Strachey. New York: W. W. Norton, 1961.

Freud, Sigmund. "The Dissolution of the Oedipus Complex." In *The Complete Psychological Works of Sigmund Freud, Volume XIX*, edited and translated by James Strachey, 173–79. London: Hogarth and the Institute of Psychoanalysis, 1961.

Freud, Sigmund. "Fetishism." In *The Complete Psychological Works of Sigmund Freud, Volume XXI*, edited and translated by James Strachey, 149–57. London: Hogarth and the Institute of Psychoanalysis, 1964.

Freud, Sigmund. "Mourning and Melancholia." In *The Complete Psychological Works of Sigmund Freud, Volume XIV*, edited and translated by James Strachey, 243–58. London: Hogarth and the Institute of Psychoanalysis, 1957.

Ganz, Caryn. "The Curious Case of Nicki Minaj." *Out*, September 12, 2010. https://www.out.com/entertainment/music/2010/09/12/curious-case-nicki-minaj.

Gill, Jon. "From 'Blackness' to Afrofuture to 'Impasse': The Figure of the Jimi Hendrix / Richie Havens Identity Revolution as Faintly Evidenced by the Work of Kendrick Lamar and More than a Head Nod to Lupe Fiasco." In Driscoll, Pinn, and Miller, *Kendrick Lamar and the Making of Black Meaning*, 191–211.

Gill, Jon. *Underground Rap and Religion: A Theopoetic Examination of a Process Aesthetic Religion*. New York: Routledge, 2020.

Gilmore, Ruth. *Golden Gulag: Prisons, Surplus, Crisis, and Opposition in Globalizing California*. Berkeley: University of California Press, 2007.

Gilroy, Paul. *Darker than Blue: On the Moral Economies of Black Atlantic Culture*. Cambridge, MA: Harvard University Press, 2011.

Girard, René. *Violence and the Sacred*. Translated by Patrick Gregory. Baltimore: Johns Hopkins University Press, 1979.

Givens, Jarvis. *Fugitive Pedagogy: Carter G. Woodson and the Art of Black Teaching*. Cambridge, MA: Harvard University Press, 2021.

Glaude, Eddie. *Exodus! Religion, Race, and Nation in Nineteenth-Century Black America*. Chicago: University of Chicago Press, 2000.

Glissant, Édouard. *Poetics of Relation*. Translated by Betsy Wing. Ann Arbor: University of Michigan Press, 1997.

Gomez, Michael. *Black Crescent: The Experience and Legacy of African Muslims in the Americas*. Cambridge: Cambridge University Press, 2005.

Gordon, Lewis. *Existentia Africana: Understanding Africana Existential Thought*. New York: Routledge, 2000.

Gordon, Lewis, and Jane Anna Gordon. *Of Divine Warning: Disaster in a Modern Age*. New York: Routledge, 2010.

Gray, Biko. *Black Life Matter: Blackness, Religion, and Subject*. Durham, NC: Duke University Press, 2022.

Gray, Biko. "The Traumatic Mysticism of Othered Others." *Correspondences: Journal for the Study of Esotericism* 7, no. 1 (2019): 201–37.

Griffin, Farah Jasmine. *"Who Set You Flowin'?": The African American Migration Narrative*. New York: Oxford University Press, 1996.

Griffith, Marie. *God's Daughters: Evangelical Women and the Power of Submission*. Berkeley: University of California Press, 2000.

Guillory, Margarita. "Can I Be Both? Blackness and the Negotiation of Binary Categories in Kendrick Lamar's *Section.80*." In Driscoll, Miller, and Pinn, *Kendrick Lamar and the Making of Black Meaning*, 25–36.

Gumbs, Alexis. *Spill: Scenes of Black Feminist Fugitivity*. Durham, NC: Duke University Press, 2016.

Halliday, Aria. "Miley, What's Good? Nicki Minaj's Anaconda, Instagram Reproductions, and Viral Mimetic Violence." *Girlhood Studies* 11, no. 3 (Winter 2018): 67–83.

Hammonds, Evelynn. "Black (W)holes and the Geometry of Black Female Sexuality." *differences* 6, nos. 2–3 (Summer–Fall 1994): 126–45.

Harris, Trudier. "Porch-Sitting as a Creative Southern Tradition." *Southern Cultures* 2, no. 3–4 (1996): 441–60.

Harrison, Deshaun. *Belly of the Beast: The Politics of Anti-Fatness as Anti-Blackness*. Berkeley, CA: North Atlantic Books, 2021. Kindle.

Hartman, Saidiya. *Lose Your Mother: A Journey Along the Atlantic Slave Route*. New York: Farrar, Straus and Giroux, 2007.

Hartman, Saidiya. *Scenes of Subjection: Terror, Slavery, and Self-Making in Nineteenth-Century America*. New York: Oxford University Press, 1997.

Hartman, Saidiya. "Venus in Two Acts." *Small Axe* 12, no. 2 (2008): 1–14.

Hartman, Saidiya. *Wayward Lives, Beautiful Experiments: Intimate Histories of Riotous Black Girls, Troublesome Women, and Queer Radicals*. New York: W. W. Norton, 2019.

Hartman, Saidiya, and Frank Wilderson III. "The Position of the Unthought." *Qui Parle* 13, no. 2 (Spring–Summer 2003): 183–201.

Hegel, Georg Wilhelm Friedrich. *Lectures on the Philosophy of Religion: One-Volume Edition: The Lectures of 1827*. Edited by P. C. Hodgson, translated by R. F. Brown, P. C. Hodgson, and J. M. Stewart. Berkeley: University of California Press, 1988.

Hills, Darrius. "Loving You Is Complicated: Black Self-Love and Affirmation in the Rap Music of Kendrick Lamar." In Driscoll, Pinn, and Miller, *Kendrick Lamar and the Making of Black Meaning*, 187–89.

Hodge, Daniel White. *The Soul of Hip Hop: Rims, Timbs, and a Cultural Theology*. Downers Grove, IL: IVP, 2010.

Holloway, Karla. *Passed On: African American Mourning Stories*. Durham, NC: Duke University Press, 2003.

Hollywood, Amy. *Acute Melancholia, and Other Essays: Mysticism, History, and the Study of Religion*. New York: Columbia University Press, 2016.

Hollywood, Amy. *Sensible Ecstasy: Mysticism, Sexual Difference, and the Demands of History*. Chicago: University of Chicago Press, 2001.

hooks, bell. *Black Looks: Race and Representation*. Boston: South End Press, 1992.

Hurston, Zora Neale. "Art and Such." In *Reading Black, Reading Feminist: A Critical Anthology*, edited by Henry Louis Gates, 21–26. New York: Plume, 1995.

Irigaray, Luce. *An Ethics of Sexual Difference*. Translated by Carolyn Burke and Gillian Gill. Ithaca, NY: Cornell University Press, 1993.

Jackson, Zakiyyah. *Becoming Human: Matter and Meaning in an Anti-Black World*. New York: NYU Press, 2020.

James, Joy. "F**ck the Police State: Rap, Warfare, and the Leviathan." In *Hip Hop and Philosophy: Rhyme 2 Reason*, edited by Derrick Darby and Tommie Shelby, 65–76. Chicago: Open Court, 2005.

JanMohamed, Abdul. *The Death-Bound Subject: Richard Wright's Archeology of Death*. Durham, NC: Duke University Press, 2005.

Jennings, Willie. "Building Landscapes: Secularism, Race, and the Spatial Modern." In *Race and Secularism in America*, edited by Jonathon Kahn and Vincent Lloyd, 207–38. New York: Columbia University Press, 2016.

Johnson, Sylvester. *African American Religions, 1500–2000: Colonialism, Democracy, and Freedom*. Cambridge: Cambridge University Press, 2015.

Jones, Andrea Sun-Mee. "What the Doing Does: Religious Practice and the Problem of Meaning." *Journal of Cultural and Religious Theory* 6, no. 1 (December 2004): 86–107.

Jones, Douglas. *The Captive Stage: Performance and the Proslavery Imagination in the Antebellum North*. Ann Arbor: University of Michigan Press, 2014.

Jones, William R. *Is God a White Racist? A Preamble to Theology*. Boston: Beacon Press, 1997.

Jordan, Winthrop D. *White over Black: American Attitudes Toward the Negro, 1550–1812*. Chapel Hill: UNC Press, 2013.

Joya, Preciosa de. "A Vision of Hell: Walter Benjamin's Angelus Novus and the Catastrophe of Progress." *Budhi: A Journal of Ideas and Culture* 18, no. 1 (2014): 18–53.

Judy, Ronald. "On the Question of Nigga Authenticity." *boundary 2*, 21, no. 3 (Autumn 1994): 211–30.

Kant, Immanuel. *Observations on the Feeling of the Beautiful and Sublime, and Other Writings*. Edited and translated by Patrick Frierson and Paul Guyer. Cambridge: Cambridge University Press, 2011.

Kearney, Richard. *Strangers, Gods, and Monsters: Interpreting Otherness*. New York: Routledge, 2002.

Keetley, Dawn. "Zombie Republic: Property and Propertyless Multitude in Romero's *Dead* Films and Kirkman's *The Walking Dead*." *Journal of the Fantastic in the Arts* 25, no. 2–3 (Spring–Fall 2014): 295–312.

Kelley, Robin D. G. *Race Rebels: Culture, Politics, and the Black Working Class*. New York: Free Press, 1996.

Khabeer, Su'ad Abdul. *Muslim Cool: Race, Religion, and Hip Hop in the United States*. New York: NYU Press, 2016.

King, Tiffany. *Black Shoals: Offshore Formations of Black Studies*. Durham, NC: Duke University Press, 2019.

King, Tiffany. "The Labor of (Re)reading Plantation Landscapes Fungible(ly)." *Antipode* 48, no. 4 (2016): 1022–39.

Kitwana, Bakari. *Why White Kids Love Hip Hop: Wankstas, Wiggers, Wannabes, and the New Reality of Race in America*. New York: Civitas Books, 2005.

Kristeva, Julia. *Powers of Horror: An Essay on Abjection*. Translated by Leon Roudiez. New York: Columbia University, 1982.

Lacan, Jacques. *The Four Fundamental Concepts of Psychoanalysis*. Edited by Jacques-Alain Miller. Translated by Alan Sheridan. New York: W. W. Norton, 1981.

Lacan, Jacques. "The Signification of the Phallus." In *Écrits: The First Complete Edition in English*, translated by Bruce Fink, 575–84. New York: W. W. Norton, 2006.

Lane, Nikki. "Ratchet Lives Matter: Megan Thee Stallion, Intra-Racial Violence, and the Elusion of Grief." *Journal of Linguistic Anthropology* 31, no. 2 (2021): 293–97.

Leonard, Keith. "First Questions: The Mission of Africana Studies: An Interview with Hortense Spillers." *Callaloo* 30, no. 4 (Fall 2007): 1054–68.

Levinas, Emmanuel. *Totality and Infinity: An Essay on Exteriority*. Translated by Alphonso Lingis. Boston: Martinus Nijhoff Publishers, 1979.

Lloyd, Vincent. "Introduction: Managing Race, Managing Religion." In *Race and Secularism in America*, edited by Jonathon Kahn and Vincent Lloyd, 1–22. New York: Columbia University Press, 2016.

Lofton, Kathryn. *Consuming Religion*. Chicago: University of Chicago Press, 2017.

Lomax, Tamura. *Jezebel Unhinged: Loosing the Black Female Body in Religion and Culture*. Durham, NC: Duke University Press, 2018.

Long, Charles. *Ellipsis: The Collected Writings of Charles Long*. New York: Bloomsbury, 2018.

Long, Charles. *Significations: Signs, Symbols, and Images in the Interpretation of Religion*. Aurora, CO: Davies Group, 1999.

Lott, Eric. *Love and Theft: Blackface Minstrelsy and the American Working Class*. New York: Oxford University Press, 1993.

Love, Bettina. "Good Kids, Mad Cities: Kendrick Lamar and Finding Inner Resistance in Response to FergusonUSA." *Cultural Studies/Critical Methodologies* 16, no. 3 (March 2016): 1–4.

Lubiano, Wahneema. "Black Nationalism and Black Common Sense: Policing Ourselves and Others." In *The House That Race Built: Black Americans, U.S. Terrain*, edited by
Wahneema Lubiano, 232–52. New York: Pantheon, 1997.

Lum, Kathryn. *Heathen: Religion and Race in American History*. Cambridge, MA: Harvard
University Press, 2022.

Lynch, Gordon. *On the Sacred*. New York: Routledge, 2014.

Malone, Eddie. "Long-Lost Brothers: How Nihilism Provides Bigger Thomas and Biggie
Smalls with a Soul." *Journal of Black Studies* 46, no. 3 (April 2015): 297–315.

Marriott, David. *Of Effacement: Blackness and Non-Being*. Stanford, CA: Stanford University
Press, 2023.

Marriott, David. *On Black Men*. New York: Columbia University Press, 2000.

Marriott, David. *Whither Fanon? Studies in the Blackness of Being*. Stanford, CA: Stanford
University Press, 2018.

Marx, Karl. *Capital: A Critique of Political Economy*. Vol. 1. Edited by Frederick Engels.
Translated by Samuel Moore and Edward Aveling. Moscow: Progress Publishers,
1887.

Masuzawa, Tomoko. "Tracing the Figure of Redemption: Walter Benjamin's Physiog-
nomy of Modernity." *MLN* 100, no. 3 (April 1985): 514–36.

Matory, *The Fetish Revisited: Marx, Freud, and the Gods Black People Make*. Durham, NC:
Duke University Press, 2018.

McCarthy, Jesse. *Who Will Pay Reparations on My Soul? Essays*. New York: Liverlight, 2021.

McCutcheon, Russell. *Manufacturing Religion: The Discourse on Sui Generis Religion and the
Politics of Nostalgia*. New York: Oxford University Press, 2003.

McKittrick, Katherine. *Demonic Grounds: Black Women and the Cartographies of Struggle*.
Minneapolis: University of Minnesota Press, 2006.

McKnight, Michael. *The Five Percenters: Islam, Hip-Hop, and the Gods of New York*. London:
Oneworld, 2013.

McMillan, Uri. *Embodied Avatars: Genealogies of Black Feminist Art and Performance*. New York:
NYU Press, 2012.

McMillan, Uri. "Nicki-Aesthetics: The Camp Performance of Nicki Minaj." *Women and
Performance: A Journal of Feminist Theory* 24 (May 2014): 79–87.

Miller, Monica. "Can Dead Homies Speak? The Spirit and Flesh of Black Meaning." In
Driscoll, Pinn, and Miller, *Kendrick Lamar and the Making of Black Meaning*, 159–74.

Miller, Monica. "God of the New Slaves or Slave to the Ideas of Religion and God?" In
Bailey, *Cultural Impact of Kanye West*, 167–79.

Miller, Monica. *Religion and Hip Hop*. New York: Routledge, 2013.

Miller, Monica, and Anthony Pinn, eds. *The Hip Hop and Religion Reader*. New York: Routledge, 2015.

Miller, Monica, Anthony Pinn, and Bernard Freeman, eds. *Religion in Hip Hop: Mapping the
New Terrain in the US*. New York: Bloomsbury, 2015.

Miyakawa, Felicia. *Five Percenter Rap: God Hop's Music, Message, and Black Muslim Message*.
Bloomington: Indiana University Press, 2005.

Morgan, Joan. *She Begat This: 20 Years of "The Miseducation of Lauryn Hill."* New York: Simon
and Shuster, 2018.

Morgan, Joan. *When Chickenheads Come Home to Roost: A Hip-Hop Feminist Breaks It Down*. New York: Simon and Shuster, 2016. Kindle.

Morrison, Toni. *Jazz*. New York: Plume, 1992.

Moten, Fred. *Black and Blur*. Durham, NC: Duke University Press, 2017.

Moten, Fred. "Black Op," PMLA 123, no. 5 (October 2008): 1743–47.

Moten, Fred. "The Case of Blackness." *Criticism* 50, no. 2 (Spring 2008): 177–218.

Moten, Fred. *In the Break: The Aesthetics of the Black Radical Tradition*. Minneapolis: University of Minnesota Press, 2003.

Moten, Fred, and Stefano Harney. *The Undercommons: Fugitive Planning and Black Study*. New York: Minor Compositions, 2013.

Muñoz, José Esteban. *Cruising Utopia: The Then and There of Queer Futurity*. New York: NYU Press, 2009.

Nash, Jennifer. *The Black Body in Ecstasy: Reading Race, Reading Pornography*. Durham, NC: Duke University Press, 2014.

Neal, Mark Anthony. "Trafficking in Monikers: Jay-Z's Queer Flow." *Palimpsest* 2, no. 2 (2013): 156–61.

Nelson, Angela. "'God's Smiling on You and He's Frowning Too': Rap and the Problem of Evil." In Miller and Pinn, *Hip Hop and Religion Reader*, 129–39.

Newport, Frank. "Americans Say Reagan Is the Greatest US President." *Gallup*, February 18, 2011. https://news.gallup.com/poll/146183/americans-say-reagan-greatest-president.aspx.

Nietzsche, Friedrich. *The Gay Science*. Translated by Walter Kauffmann. New York: Vintage Books, 1974.

Nietzsche, Friedrich. *Untimely Meditations*. Translated by R. J. Hollingdale. Cambridge: Cambridge University Press, 1997.

Nietzsche, Friedrich. *The Will to Power*. Translated by Walter Kaufmann and R. J. Hollingdale. New York: Vintage Books, 1968.

Okiji, Fumi. *Jazz as Critique: Adorno and Black Expression Revisited*. Stanford, CA: Stanford University Press, 2018.

Otto, Rudolf. *The Idea of the Holy*. Translated by John Harvey. New York: Oxford University Press, 1958.

Park, Robert. *Race and Culture*. Glencoe, IL: Free Press, 1980.

Perkinson, James. "Tupac Shakur as Ogou Achade: Hip Hop Anger and Postcolonial Rancour Read from the Other Side." *Culture and Religion: An Interdisciplinary Journal* 10, no. 1 (March 2009): 63–79.

Perry, Imani. *Prophets of the Hood: Politics and Poetics in Hip Hop*. Durham, NC: Duke University Press, 2004.

Peterson, James. *The Hip Hop Underground and African American Culture*. New York: Palgrave Macmillan, 2014.

Peterson, James. "A PARTICULAR PAC: Ontological Ruptures and Posthumous Presence of Tupac Shakur." In Miller et al., *Religion in Hip Hop*, 71–86.

Pietz, William. "The Problem of the Fetish, I." *Anthropology and Aesthetics* 9 (Spring 1985): 5–17.

Pinn, Anthony. *Deathlife: Hip Hop and Thanatological Narrations of Blackness*. Durham, NC: Duke University Press, 2024.

Pinn, Anthony. "'Handlin' My Business': Exploring Rap's Humanist Sensibilities." In Pinn, *Noise and Spirit*, 85-104.

Pinn, Anthony. *Interplay of Things: Religion, Art, and Presence Together*. Durham, NC: Duke University Press, 2021.

Pinn, Anthony. "Introduction: Making a World with a Beat: Musical Expression's Relationship to Religious Identity and Experience." In Pinn, *Noise and Spirit*, 1-28.

Pinn, Anthony, ed. *Noise and Spirit: The Religious and Spiritual Sensibilities of Rap Music*. New York: NYU Press, 2003.

Pinn, Anthony. *Terror and Triumph: The Nature of Black Religion*. 20th anniversary ed. Minneapolis: Fortress, 2022.

Pinn, Anthony, and Christopher M. Driscoll. "Introduction: K.Dotting the American Cultural Landscape with Black Meaning." In Driscoll, Pinn, and Miller, *Kendrick Lamar and the Making of Black Meaning*, 1-16.

Pough, Gwendolyn. *Check It While I Wreck It: Black Womanhood, Hip Hop Culture, and the Public Sphere*. Boston: Northeastern University Press, 2004.

Puar, Jasbir. *Terrorist Assemblages: Homonationalism in Queer Times*. Durham, NC: Duke University Press, 2007.

Puar, Jasbir, and Amit Rai. "Monster, Terror, Fag: The War on Terrorism and the Production of Docile Patriots." *Social Text* 20, no. 3 (2002): 117-48.

Quashie, Kevin. *The Sovereignty of Quiet: Beyond Resistance in Black Culture*. New Brunswick, NJ: Rutgers University Press, 2012.

Quinn, Eithne. *Nuthin' but a "G" Thang: The Culture and Commerce of Hip Hop*. New York: Columbia University Press, 2005.

Rabaka, Reiland. *Hip Hop's Inheritance: From the Harlem Renaissance to the Hip Hop Feminist Movement*. New York: Rowman and Littlefield, 2011.

Rabin, Nathan. "Lupe Fiasco: Food and Liquor." *The AV Club*, September 20, 2006. https://www.avclub.com/lupe-fiasco-food-and-liquor-1798201991.

Rae, Gavin. "Questioning the Phallus: Jacques Lacan and Judith Butler." *Studies in Gender and Sexuality* 21, no. 1 (March 2020): 12-26.

Ralph, Michael, Aisha Beliso-De Jesús, and Stephen Palmié. "Saint Tupac." *Transforming Anthropology* 25, no. 2 (October 2017): 90-102.

Reed, Adolph. *W. E. B. Du Bois and American Political Thought: Fabianism and the Color Line*. New York: Oxford University Press, 1997.

Rifkin, Mark. *Beyond Settler Time: Temporal Sovereignty and Indigenous Self-Determination*. Durham, NC: Duke University Press, 2017.

Roberts, Tyler. *Encountering Religion: Responsibility and Criticism After Secularism*. New York: Columbia University Press, 2017.

Robinson, Cedric. *Black Marxism: The Making of the Black Radical Tradition*. Chapel Hill: UNC Press, 2021.

Robinson, Zandria. *This Ain't Chicago: Race, Class, and Regional Identity in the Post-Soul South*. Chapel Hill: UNC Press, 2014.

Rollefson, J. Griffith. *Flip the Script: European Hip Hop and the Politics of Postcoloniality*. Chicago: University of Chicago Press, 2017.

Rose, Tricia. *Black Noise: Rap Music and Black Culture in Contemporary America*. Middletown, CT: Wesleyan University Press, 1994.

Rubin, Gayle. "The Traffic of Women: Notes on the Political Economy of Sex." In *Toward an Anthropology of Women*, edited by Rayna Reiter, 157–210. New York: Monthly Review Press, 1975.

Said, Edward. "Orientalism Reconsidered." *Race and Class* 27, no. 2 (1985): 1–15.

Sartre, Jean-Paul. *Anti-Semite and Jew: An Exploration of the Etiology of Hate*. Translated by George J. Becker. 1948. Reprint, New York: Schocken Books, 1976.

Saucier, P. Khalil, and Tryon Woods. "Hip Hop Studies in Black." *Journal of Popular Music Studies* 26, no. 2–3, (2014): 268–94.

Schmitt, Carl. *Political Theology: Four Chapters on the Concept of Sovereignty*. Translated by George Schwab. Chicago: University of Chicago Press, 2005.

Sexton, Jared. "The Social Life of Social Death: On Afro-Pessimism and Black Optimism." *Intensions* 5 (Fall–Winter 2011): 23–28.

Shange, Savannah. "A King Named Nicki: Strategic Queerness and the Black Femmecee." *Women and Performance: A Journal of Feminist Theory* 24, no. 1 (2014): 29–45.

Sharpe, Christina. "Black Studies: In the Wake." *Black Scholar* 44, no. 2 (Summer 2014): 59–69.

Sharpe, Christina. *In the Wake: On Blackness and Being*. Durham, NC: Duke University Press, 2016.

Sharpe, Christina. *Monstrous Intimacies: Making Post-Slavery Subjects*. Durham, NC: Duke University Press, 2009.

Sharpley-Whiting, T. Denean. *Frantz Fanon: Conflicts and Feminisms*. Lanham, MD: Rowman and Littlefield, 2000.

Shulman, George. *American Prophecy: Race and Redemption in American Political Culture*. Minneapolis: University of Minnesota Press, 2008.

Smalls, Shanté. *Hip Hop Heresies: Queer Aesthetics in New York City*. New York: NYU Press, 2022.

Sorett, Josef. "'Believe Me, This Pimp Game Is Very Religious': Toward a Religious History of Hip Hop." *Culture and Religion* 10, no. 1 (March 2009): 11–22.

Sorett, Josef. *Black Is a Church: Christianity and the Contours of African American Life*. New York: Oxford University Press, 2023.

Spence, Lester. *Knocking the Hustle: Against the Neoliberal Turn in Black Politics*. New York: Punctum Books, 2015.

Spence, Lester. *Staring in the Darkness: The Limits of Hip Hop and Black Politics*. Minneapolis: University of Minnesota Press, 2011.

Spencer, Jon Michael. *Protest and Praise: Sacred Music of Black Religion*. Minneapolis: Fortress, 1990.

Spillers, Hortense. "Mama's Baby, Papa's Maybe: An American Grammar Book." *Diacritics* 17, no. 2 (Summer 1987): 64–81.

Stallings, L. H. *Funk the Erotic: Transaesthetics and Black Sexual Cultures*. Champaign: University of Illinois Press, 2015.

Stern, Adam. *Survival: A Theological Political Genealogy*. Philadelphia: University of Pennsylvania Press, 2021.

Stewart, Lindsey. *The Politics of Black Joy: Zora Neale Hurston and Neo-Abolitionism.* Evanston, IL: Northwestern University Press, 2021.

Stoever, Jennifer. *The Sonic Color Line: Race and the Cultural Politics of Listening.* New York: NYU Press, 2016.

Sullivan, Mecca. "Fat Mutha: Hip Hop's Queer Corpulent Poetics." *Palimpsest* 2, no. 2 (2013): 200–213.

Tate, Greg. *Flyboy 2: The Greg Tate Reader.* Durham, NC: Duke University Press, 2016.

Taylor, Mark Lewis. "Bringing Noise, Conjuring Spirit." In Pinn, *Noise and Spirit,* 107–30.

Thomas, Michael. "Singing Experience in *Section.80.*" In Driscoll, Pinn, and Miller, *Kendrick Lamar and the Making of Black Meaning,* 51–66.

Tinsley, Omise'eke Natasha. *Ezili's Mirrors: Imagining Black Queer Genders.* Durham, NC: Duke University Press, 2018.

Turner, Richard Brent. *Islam in the African-American Experience.* Bloomington: Indiana University Press, 2003.

Turner, Victor. *The Ritual Process: Structure and Anti-Structure.* Ithaca, NY: Cornell University Press, 1977.

Utley, Ebony. *Rap and Religion: Understanding the Gangsta's God.* Santa Barbara, CA: Praeger, 2012.

Volf, Miraslov. "Wheaton Professor's Suspension Is About Anti-Muslim Bigotry, Not Theology." *Washington Post,* December 17, 2015. https://www.washingtonpost.com/news/acts-of-faith/wp/2015/12/17/wheaton-professors-suspension-is-about-anti-muslim-bigotry-not-theology.

Warren, Calvin. "Black Nihilism and the Politics of Hope." *New Centennial Review* 15, no. 1 (Spring 2015): 215–48.

Warren, Calvin. *Ontological Terror: Blackness, Nihilism, and Emancipation.* Durham, NC: Duke University Press, 2018.

West, Cornel. *Race Matters.* New York: Vintage Books, 2001.

White, Carol Wayne. *Black Lives and Sacred Humanity: Toward an African American Religious Naturalism.* New York: Fordham University Press, 2016.

Wilderson, Frank. *Afropessimism.* New York: Liveright, 2021.

Wilderson, Frank. *Red, White, and Black: Cinema and the Structure of U.S. Antagonisms.* Durham, NC: Duke University Press, 2010.

Wilderson, Frank, and Percy Howard. "Frank B. Wilderson, 'Wallowing in the Contradictions,' Part I." *A Necessary Angel* (blog), July 9, 2010. https://percy3.wordpress.com/2010/07/09/frank-b-wilderson-"wallowing-in-the-contradictions"-part-1.

Winters, Joseph. *Hope Draped in Black: Race, Melancholy, and the Agony of Progress.* Durham, NC: Duke University Press, 2016.

Winters, Joseph. "How Protesting Black Bodies Are Imagined as a Threat to National Pride." *Religion Dispatches,* September 22, 2016. http://religiondispatches.org/colin-kaepernick-and-the-ambivalent-sacred-black-bodies-as-an-imagined-source-of-disorder.

Wolin, Richard. *Walter Benjamin: An Aesthetic of Redemption.* Berkeley: University of California Press, 1994.

Wood, Amy Louise. *Lynching and Spectacle: Witnessing Racial Violence in America, 1890–1940.* Chapel Hill: UNC Press, 2009.

Wynter, Sylvia. "Afterword: Beyond Miranda's Meanings: Un/Silencing the Demonic Ground of Caliban's Woman." In *Out of the Kumbla: Caribbean Women and Literature*, edited by Carol Boyce Davies and Elaine Savory Fido, 355–72. Trenton, NJ: Africa World Press, 1990.

Wynter, Sylvia. "1492: A New World View." In *Race, Discourse, and the Origin of the Americas: A New World View*, edited by Vera Lawrence Hyatt and Rex Nettleford, 5–55. Washington, DC: Smithsonian Institution Press, 1995.

Wynter, Sylvia. "Unsettling the Coloniality of Being/Power/Truth/Freedom: Towards the Human, After Man, Its Overrepresentation—an Argument." *CR: New Centennial Review* 3, no. 3 (2003): 257–337.

Zeller, Ben. "Why Kaepernick's Refusal to Stand Is an Act of Religious Dissent." *Religion Dispatches*, August 31, 2016. http://religiondispatches.org/why-kaepernicks-refusal-to-stand-was-an-act-of-religious-dissent.

Index

fetish, 140–41
Feuerbach, Ludwig, 59
Fiasco, Lupe. *See* Lupe Fiasco
50 cent (Curtis James Jackson III), works of:
    The 50th Law, 59; *Get Rich or Die Tryin',* 58–59;
    "Many Men (Wish Death)," 57–58
Fisk Jubilee Singers, 47
flag symbolism, 15, 156n63
Flatbush Zombies, 109
Floyd, George, 132
Floyd-Thomas, Juan, 89, 90
Freud, Sigmund, 41, 59; on death drive, 58; on
    fetishes, 140, 141
Fugees, 60
funk, 31–32, 54

gangsta rap, 8–9, 127, 154n25; Arrested Develop-
    ment and, 54; Quinn on, 26–27. *See also* rap
    music
gang wars, 101
Garden of Eden, 139
Gates, Bill, 25
Geertz, Clifford, 155n37
gender norms, 59, 135–36; Fanon on, 168n54;
    female/femme body and, 29; Jackson on,
    123; Madonna/whore binary of, 5; Perry on,
    107–8; Spillers on, 122–23; storytelling and,
    97–108. *See also* masculinity; misogyny
Ghostface Killah (Dennis David Coles), 38,
    49, 56–57
Gilmore, Ruth, 53
Gilroy, Paul, 75
Giuliani, Rudolph, 63
Glaude, Eddie, 44–45
Glissant, Édouard, 20, 46
golden-age tropes, 70–71
Gotti, John, 63
Grandmaster Flash and the Furious Five,
    49–55, 62–64, 81
Gray, Biko, 32
Gremlins (film), 110–11
Griffin, Farrah Jasmine, 56
griots, 150
Guillory, Margarita, 99
Gumbs, Alexis, 149

Halliday, Aria, 137
Hammonds, Evylynn, 162n7

Harrell, Haylee, 168n64
Harris, Trudier, 76
Harrison, Deshaun, 128
Hartman, Saidiya, 20, 45, 49, 85; on gender
    norms, 166n111; on slavery, 95; on "terrible
    spectacle," 136; "Venus in Two Acts," 85, 108;
    Wilderson and, 77–78, 83–84
Havens, Richie, 165n83
Hawkins, Larycia, 91
Hegel, G. W. F., 40
Heidegger, Martin, 64–65
Hendrix, Jimi, 165n83
hierophany, 13
Hill, Lauryn, 59–61, 71
hip hop, 49, 74, 149–50; Blaxploitation films
    and, 64; commodification of, 25–28; corpo-
    ratization of, 26; death of, 14, 43, 68–74; defi-
    nitions of, 152, 154n24; New York City roots
    of, 14; origins of, 24; as youth rebellion, 21.
    See also individual artists
hip hop industry, 24–25, 33, 69–70
HIV/AIDS, 37–38, 100
Holloway, Karla, 56
Hollywood, Amy, 112
homosocial intimacy, 67
hooks, bell (Gloria Watkins), 59, 142–43,
    170n115
Horkheimer, Max, 69–70, 81
Howard, Percy, 86
humanism, 85
Hurston, Zora Neale, 46–47

Ice Cube (O'Shea Jackson), 26
Ice-T (Tracy Lauren Marrow), 26
indigenous genocide, 7, 93, 94, 95
Iraq War, 92
Irigaray, Luce, 154n17
Islam, 89–91, 146
Israel, 92, 117

Jackson, Ayanna, 6
Jackson, Zakiyyah, 34, 111, 119, 122
Jaco, Ayesha, 88–89
Jafa, Arthur, 20
Jakes, T. D., 8
Jay-Z (Shawn Corey Carter), 25, 133–34
jazz music, 31–32, 96, 149
Jean Grae (Tsidi Ibrahim), 109

www.ingramcontent.com/pod-product-compliance
Lightning Source LLC
Jackson TN
JSHW021628160725
87746JS00001B/2